SPEAKING FOR RESULTS

SPEAKING FOR RESULTS
COMMUNICATION BY OBJECTIVES

John E. Baird, Jr.
formerly
The University of Michigan

1817

HARPER & ROW, PUBLISHERS, NEW YORK
Cambridge, Hagerstown, Philadelphia, San Francisco,
London, Mexico City, São Paulo, Sydney

Sponsoring Editor: Alan M. Spiegel
Project Editor: Robert Ginsberg
Designer: Michel Craig
Production Manager: Jeanie Berke
Compositor: Bi-Comp, Incorporated
Printer and Binder: Halliday Lithograph Corporation
Art Studio: Vantage Art Inc.

Speaking for Results: Communication by Objectives

Library of Congress Cataloging in Publication Data
Baird, John E
   Speaking for results.

   Includes index.
   1. Public speaking.   I. Title.
PN4121.B316   808.5'1   80-24026
ISBN 0-06-040457-4

To Linda

CONTENTS

PREFACE

When you give a speech, you do so for a reason. Occasionally, you do so because you are required to; more often, you do so because there is something you want to accomplish. You may want to teach people something—to give them information. A progress report presented to a group of business executives, for example, seeks to "teach" these listeners something, just as a lecture is designed to teach a class or a sermon is designed to teach a congregation. You may want to change people's minds, as when a young engineer tries to convince his or her superiors not to scrap a proposed project, or when a Republican candidate attempts to garner the support of a group of Democrats. You may want to cause people to act, just as a union organizer tries to convince people to sign union authorization cards. Or you may simply wish to keep your audience entertained for a few minutes. Whatever your purpose, the point is this: Public speeches are tools designed to achieve something, and good public speeches are "good" because they achieve (within ethical guidelines) the speaker's objectives.

Public speeches are among the most powerful forces in our society, and in our lives. Speeches determine who our political, educational, religious, and business leaders are to be, and our own speeches often determine whether we are to be among those leaders. Whenever we find ourselves in a position allowing us to deliver a speech, we truly have an opportunity at hand. When we give a speech, we have a chance to influence people—to change their beliefs, their attitudes, and their behaviors. In effect, we have an opportunity to determine the future. Obviously, you have a tremendous advantage in life if you are able to deliver effective public speeches.

This book is intended to enable you to improve your public speaking skills. As we seek improvement in speaking, we will take an approach called "speaking by objectives." The "by objectives" part of this approach is not particularly original—for years people have applied objectives to management, education, and other fields of endeavor. However, the systematic objectives-oriented approach to communication taken in this book *is* unique, for no other text uses a step-by-step system of establishing main, primary, and secondary objectives and speaking strategies as the central method for developing and delivering speeches. Chapter 1 sets out what I believe to be the advantages inherent in this objectives-based approach.

The book is divided into five parts. In Part I you will be given information about the nature of communication and the nature of audiences that serves as the basis for the principles presented in the rest of the book. In Part II, techniques for presenting speeches are outlined as we examine methods of coping with stagefright and study strategies of speech delivery. In Parts III and IV, we turn to the preparation of speech materials. Part III discusses preparational techniques for informative speeches; Part IV presents methods for preparing effective persuasive messages. Finally, Part V discusses techniques for preserving the positive impact of the speech and presents methods of handling question-and-answer sessions smoothly. Throughout we will adhere to the "by objectives" approach: Every chapter begins with a list of chapter objectives, and Chapters 3 through 11 each present a primary objective that must be achieved if the overall speaking objective is to be accomplished. For each of those chapters, secondary objectives and corresponding strategies are listed at the chapter's beginning.

In the years that I have taught public speaking skills to almost anyone who would listen, I have found three common misconceptions about public speaking. Since those misconceptions ultimately inspired me to write this book, let me describe and respond to them briefly.

1. *"Real" people do not give public speeches.* This I heard primarily from students in universities, who apparently did not consider themselves "real" people. They could not have been more wrong. In every occupation I have encountered as a teacher, businessman, and consultant, I have seen people give formal and informal public speeches. They report the progress of their projects, they announce upcoming events, they argue their viewpoints, they try to stir up their coworkers, they introduce other speakers, they try to entertain their listeners—they deliver speeches to fulfill a multitude of purposes. "Real" people *do* give public speeches, and they give them frequently.

2. *Public speaking is a relatively unimportant form of communication.* Many people think that since we give speeches less often than we engage in conversations, attend group meetings, participate in interviews, and so on, public speaking is relatively less important than these other communication types. Again, I disagree. It is true that we give speeches less often than we do those other things, but when one considers the consequences of those speeches, the true importance of public speaking becomes evident. When we present a speech, it is usually to influential people— people who can affect our future and the future of the things with which we are concerned. In any profession, people who give effective presentations rapidly gain reputations as being competent and articulate, and they frequently are rewarded as a consequence. Conversely, people who consistently give poor presentations, even if they are competent in other respects, come to be regarded as dull, uninspired individuals whose potential is limited. I am not advocating that these judgments should be made, nor am I saying that in every instance credibility is solely a function of public speeches. But my experience has shown me that one's reputation among one's superiors and coworkers is significantly influenced by the quality of the public presentations one makes. The speeches you deliver *are* important, particularly in terms of the consequences they produce for you.

3. *Good speakers are born, not made.* Let's acknowledge something right now: There *are* certain attributes (such as intelligence, a pleasant voice, or physical attractiveness) that enhance your effectiveness as a public speaker and that are acquired (at least partially) via heredity. But the most important elements of effective public speaking are skills, not attributes, and you can acquire those skills through study and practice. Good speakers develop through their own efforts, not through heredity.

We arrive then at the three conclusions that form the foundation for this book: (1) You *will* deliver public speeches in the future; (2) those speeches *will* have an important impact on your own future and the futures of those who listen to you; and (3) you *can* learn how to give those speeches effectively. The importance of studying public speaking is derived from the truth of these conclusions.

It is traditional, of course, to acknowledge in the Preface those people who contributed to the completion of the text. As a respecter of tradition, I will mention the people who played a central role in the completion of this book. Alan Spiegel, Speech Communication Editor for Harper & Row, provided guidance, support, and a few cornball jokes to use at the beginning of the chapters after I had run out of jokes of my own. Cathy Carmichael and Kathy Eikum typed parts of the manuscript and, more importantly, covered for me while I wrote the book on company time. Howard Thompson, my boss while this was written, saw through the cover, but he still was kind enough to allow me to write anyway. Leslie Nathanson and Herb Melnick gave me opportunities to learn new things about communication and human behavior, and much of what I learned is presented in this book. And Linda Fredericks gave me encouragement, sympathy, time, and above all, friendship. It is to her that this book is dedicated.

JOHN E. BAIRD, JR.

SPEAKING FOR RESULTS

PART I
INTRODUCTION

Look, for a moment, into the future. At some point, perhaps very soon, you will need to convince someone to do something that will have an important impact upon your life. If you are not presently employed (or if you are dissatisfied with your current position), you will need to convince some recruiter-employer that he or she would have a far better organization if you were a part of it. If you do have a job at present, you may have to convince your employer that your services are far more valuable than your current compensation might indicate (that is, you deserve a raise). If people work for you, you will have to instruct them in proper work methods and to convince them that hard work is beneficial to their own futures (and, of course, to your performance as a manager). Indeed, virtually every day from this moment until the end of your life, you will have to convince someone to do something and, most likely, inform them of what to do and how to do it. You will have to achieve these things, of course, through communication.

Perhaps you now are thinking to yourself, "Big deal. People communicate all the time. I communicate all the time. So what?" To tell you "so what," let me tell you just a little bit about how I make my living (not that my life is all that fascinating; I just want to make a point). I work for a management consulting firm as a full-time consultant. In this capacity, I am hired by organizations of various types to do three things: to analyze the type and extent of problems the organization has, to develop solutions to those problems, and to implement those solutions so that the morale and productivity of the organization are increased. The end products of my efforts should be happier employees and a more profitable operation.

To analyze an organization's problems, my colleagues and I use two basic techniques: interviews with supervisors and managers in which they are asked to report their own and their employees' problems and concerns, and questionnaires that ask all employees in the organization to indicate their perceptions and attitudes of specific elements of their work life. From these information-gathering tools, several rather interesting conclusions have been drawn:

1. Most supervisors and managers think they communicate pretty well with their subordinates.
2. Most supervisors and managers think that their immediate superiors do not communicate very well with them.
3. Most nonsupervisory employees feel that supervisors and managers in their organization do not communicate very well.
4. When asked what the primary problem in their organization is, most managers, supervisors, and employees give the same answer: "Communication."
5. When asked whether they meet regularly, supervisors and employees generally answer, Yes. When asked whether those meetings provide the information employees want and need to know, supervisors answer, Yes, but employees say No.
6. When asked whether their communication efforts are generally successful, most company managers will indicate that they are. When asked to provide proof of that success, these managers will say things like, "Look how clearly written this report/memo/letter/proposal (select one) is," or "This newsletter/magazine won the IBCAW 'best composition' award." Rarely will they talk in terms of the impact of their communication upon their employees.

From all of this, we can conclude that: (1) most people think they communicate pretty well; (2) many of those people are dead wrong; (3) too few people take the trouble to determine how well they actually are communicating; and (4) communication is one of the major weaknesses in today's organization, whether that organization is an industry, a hospital, an educational institution, a religious organization, a financial institution, a publishing house, or any of the other types of organizations with which the people in my company have worked. So back to your question, "So what?" If you asked the question, you probably are one of the people who need this book the most. The worst communicators typically are those who are most confident that they communicate well.

Communication, then, is important, and communication skills are a major determinant of your own ability to succeed in your future endeavors. However, you should beware of taking these principles too far. There are two other things which I have observed in my client organizations, and these things are just as troublesome as are the problems described above. Specifically, many people assume either or both of the following:

1. All of the problems they face in their organization are communication problems.
2. All of the problems in their organization can be solved by more and better communication.

While these assumptions keep management consultants in business, they also are dead wrong. Sometimes people communicate perfectly well; they simply disagree. However, rather than recognize the disagreement, the people assume that "communication has broken down." On the other hand, managers often conclude that, because absenteeism is high and productivity low, they have a communication problem. By conducting more meetings and by training their supervisors to communicate "better," they believe they can solve these problems. In truth, these problems may stem from lax policies or poor production techniques, so that no amount of communication can solve them. Yet "communication" is an easy scapegoat, and improving communication seems an easy solution.

The truth, of course, lies somewhere between "communication is easy—I do it all the time," and "solving our communication problems will cure all of our ills." Communication *is* important. Communication *is not* the answer to the world's problems. But communication *will* help you to succeed if you know how to use it.

In this book, we will examine ways you can use communication to achieve your goals. In the first part of the book, we will consider some of the fundamental elements of successful communication. We will discuss the process itself, and then we will consider the people to whom we communicate: our receivers. After all, our success is a function of those receivers; the recruiter either does or does not hire us, our boss either gives or refuses our raise, our employees either work hard or goof off, and so on. To judge our success, we must understand and observe our listeners. Then, in subsequent sections, we will study the specific strategies you can use in order to become a successful communicator. Then, when you answer in an interview or on a questionnaire that you communicate well, you will be one of the few people I have encountered who is right.

CHAPTER 1
AN INTRODUCTION TO COMMUNICATION BY OBJECTIVES

CHAPTER OBJECTIVES

After studying this chapter, you should be able to:

- Explain the importance of communication in human activity
- Provide your own definition of the concept *communication*
- Draw your own model of communication
- Explain the "process" nature of communication
- Explain why communication is a function of the receiver
- Explain why communication is irreversible and unrepeatable
- Explain why communication imposes responsibility
- Set your objective for communicating in a public speech
- Apply the criteria for communication objective statements to your own speaking objective
- Explain the stages of situational analysis, goal setting, goal planning, presentation, and preservation

INTRODUCTION

Of all the activities or behaviors you conduct during your lifetime, which do you do the most often? Work? Stewart and Cash (1978) estimate that we spend only about one-third of our time working. Sleep? Most people spend about one-third of their time doing that, too, although some seem able to combine the two activities. How about a more specific analysis of our behaviors? Breathing, for example. Most of us do that continually. Circulating blood throughout our bodies also occupies much of our time. But those activities occur involuntarily—we rarely devote conscious effort to keeping our heart and lungs going. No, on the conscious level, there is one activity in which we engage almost constantly, from the moment we are born until the instant we die. That activity is communication.

But if we communicate all of the time, with ourselves or with others, why should we worry about it? Why devote time and effort to something we've done for years? After all, we don't read books titled *How to Work Your Lungs* or *How to Keep Your Heart Pumping*. The reason we should worry about communication is that often we don't do it very well. Hearts and lungs are either-or propositions: either they work, or we're dead. Communication is not either-or: we can communicate badly and still get by, stumbling along from one misunderstanding to the next, wondering why life never seems to go the way we want. But to succeed in life, no matter what our standards of success are, we must be able to communicate reasonably well, and the better we communicate, the better our chances for success.

In my experiences as college professor and businessman, I have seen a great number of successes and an equal number of failures. Surprisingly, I have seen very little difference between those who succeeded and those who failed. Intelligence makes little difference: smart people fail about as often as dumb ones. Motivation means little: I've known managers who were fired even though they worked 12 to 16 hours a day. The key element seems to be communication. I've seen highly motivated, near geniuses lose their jobs because they could not work well with people, and I've known some not-so-motivated, not-so-bright individuals who made millions because they could sell a fur coat to a polar bear.

The importance of studying communication therefore is twofold. First, we communicate continuously: with ourselves in our thought processes, and with others in both formal and informal settings. Communication thus occupies a central point in our daily lives. Second, the consequences of communication are enormous. All of our relationships with other people are dependent upon communication. All of our achievements depend, to some degree, on the willingness of others to listen to us, to believe in us, and to do as we ask. If we communicate well, we probably will be able to establish and maintain desirable personal and professional relationships; if we communicate badly, we probably will be doomed to a life filled with unhappy relationships and unsuccessful ventures. Physical survival may not depend upon our ability to communicate, but happiness and achievement certainly do.

The purpose of this text, simply put, is to enable you to make yourself a better communicator. But let's think about that for a second. Note that I did not say, "The purpose of this text is to make you a better communicator." I can't do that. Only you can improve your communication skills. But there are two things I can do. First, I can help you explore the communication process, showing you how it works, and why. Second, based upon that exploration I can suggest specific behaviors that, under certain circumstances, seem to produce predictable responses in other people. It then falls to you to analyze your own situation, to decide what responses you want from others, and to select and develop your skills in the behaviors most likely to get those responses. So this book serves as a guide by which you can make decisions concerning your own behavior. The real work of developing your communication skills is left to you. But the rewards you will reap through communicating effectively will make the effort worthwhile.

This first chapter will introduce to you the nature of human communication. We will try to define the communication process—something a lot of people have tried to do in the past but to no one's satisfaction—so that we have some common starting

point; we will examine some models of that process; we will note some characteristics of communication; and then we will discuss "communication by objectives," the
approach this text takes to the development and implementation of communication
strategies and skills. These considerations will serve as the foundation upon which the
remainder of this text will be built.

COMMUNICATION DEFINED

Since we are talking about communication, it seems only reasonable to begin with
the question, what is communication in the first place? Unfortunately, the answer to
that question is not easily presented. Everyone thinks he or she knows what communication is, but when they are asked to communicate the meaning of communication, words fail them. To illustrate, consider the following definitions, presented
chronologically, of the communication process:

> *Communication is the eliciting of response and successful human speech
> communication is the eliciting of the desired response through verbal sym-
> bolization. (Zelko and Dance, 1965, p. 5)*

> *Human communication is a subtle set of processes through which
> people interact, control one another and gain understanding. (Smith, 1966,
> p. v)*

> *Communication is social interaction through symbols and message sys-
> tems. (Gerbner, 1966, p. 99)*

> *Communication has as its central interest those behavioral situations in
> which a source transmits a message to a receiver(s) with conscious intent to af-
> fect the latter's behaviors. (Miller, 1966, p. 92)*

> *Communication is a social function . . . a sharing of elements of behav-
> ior, or modes of life, by the existence of sets of rules. . . . Communication is
> not the response itself but is essentially the relationship set up by the transmis-
> sion of stimuli (signs) and the evocation of responses. (Cherry, 1966, pp. 6–7)*

> *Speech is ongoing multisymbolic behavior in social situations carried on
> to achieve communication. We define communication as a social achieve-
> ment in symbolic behavior. (Baird & Knower, 1968, p. 3)*

> *The sequence of events which must occur to produce a communication
> event may be viewed as involving a minimum of five sequential ingredients:
> (1) a generator of a (2) stimulus which is (3) projected to a (4) perceiver which
> (5) responds discriminatively (assigns meaning). (Goyer, 1970, p. 8)*

> *Communication is an ongoing process. Ideas originate in an individual's
> cognitive framework; they are coded and sent through some channel or chan-*

nels; the messages are received and decoded by another person who responds according to his own cognitive framework. (Fausti & McGlone, 1972, p. 22)

Communication occurs whenever persons attribute significance to message-related behavior. (Mortensen, 1972, p. 14)

Communication is the process involving the transmission and reception of symbols eliciting meaning in the minds of the participants by making common their life experiences. (Baird, 1977, p. 6)

Intentional Communication is a transactional process involving a cognitive sorting, selecting, and sending of symbols in such a way as to help a listener elicit from his or her own mind a meaning or response similar to that intended by the communicator. (Ross, 1977, p. 11)

We could review more definitions—in fact, Dance (1970) noted a decade ago that, at that time, over 95 attempts at clarifying communication had appeared in print. But the point is all too clear. No one really knows what communication is.

Rather than add to the already mountainous pile of definitions, let's try to extract some of the more cogent points which most definitions offer. Perhaps by reviewing those points, we can arrive at some understanding of human communication.

1. Communication involves meaning. It occurs when someone forms a meaning or an idea in his or her mind.

2. Communication involves responses. The meaning one forms must be a consequence of something that occurs around him or her—some stimulus in his or her environment. If the meaning that occurs in our minds happens in response to a stimulus external to us, we have been communicated with. If that meaning occurs through our own ponderings and ruminations without help from the environment, we are simply thinking.

3. Communication involves symbols. Meaning exists nowhere except in our own minds. Words, for example, don't "mean" anything. Instead, they stand for things—they symbolize meanings because we have agreed on their symbolic value. Thus, when you read this book, hear spoken words, observe someone's behaviors, and so on, you are not reading, hearing, or observing meanings, you are receiving symbols. When you interpret those symbols in your mind, then and only then does meaning occur.

4. Communication may be intentional or unintentional. If you deliberately send a message to someone, perhaps by saying something to him, you intend to communicate with him. If, however, he observes you without your knowing it, or if he sees or hears things you are unconsciously doing or saying, you still are communicating with him, even though you don't mean to. Much of "body language," for example, is unintentional communication whereby, presumably, people allow their "true" feelings to leak our without being aware of it.

5. Communication may be successful or unsuccessful. You judge the success of your communication by its results. If you got the response you wanted, you probably were successful. If you did not get the desired response, you probably communicated

What You Say

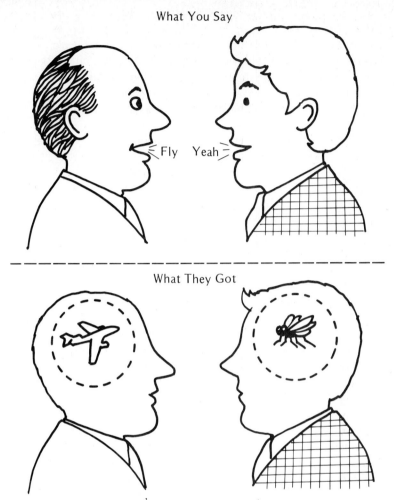

What They Got

The Results of Communication Are Difficult to Judge

unsuccessfully. But understand two things. First, this applies only to intentional communication; unintentional communication obviously is not designed to produce results in the first place. Second, these results are often hard to measure. How can you determine if someone truly understood you (as opposed to merely thinking he understood you)? How can you see if you changed someone's mind? Often, you can't judge these things, so that you really don't know whether or not you communicated successfully. Nevertheless, we will be guided by the principle that successful communication is communication that achieves the results we desire.

   6. Communication is a tool. In the past, a great deal of emphasis was placed upon the ''art'' of speaking, as though communication were something to be admired for its own sake. ''Scholars'' in communication taught people to speak in melodious tones and to use carefully planned gestures as they dramatized their ideas. While the result often was very unnatural, artificial speaking, some people still feel that we should be concerned primarily with the artistry of communication. I disagree. In my view, communication has the same qualities as a hammer. It's good if it works; if it doesn't, then no matter how beautiful it looks, it's worthless. When we communicate, we should do so with some purpose in mind. "Artistic" communication is desirable when it helps us achieve that purpose. However, when our primary concern is simply to appear "artistic," then we have lost sight of the principle that communication is a tool.

These six points seem to reflect the ideas contained in most definitions of communication. People generally agree that communication involves symbols that, intentionally or unintentionally, produce meaningful responses in people's minds. They also seem to agree, although perhaps to a lesser extent, that communication is a tool that may be used with varying degrees of success. Our purpose in this book, then, is to discover ways of intentionally using symbols to achieve the responses we desire.

COMMUNICATION ILLUSTRATED

An alternative to defining communication is to represent the communication process with a model. In essence, a model is an abstraction of the thing with which we are concerned. A model airplane, for example, represents the full-size object, but presents only the most general parts. Similarly, a communication model represents the process of communication by presenting its important parts in some abstract form.

Models do serve some useful functions. They serve to illustrate the components of communication, and they can present those components in an organized fashion. But models also have shortcomings. They necessarily leave out some parts of the communication process, because communication is composed of an infinite number of parts. They represent some aspects of communication only in a very general, abstract fashion, because much of communication is psychological and, as a consequence, cannot accurately be represented in a model. Yet models give us another perspective on the communication process, so that examining a couple of them is worth our while.

Not surprisingly, there are nearly as many models as there are definitions of communication. Some use only words; some use words in boxes; some use words, boxes, and arrows; some substitute circles for the boxes; some even use drawings of faces, brains, ears, mouths, and other things involved in human communication. Rather than bombard you with the entire menagerie of words, boxes, circles, arrows, eyes, ears, noses, and throats, I will simply offer three models which are representative of the most common approaches to illustrating communication.

Perhaps the simplest model is the verbal representation developed by Lasswell (1948). In his view, communication can be represented by five questions:

Who?
Says what?
In what channel?
To whom?
With what effect?

Figure 1-1: A Linear-Graphic Communication Model

We can translate these questions into five elements of the communication process: the source (who?), the message (says what?), the medium (in what channel?), the receiver (to whom?), and the result (with what effect?). We also can observe the order in which these parts enter into the communication process: the source says a message that passes through a medium to a receiver, who receives it and reacts. Although the multitude of models developed after Lasswell's have elaborated upon this process, virtually all of them have been built upon this five-part, five-step system.

A second sort of model attempts to represent pictorially the communication process as it moves from start to finish. Since these models view communication as a linear progression through a series of stages, we will call them *linear-graphic* models. Figure 1-1 presents a model that typifies the linear-graphic approach.

Like Lasswell's model, the linear-graphic model begins with the source, or the person who initiates communication with someone else. But inside the source, certain things unmentioned by Lasswell occur. First, he or she forms some thought, has some idea, or in some way develops meaning in his or her mind. But that meaning is abstract, and as an abstraction it cannot be sent to other people. Thus, the source encodes that meaning, placing it in some symbolic form (typically words) that represents the abstract thought in his or her mind. Those symbols then are transmitted or sent in the general direction of the receiver.

The transmitted symbols comprise the message a source sends a receiver. But in order for the message to reach a receiver, it must pass through some sort of channel. Briefly, a channel is anything that carries a message from a source to a receiver. The air carrying sound waves and light waves between people is a channel, as are radio devices, television systems, telephone wires and receivers, and so on. Again, all things carrying messages between people are communication channels.

In every communication event there exists yet another element of communication, *noise*. In my view, noise is any and all message elements besides the message sent by the source. Static received on a radio is noise, perhaps obscuring the message sent by the radio station. On a long-distance telephone call, the "hiss" you hear is noise, as are other voices on other lines, commotion in the background of the person to whom you are talking, commotion going on around you, and so on. Noise is always present in both the channel through which the source sends the message (as with static received over the radio) and in other channels with which the receiver is surrounded (such as the commotion going on around him or her during a telephone call).

Usually, communication scholars acknowledge only one kind of noise: the harmful kind that makes the message more difficult for the receiver to pick up or interpret. Radio static, television interference, and background commotion all fall into this category. But there is a second kind of noise that is even more important: noise that is helpful to the message, adding to its impact on the receiver. Consider your friendly local supermarket. Probably it has taped background "muzak" playing through its sound system most of the time. That music is noise, deliberately added to the setting to make shopping a more pleasant experience for you. Theoretically, it relaxes you, making you more receptive to the visual messages on the products lining the aisles.

Or consider magazine advertisements. Standing next to the car being advertised (the message) is a lovely young woman dressed in a revealing gown (the noise). She is not for sale—the car is. So why is she there? The reason is that she causes male readers to fool themselves. They subconsciously think, "Hey, if I buy this, I'll get that." Life doesn't work that way, of course, but advertisers don't care. Such advertisements sell cars, and that's why the noise is deliberately placed in the channel.

But what has all of this to do with you? Just this: if you are to communicate with maximum effect, you must not only transmit well-formulated messages, you also must take into account and, when possible, control noise. In public speaking, everything around you is noise: the podium, the blackboards (if any), the setting, and so on. You can use these things to enhance your message, if you know what you are doing. When we discuss the delivery of public speeches in a later chapter, we will see specific ways of using noise to our advantage.

When the message has passed through communication channels, it arrives at the receiver—the person with whom the source is communicating. The receiver first of all receives the message through one of his or her five senses: hearing it, seeing it, feeling it, tasting it, or smelling it. But the message still is in the symbolic form, so the receiver must convert it into an abstract idea. Through the interpretation process, then, the receiver arrives at some meaning and, in so doing, completes the communication event.

This linear-graphic approach to communication does show us some important things. First, it demonstrates the major parts of communication and the order in which they occur. Second, it illustrates the psychological nature of communication—the formation and encoding of an idea by a source, and the decoding and interpretation of the idea by a receiver. And third, it gives us the key for determining the quality of communication. If communication is perfect, the idea the source had and the idea the receiver formed will exactly match. As communication becomes less perfect, the source's idea and the receiver's idea become less alike. When communication is awful, the two ideas differ entirely. So the ultimate goal of communication is to produce ideas in the receiver's mind that are identical to our own, and the more closely we approach this goal, the more successfully we have communicated.

Unfortunately, there also are some problems associated with the linear-graphic approach. The primary problem is that this approach views communication as a one-way event in which a source sends a message to a receiver, and that's the end. Nothing happens after the receiver interprets the message. In addition, this approach does not allow sources and receivers to switch roles. A source only sends messages, a receiver only receives them, and never the twain shall meet. Obviously, the real world is not like that. We simultaneously send and receive messages, and we respond to the messages which others send us. So we need something more complete than the linear-graphic model if we are to represent the communication process accurately.

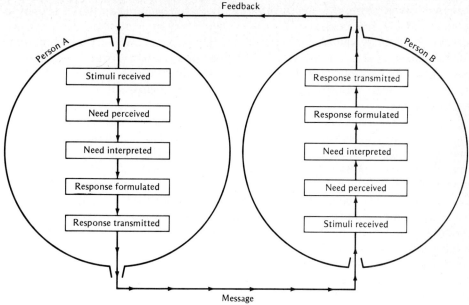

Figure 1-2: A Circular-Graphic Communication Model

Figure 1-2 presents a *circular-graphic* model of communication. Recently, communication theorists have taken to using this sort of model to represent communication between people. This sort of model adds another important element of the communication process, *feedback*. In essence, feedback is the reverse of the communication process described above. While the source is sending messages to the receiver, the receiver simultaneously is sending messages back to the source. While you give a speech, for example, the members of the audience are sending messages back to you: nodding their heads in agreement, shaking their heads in disagreement, bowing their heads in slumber, and so on. Communication therefore is two-way, as the participants simultaneously are sources and receivers.

But communication is even more involved than that. When we communicate with someone, we usually have a reason for doing so. That is, we perceive a need to communicate. That need may be simply to recognize someone's presence (as when we say "Hi" to someone we pass in a hallway), or to fill time (perhaps with "small talk" at a party), or to accomplish some monumental goal (such as impressing our boss to keep our job). In any case, we perceive some need, and our communication is in response to it. Moreover, when we speak to someone, it causes him or her to perceive a need. The need may be simply to listen, or to pretend to be listening, or to listen and respond, or to leave and thus avoid communicating, or to perform some other behavior. But that person has to do something as a response to our communication attempts. His or her choice of response—listening, speaking, leaving, or whatever—then becomes another need to us, as we must decide how to respond to this response. And so it goes, each of us causing the other to feel a need to respond, until one of us finally feels a need to quit, and we end the encounter.

While the circular-graphic model of communication is a substantial improvement over the linear-graphic approach, it still represents an incomplete view of the communication process. As we saw earlier, communication is a tool—it is used to accomplish things. Specifically, it is used, intentionally or unintentionally, to change the beliefs, attitudes, values, and behaviors of the people involved in the communication. Because of their interaction, these people come to think differently, feel differently, and act differently toward each other and toward their environments. A model of communication should somehow illustrate these changes; the circular-graphic models do not.

Figure 1-3 offers a *process* model of communication that demonstrates, although only in a very abstract way, that communication is transactive—that is, it involves changes produced in each person by the other. The model is spiral shaped to indicate that each person changes, becoming a slightly different person, as he or she communicates through time. Within each person are beliefs (B), attitudes (A), values (V), and potential behaviors (Bp) which also change while the interaction occurs, and from these things spring actual behaviors (Ba) or responses that are transmitted to and produce changes in the other person. Thus, this model illustrates to a degree the mutual influence which occurs in communication.

COMMUNICATION CHARACTERIZED

Earlier in this chapter, we saw some attributes of communication: it involves meanings, responses, and symbols, it may or may not be intentional or successful, and it is a tool. Now that we have examined some communication models, we can specify even further the characteristics of communication and thereby gain a clearer understanding of what "effective communication" means.

Communication Is a Process

Although this statement appears simple, it implies a complicated subset of communication characteristics. Communication really is a process within a process which controls other processes. Confused? Let's consider the three elements of that statement.

First, communication itself is a process because it involves continuous change. As people send messages back and forth, their behaviors change as they respond to each other. What one says is influenced by what the other has just done; what the other has done reflects the first person's previous behaviors. Thus, communication is a process because it consists of continually changing behaviors.

Second, communication is a process within a larger process: the ongoing chain of events comprising human history. What you say or what happens in any communication encounter is determined by a whole series of events leading up to the encounter and determines a whole series of events following the encounter. Imagine you are giving a briefing to top management in your company, summarizing for them the progress of a project in which you have been involved. What you say in that briefing represents the culmination of your entire life—your birth, background, education, and so on—as well as the specific progress of the particular project under consideration. Had anything occurred differently in your life, you might not even be in that situation, much less saying the things you are saying now. Moreover, what you say will trigger a whole series of events. If your briefing is well liked, then promotions,

KEY
R = Received
B = Belief
A = Attitude
V = Value
Bp = Behavior potential
Ba = Actual behavior (response)

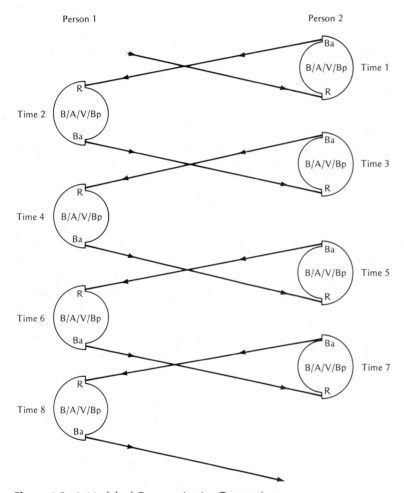

Figure 1-3: A Model of Communicative Transactions

raises, increased project funding, increased responsibility for you, and so on could follow; if your briefing goes poorly, professional disaster for you and the collapse of your project could result. Indeed, every time you communicate, you influence to some degree the events that will occur in the future. So choose carefully what you say. Your words, like a stone thrown into a quiet pool, will produce a series of ripples influencing significantly the events which occur in the future.

Third, communication is a process that controls another process. Carl Rogers, the noted psychologist, claims that people always are involved in the process of "becoming." He argues that we are constantly changing, becoming someone slightly different, until the moment we die. A primary determinant of this process is communication with others. Through interactions with other people—parents, friends, acquaintances—we develop our personalities, our knowledge, our self-concept, and so on. Research in child development, for example, demonstrates that children who receive positive messages from their parents tend to develop high self-esteem, while children whose parents give them primarily negative messages tend to form low self-images. Similarly, when people develop personality disorders, they often seek assistance from professional psychologists who try to "straighten them out"—through communication. The process of communication thus works within the process of human events to influence people's process of development.

Communication Is a Function of the Receiver

This second characteristic of communication seems odd. When we think of communication, we typically think of it in terms of sources. We talk about speakers' stagefright, we study methods of constructing speeches, we examine source credibility, and we dissect speakers' delivery techniques. It would be only natural for us to assume that sources are the most important element of the communication process. In fact, that assumption would be terribly wrong. In my view, the source probably is the least important part of communication; the most important is the receiver. To see why, consider the following two principles:

1. Communication occurs only when someone receives the message.

Philosophers are fond of asking the question, "If a tree falls in the forest and no one is there to hear it, does it make any noise?" While this question is unlikely to generate the most exciting conversation in the world, it does suggest a parallel question relating to communication: "If a message is sent and no one is there to receive it, is there any communication?" The answer clearly is No. We can send messages until we are blue in the face, but if no one receives them, we have not communicated. Therefore, we must have a receiver if we are to communicate.

2. All behavior is potentially communicative.

In a sense, this principle represents the other side of the coin. Just as you must have a receiver to communicate, so it is that any time you have a receiver—any time someone is watching you and interpreting your actions—you are communicating whether you want to or not. Consider a typical business meeting. Sitting around the conference table is a group of executives who are simply trying to stay awake while the speaker drones on. The last thing on their minds, probably, is communicating messages to someone else. Yet if you watch them, their slumped postures, drooping eyelids, and twiddling thumbs give you a very clear message: "I'm bored out of my mind and can hardly wait to leave." While you need not become a raving paranoic, then, you should realize this: anything you do, intentionally or unintentionally, is potentially communicative. If someone is watching, you are communicating; if no one is paying attention to you, then you are not communicating. For this reason, we must conclude that communication is a function of the receiver.

Communication Is Irreversible and Unrepeatable

This principle stems from the concept of change described above. When you say something to someone, it changes him (or her)—his thoughts, his ideas, his feelings toward you or toward others, and so on. When that change has been achieved, the person is slightly different than he was before you spoke. This leads to the dual principle we face here. Communication is irreversible, because once you have spoken, you have changed the receiver. Or once someone has spoken to you, you have changed a little bit, too. There is no way that you or he can be changed back into the exact same person you were or he was before. Communication is also unrepeatable. Because of the continuous change involved in the people who communicate, the participants in communication always are becoming slightly different people. The source who spoke seconds ago is different than the person speaking right now; the receiver hearing the words is slightly changed from the person he or she was moments ago. Because the people are changing, the meanings of the words they send and receive also change. Thus, you cannot repeat communication acts. You can say the same words, but they take on slightly different meanings because the people are a bit different.

Communication Imposes Responsibility

Look at the impact your communication has. You change the people you talk to; you trigger a series of future events. Your influence is tremendous. And that imposes a tremendous responsibility upon you. You have the power to help or harm, to lead or mislead, to improve or destroy. To a large degree, the ultimate impact of your communication is determined by the degree to which you communicate ethically. Ethical communication, I believe, is more likely to yield positive results than is unethical communication. But what is ethical communication in the first place? Frankly, that's difficult to answer, partly because there are so many answers from which to choose. The legal perspective offers the opinion that, if it's legal, it's ethical; the utilitarian perspective holds that anything which does the greatest good for the greatest number of people is ethical; religious perspectives argue that ethical communication is that which conforms to the teachings of various religions. Many people prefer the ontological approach, which suggests that since the thing which makes us uniquely human is our capacity to reason, any communication which hampers our reasoning abilities is unethical. Thus, it would be unethical to give someone false information, incomplete (and thus misleading) information, information misleading him or her about our identity or intentions, and so on—anything that would cause someone to arrive at an erroneous conclusion. I like that perspective, and in accordance with it, I offer you this principle: it is your responsibility as a communicator to provide your receivers with the most complete and accurate information you have so that they can make the best decisions possible.

These, then, are some, although certainly not all, of the important characteristics of communication. Doubtless we will discover others as we analyze communication throughout this book; nevertheless, they need to be kept in mind from the outset.

Although the realm of communication may be subdivided in any number of ways, most theorists seem to feel that oral communication should be distinguished from written, and that oral communication consists of five general types:

Intrapersonal communication, in which an individual communicates with himself or herself, usually by thinking but occasionally aloud.

Interpersonal communication, in which two individuals communicate with each other face to face (as in a job interview or an informal conversation between acquaintances).

Group communication, in which several people meet face to face to discuss whatever matters may be at hand, and in which those people share the source and receiver roles.

Public communication (or public speaking), in which one speaker presents a message to a group of receivers in a face-to-face setting. While the receivers occasionally may adopt the source role, generally the speaker does most or all of the talking.

Mass communication, in which one speaker transmits a message to a group of receivers via some mass medium, such as radio or television. Since the source and receivers are not face to face, the source and receiver roles are not exchanged, and any feedback which is sent by the receivers to the source occurs on a delayed basis (as when, for example, viewers send fan mail to a television personality).

Our concern in this text is public communication. While all of the oral communication forms listed above play important roles in our lives, public speaking holds a particularly prominent place in all elements of society. Educators rely primarily upon public lectures to convey information to students; religious leaders use public sermons to convert and maintain their followers; politicians use public speeches to gain support for themselves and their causes; businesspersons use public presentations to coordinate and promote their ventures. Indeed, no matter what course your life and career may take, you almost certainly will rely upon public speeches to achieve the success you desire. My purpose in this text, then, is to assist you in developing the skills you need to communicate effectively in public speaking situations.

Earlier in this chapter, we examined the elements of human communication. It is worthwhile at this point to review those elements, this time as they occur in public speaking settings. Figure 1-4 illustrates the principles described below.

We already know that communication begins with the source. In public speaking the same principle holds, of course, but several subprinciples demand attention.

1. The source in a public speaking setting is more likely than in other settings to suffer from "communication apprehension" or stagefright. Often, then, our first task as speakers is to gain control of our own thoughts and emotions before we can even begin to think about controlling the thoughts and emotions of our listeners.

2. Since the actions of the source are under close scrutiny by the audience, and since in our society there are some rather strict stereotypes concerning "good" public

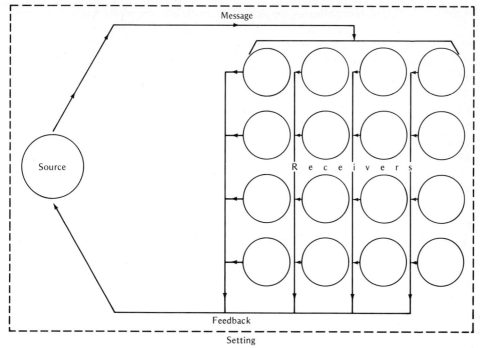

Figure 1-4: A Model of Public Speaking

speakers, the manner in which the source delivers his or her message to the audience is particularly important. Consequently, we will devote considerable attention in this text to the vocal and physical delivery of public speeches.

3. The feelings of the audience toward the speaker are important determinants of their acceptance of the speaker's message. That is, your "credibility" as a speaker in the eyes of a particular audience determines to a large degree the extent to which you will communicate successfully with them. The concept of source credibility thus is a third speaker-related topic we will consider in this text. Again, stagefright, delivery, and credibility are important elements of any communication situation, but they play particularly vital roles in public speaking.

As in all communication forms, public speaking involves receivers. In fact, public speaking typically involves many receivers, and it is this characteristic of public speaking which causes us the most trouble. Our task in giving a speech is to exert influence over our listeners, and in order to exert such influence, our message must be adapted as closely as possible to the beliefs, attitudes, and values those listeners hold. The greater the number of receivers, the more difficult this job becomes. In this respect, then, public speaking may be the most difficult form of communication to perform successfully as it requires us to analyze thoroughly the characteristics of all our receivers. In a later chapter, we will consider in some detail the techniques we can use to analyze audiences.

Communication always occurs in some setting, and this element also influences our capacity to succeed in public speaking. The social, psychological, physical, and historical characteristics of the setting and occasion must be analyzed and responded to if we are to achieve the sorts of results we desire. Again, techniques for the analysis of public speaking settings will be examined in a later chapter.

4. Public speaking involves the message itself—the speech which we present to our audience. Typically, speeches consist of three parts: an *introduction,* which captures the attention of the audience, motivates them to listen, establishes the speaker's credibility, and provides an orientation to the speaker's topic; a *body,* which presents in a carefully organized pattern the main points, subpoints, and specific pieces of information and reasoning which the speaker wants the audience to understand and accept; and a *conclusion,* which summarizes the main ideas of the speech and provides a strong finish to the speaker's remarks. Except in unusual cases, such messages are prepared well in advance of their presentation to the audience, although the speaker may revise the message as he or she presents it in order to respond to the feedback obtained from the audience.

5. Finally, public speaking, like all forms of communication, involves feedback from the receivers. While the speaker is talking, the audience are reacting. By "reading" such nonverbal audience reactions as head nods, eye contact, bodily movements, and so on, the perceptive speaker can gauge listeners' understanding and acceptance of the message and, if necessary, revise that message so that it more closely adapts to the psychological characteristics of the audience. This element of public speaking also will receive our attention in a later chapter.

Clearly, public speaking poses some unique challenges to those of us who would influence others. Successful public speaking depends upon our ability to develop the skills necessary to meet those challenges as we seek to use public speaking to obtain the things we want out of life.

COMMUNICATION BY OBJECTIVES

In recent years, theorists and practitioners in a variety of fields have shown increasing concern for the use of specific objectives as guides and goals for human behavior. Management theorists, for example, have developed "management by objectives," a system whereby supervisors and subordinates cooperatively develop specific, measurable objectives which govern the subordinates' subsequent activities. In education, administrators and teachers have instituted "behavioral objectives" to guide teachers' efforts and assess students' successes. Similarly, "behavior modification" has been developed by psychologists, therapists, and others as a device for achieving specific behavioral change objectives in patients and clients. Indeed, a tremendous number of disciplines have realized that objective-directed activities are more efficient, effective, and productive than are activities engaged with no preset objectives to guide them.

This book applies the objectives approach to communication. Remember the points we saw earlier in this chapter: communication is a tool, it involves responses, it may be unsuccessful or successful, and so on. Communication by objectives (C.B.O.) is based upon these ideas. It holds that the objective of communication is to produce a specific response in the receivers. If you are able to produce that response, you have met your objectives and succeeded; if not, you have failed to some degree. In preparing messages, then, we must ask ourselves two basic questions: "What response do we want?" and "How can we use the tool of communication to get it?" Then we systematically go about constructing appeals aimed toward the achievement of our objective.

Several advantages grow out of the communication-by-objectives approach. First, it treats communication as a process of influence: it recognizes that all participants in communicative acts exert influence over each other and places primary emphasis upon the behaviors which achieve that influence. Second, it views communication as a means, not an end. Too often, people lose sight of the utility of communication, viewing it as an act to be admired for its own sake rather than as a tool to be used to achieve results. Communication by objectives encourages artistry in communication, but artistry with purpose—eliciting desired responses. Third, an objectives-based approach assures systematic preparation. Rather than doing what "feels right," we are required to consider all aspects of the communicative situation and develop strategies which best adapt to them. Finally, communication by objectives guarantees thorough preparation by requiring us to answer specific questions about all elements of the communicative situation as we prepare to deliver the message. For all of these reasons, then, we are going to follow a communication-by-objectives approach.

C.B.O. and Public Speaking

While communication by objectives may be applied to any communication situation, it applies most directly to public communication. We can establish objectives for a meeting, an interview, or a conversation, but the exchange of source-receiver roles which occurs in those settings makes preparation for achievement of our objective rather difficult. In public speaking, however, we control to a maximum extent the flow of communication; thus, we are able to map out and follow a strategy for the achievement of our objectives.

Generally, the objectives we will seek to achieve in our public speeches can be divided into three categories:

1. Informative.   If we seek to provide our listeners with new information, our objective falls into this category. For example, "I want the company's board of directors, when I have finished speaking, to understand the results of the employee opinion surveys which I will present to them" or "I want my department to be able to complete their travel expense reports when I have finished showing them how" are typical instances of informative objectives.

2. Persuasive.   If we seek to change, either in direction or strength, the attitudes or behaviors of our listeners, our objective is persuasive. Examples include: "I want this football team to play with more intensity in the second half than they did in the first, because winning the game depends on it" or "I want this social club to vote for me in the next election" or "I want this congregation to renounce even more strongly the temptations of the world" or "I want this rifle club to change their minds and support gun control." As these examples illustrate, persuasive objectives differ from informative objectives in that they seek to produce a change in the audience.

Informative messages add information; persuasive messages try to intensify listeners' feelings or behaviors or to reverse them.

3. *Entertaining.* Occasionally, we may seek only to provide our listeners with momentary entertainment. We don't want to teach them anything or to change their attitudes or behaviors, we simply want them to have a good time while they listen to us. When a sports star, for example, speaks to some civic group, he or she typically wants only to provide the listeners with some entertainment. That entertainment may, of course, produce more positive feelings in the audience toward a particular sport, team, or player, but such attitude change is only a by-product; the main objective of the speech still is to provide amusement. Often, it is difficult to phrase an entertainment objective more specific than "I want this audience to chuckle or laugh while I tell them stories about my career." Nevertheless, even this general an objective statement causes us to focus on our listeners' responses and assists us in developing effective communication strategies.

In the remainder of this chapter, then, we will examine communication by objectives as it applies to communication in all settings. In subsequent chapters, however, we will apply the C.B.O. principles to the development of our skills in the public speaking situation.

Stages of C.B.O.

As we will apply it to public speaking in this text, communication by objectives consists of five basic stages: setting the main objective, analyzing the audience and situation, setting the primary objectives, setting the secondary objectives, and developing speaking strategies. We will consider each stage in turn.

1. Setting the Main Objective

Your main objective is the thing you want to accomplish with your speech—the specific result your speech is designed to achieve. To set that objective, you need to answer six questions.

Who (do I want to influence)?
What (do I want them to do)?
How (do I want them to do it)?
When (do I want them to do it)?
Where (do I want them to do it)?
Why (do I want them to do it)?

Then, having answered those questions, you use the answers to phrase a single, declarative statement: "I want (*who*) to (*what*), (*how, when, where*) because (*why*)." Consider some examples:

1. "I want my boss to give me a raise by increasing my check by $50 starting next month, here, because I have done a good job and deserve it."

2. "I want the people in this audience to vote for me by writing my name on the ballot on November 7 at their polling place because I'm the best person for the job."

3. "I want this guy to buy this used car by signing this contract now and here because I need the commission to feed my family."

4. "I want my congregation to demonstrate their faith and principles by living a good life, every day and everywhere, because it's the moral, right, religious thing to do."

5. "I want my subordinates to understand their jobs when they start working for me because their success and mine depend upon their abilities to do their jobs."

Each of these examples follows the pattern outlined above. However, some things about them need to be pointed out. First, note that these objectives are set by the speaker. Unlike management by objectives, where supervisors and employees cooperatively set their objectives, communication by objectives involves unilateral objective setting by the source, who takes into account the wishes of the receiver. Each of these examples, then, represents the desire of the speaker, who in turn will try to make that objective the desire of his or her receivers as well. Second, note that each example above does a good job of specifying "who" and "what," although the fourth example ("to demonstrate their faith") is a little unspecific. The "how" sections are good in the first three examples, but very fuzzy in the fourth; "living a good life" needs to be expressed in specific behaviors. The "when" and "where" sections are accounted for adequately—indeed, they may even be unnecessary in some instances. But better to put "here and now" when they could just as well be assumed than to take a chance of omitting them when they should be analyzed. Finally, the "why" sections are noteworthy. Even though each example gives only one "because," most situations will have several: "because I deserve it"; "because I want the money"; "because I want to make more than my brother"; and so on. You should list every "why" you can think of. But notice also that the "why" in the third example is probably not going to be considered a good reason by the receiver, while the reasons given in the other four probably would be accepted. One thing you will have to do is decide which "why" statements you will present to your receivers and which you will keep to yourself. And lastly, note that many of the "whys" will need proof. "I've done a good job," "I'm the best person," and so on are things which will have to be proven to your receivers if they are to respond in the way you wish.

From the considerations above, we can infer several characteristics of good objective statements.

1. *Good statements are specific.* They state who, what, how, where and why in exact, precise times. Granted, in some cases you'll have to settle for "this audience" rather than "my boss" or "feel more positively toward . . ." instead of "vote

Who? _____

What? _____

Where? _____

When? _____

How? _____

Why? _____

I want _____ to _____ .

_____ because _____ .

Figure 1-5: To Set Your Speech Objective, Fill In the Blanks

for . . ." or "as soon as possible" rather than "at 3:00 tomorrow afternoon," but as a rule, the more specific you can make your statement, the better it will be.

2. Good statements are attainable. They are realistic, achievable responses that can be elicited from the audience. "I want them to overthrow the federal government this afternoon . . ." is asking a little too much of your audience; I want them to understand the value and methods of civil disobedience . . ." is a bit more realistic.

3. Good statements are worthwhile. Really, this relates to the preceding principle. Your objective should be attainable, but not trivial. I once delivered a speech in a public speaking class on "How to Cure Your Hiccups." Had I used the C.B.O. approach (and I didn't because I hadn't thought of it yet), my objective might have been: "I want my classmates to go forth and cure their own hiccups by holding their breath, blowing into a paper bag, or scaring themselves when and where the need arises because hiccups are painful and socially unacceptable." Terrible. I deserved that D−. A good objective is one that is worth attaining, and one which requires some effort and skill on your part to accomplish.

4. Good statements are appropriate. They fit the interests and capabilities of your audience, they fit the occasion, and they fit you as a speaker. Imagine an after-dinner speech in which a linebacker for the Packers is asked to talk to a meeting of the United Mine Workers. If he selects as his objective, "I want them to learn how to drive a car defensively," he'll probably fail—that's not what this group wants this speaker to talk about, nor is it something they are likely to run right out and do. In fact, they are more likely to become hostile out of disappointment and resentment. So when you phrase an objective, keep it relevant to the audience, occasion, and yourself.

5. *Good statements are measurable.* This is the most difficult thing to achieve. Ideally, you should be able to observe the audience's responses. Do they vote for you, or don't they? Do they sign the petition you pass around, or do they tear it up? Do they give blood in the back of the room, or do they leap out of the window to avoid it? However, some things we simply cannot observe: understanding, interest, attitude change, learning, and so on. Nevertheless, the principle remains: try to phrase a measurable, observable, immediate response—something that you can use to gauge the success of your message. As we shall see in later chapters, a good "action" step in your speech will be of great assistance here.

Your first task in communicating by objectives, then, is to phrase a declarative statement of objective that states who, what, how, when, where, and why in a specific, attainable, worthwhile, appropriate, measurable fashion.

2. Analyzing the Audience and Situation

Once you have set your objective, you next need to know what you are up against—what stands between you and success. Basically, your audience determine whether you succeed or fail. But we must become more specific than that. There are characteristics of your audience which you may have to overcome, and there may be other characteristics which you can use to your advantage. Therefore, you must look at their interests, motives, knowledge, attitudes, and values to answer the question, "What must I accomplish with them to achieve my objective?" In Chapter 2, we will examine some ways of both inferring and measuring these audience characteristics.

3. Setting the Primary Objectives

When you analyze your audience, you will discover particular things about them which must be changed if you are to achieve your objective. Perhaps they are apathetic about your topic, and must be made interested; perhaps they are ignorant about your topic and must be informed; perhaps they have no confidence in you and must be convinced of your credibility; perhaps they disagree with your viewpoint and must be convinced that your ideas are correct. In effect, the answers to the question, "What must I accomplish with them to achieve my objective?", themselves become objectives which must be achieved if success is to follow. Through audience analysis, then, you set one or more "primary objectives," which, when achieved, almost automatically guarantee the achievement of your main objective.

4. Setting the Secondary Objectives

To achieve your primary objectives, you will have to accomplish certain things. Establishing credibility, for example, requires achievement of several specific subobjectives (such as demonstrating competence, trustworthiness, or good will). Giving the audience "good" reasons requires that other subobjectives (such as establishing deductive or inductive relationships) be accomplished. At this point, then, you have set the very specific objectives, which lead to achievement of the primary objectives, which lead to achievement of the main objective.

5. Developing Speaking Strategies

You know what must be done; now, how do you do it? Basically, you develop communication strategies to achieve your secondary objectives. Really, this stage comprises the heart of this book, as we seek the strategies which will initiate the chain of objective achievements which lead to our ultimate success. Aristotle, the Greek philosopher generally considered the originator of the field of rhetoric (the study of human communication), defined rhetoric as "finding all the available means of persuasion." That is what strategy development is all about—finding all the available means for achieving your secondary objectives, and hence your primary objectives, and hence your main objective.

THE PLAN OF THIS BOOK

In my view, public speeches involve three steps: *preparation* prior to speaking, *presentation* of the speech itself, and *preservation* of the positive impact which the speech had. The body of this book similarly is divided into these three steps, although their sequence has been altered. After examining audience and situational analysis (so that we can establish our primary objectives), we will consider first the objectives, both primary and secondary, you must accomplish in your presentation (and, of course, the strategies you might use to accomplish them). It seems likely that you will have to deliver a speech before you have had an opportunity to complete this entire book; consequently, we will discuss the presentational elements of speaking first. Second, we will examine the preparation stage, studying the primary objectives, secondary objectives, and speaking strategies applicable to both informative and persuasive main objectives. Finally, we will devote attention to the preservation stage: we will consider the question-and-answer session that typically follows a public speech and develop objectives and strategies through which that session can be used to preserve—indeed, to enhance—the positive impact of the speech itself.

SUMMARY

This chapter was intended to do several things. First, it sought to impress upon you the importance of communication. You should now realize that while we communicate almost all of our lives, we often do so in ways which produce results we may not want. You should also realize that by learning to communicate effectively, you can do much to achieve personal happiness and professional success. That is what this book is all about.

Second, this chapter sought to give you an understanding of the communication process by acquainting you with various definitions of communication (and their implications), models of communication, and characteristics of communication. More specifically, it was designed to help you understand the nature of public speaking—the type of communication with which this text is concerned.

Finally, this chapter attempted to explain communication by objectives, a pragmatic approach to using the tool of communication. We examined the five steps making up C.B.O., with special attention to the first step, setting the main objective.

We now are ready to begin working toward achievement of the main objectives we establish.

REFERENCES

Baird, A. and F. Knower. *Essentials of General Speech.* New York: McGraw-Hill, 1968.

Baird, J. *The Dynamics of Organizational Communication.* New York: Harper & Row, 1977.

Cherry, C. *On Human Communication.* Cambridge, Mass.: The M.I.T. Press, 1966.

Dance, F. "The 'Concept' of Communication," *Journal of Communication* 20(1970):201–210.

Fausti, R. and E. McGlone. *Understanding Oral Communication.* Menlo Park, Calif.: Cummings, 1972.

Gerbner, G. "On Defining Communication: Still Another View," *Journal of Communication* 16(1966):99.

Goyer, C. "Communication, Communicative Process, Meaning: Toward a Unified Theory," *Journal of Communication* 20(1970):8.

Lasswell, H. "The Structure and Function of Communication in Society," in *The Communication of Ideas,* ed. Lyman Bryson, p. 37. New York: Harper & Row, 1948.

Miller, G. "On Defining Communication: Another Stab," *Journal of Communication* 16(1966):88–98.

Mortensen, C. *Communication.* New York: McGraw-Hill, 1972.

Ross, R. *Speech Communication: Fundamentals and Practice.* Englewood Cliffs, N.J.: Prentice-Hall, 1977.

Smith, A., ed. *Communication and Culture.* New York: Holt, Rinehart and Winston, 1966.

Zelko, R. and F. Dance. *Business and Professional Speech Communication.* New York: Holt, Rinehart and Winston, 1965.

SUPPLEMENT

YOUR FIRST SPEECH

Probably you have seen someone deliver a speech some time during your life. Thus, you probably have at least some idea of what a "speech" is. Still, the steps through which you should proceed as you prepare and present a speech may still be a bit of a mystery to you. In this brief supplement, then, we will look at some of the things you should do as you prepare to give your first speech.

Preparing

1. Choose your topic. Select something that interests you and, if possible, your audience and that can be covered in the time allowed for your speech. Be sure, too, that the topic is appropriate to the setting and the occasion and that you either know something about the topic already or can find enough information about it to present an intelligent speech.
2. Analyze your audience. Try to judge how much your audience are likely to know about your topic and what attitudes relevant to your topic they are likely to hold. Also, try to determine what things relevant to your topic might interest your audience most. These judgments will help you to establish the things you must accomplish and the things you can use in order to give an effective speech.
3. Choose your purpose. Decide what you want to accomplish in your speech. Do you simply want to give your audience new information? Do you want to change their attitudes? Do you want to convince them to do something? Do you want to entertain them? Perhaps you want to do all of these things. In any event, you must set an objective or purpose for yourself as you prepare the speech.
4. Gather information. Through consideration of your own knowledge and experience and through research in the library, get the facts you need to present an informed speech.
5. Organize your material. Subdivide your topic into three or four main categories or ideas. Subdivide those subdivisions into two or three supporting ideas. Then use your factual materials to support or illustrate those specific ideas. Through this process, you will have developed a brief outline for your speech and, simultaneously, a set of notes you can use while speaking. For example:

GUN CONTROL
  I. The crime rate is high.
    A. Rate has increased during the past ten years.
      1. (Quotation from *Time*)
    B. Crimes of personal violence have increased even faster.
      1. (Quotation from *Time*)

II. Guns are used in most violent crimes.
   A. Murders and robberies typically involve guns.
   B. Guns are easier to use because they require less physical effort.
      1. (Quotation from *Psychology Today*)
III. Guns control should be instituted.
   A. Guns are not effective self-protection.
      1. (Quotation from *Newsweek*)
   B. Gun legislation is constitutional.
      1. (Quotation from the Second Amendment)
   C. Gun control would reduce crime.

6. Prepare an introduction. Develop an opening statement that gets attention, arouses interest, demonstrates your knowledge of or experience with the topic, and then leads into the body of the speech.
7. Prepare a conclusion. Develop a statement that reviews the main points you have covered and then tells the audience what they should believe or do. Like the introduction, the conclusion should be dramatic and motivating.

Presenting

1. Realize that some nervousness is natural. All speakers experience nervousness before they talk. Concentrate on rehearsing your speech mentally while you wait to speak.
2. When called upon, walk confidently to the front of the room, turn and look at your audience for a moment, and then begin to speak. Be deliberate as you begin; don't rush things.
3. While speaking, look at your audience as much as possible and at your notes as little as possible.
4. Be as active as you can while you talk, moving around the front of the room and using as many gestures as you can.
5. Be as varied as you can, making a conscious effort to vary your voice and gestures as much as possible.
6. Be as conversational as you can. Speak as though you were telling a story to a group of friends. In effect, be as natural as possible.
7. When you finish, again look at your audience for a brief moment after you have finished, and then walk deliberately to your seat.

Possible Topics for the First Speech

How should America cope with the energy shortage?
How might the American system of electing national officials be improved?
How might the country's crime rate be reduced?
How might the American legal system be made more fair?
How might public education be improved?
How might the plight of American cities be improved?

ASSIGNMENT: THE TWO-POINT SPEECH

Choose one of the topics listed above, or develop a topic of your own. Then decide what your purpose in the speech will be: to persuade, to inform, or to entertain. Third, subdivide your topic into two subpoints or arguments, and then gather a little information that either demonstrates the points or proves the arguments. Organize the information for each subpoint into some sensible pattern and then develop a very brief introduction and conclusion. When presented, the entire speech should last approximately three minutes.

On the form that appears on the next page, fill in (in outline form) the materials you have developed for your speech. You will be asked to complete this form for every assignment you complete throughout this text.

Name _____

Date _____

Speech Type _____

Speech Outline, Project Number _____

Speech Topic: _____

Speech Objective: _____

_____

Speech Title: _____

Introduction

    Attention:

    Motivation:

    Credibility:

      Preview

        Body

        Conclusion

Instructor's Comments:

CHAPTER 2
ANALYZING THE AUDIENCE AND SITUATION

CHAPTER OBJECTIVES

After studying this chapter, you should be able to:

- List the ways in which people can respond to proposed changes
- Explain the nature of "interests" that listeners have
- Explain the nature of "beliefs" that listeners have
- Explain the nature of "attitudes" that listeners have
- Explain the nature of "values" that listeners have
- Explain the nature of "needs" that listeners have
- Explain the interrelationships among interests, beliefs, attitudes, values, and needs
- List some speech factors that should be adjusted based upon audience analysis
- List relevant audience characteristics and the conclusions which those characteristics imply in audience analysis
- Construct dichotomous audience analysis measures
- Construct rank/order audience analysis measures
- Construct Likert-type audience analysis measures
- Construct Semantic Differential audience analysis measures
- Develop primary objectives to be accomplished during a speech

INTRODUCTION

When we communicate by objectives, our general goal is to have some impact upon our receivers. When we have finished speaking to them, we want them to possess new information or to hold different attitudes or to perform new or different behaviors. However, when we try to have an impact on people, they can react in any of five ways:

1. Rejection. The audience can simply reject what we say to them, perhaps even turn against us in the process. Obviously, we should avoid this response.

2. Resistance. Although not as severe as rejection, this response still is undesirable. Our listeners may learn our information or perform the behaviors we request, but only with a great deal of hesitancy and resentment.

3. Toleration. Receivers, seeing no reason to actively oppose us, also may see no real reason to support us. Thus, they may decide simply to humor us, going along with our statements or requests but making no strenuous effort to adopt our viewpoints. In fact, when they get out of our sight, they might well "forget" everything we told them.

4. Acceptance. If what we say makes sense, and if our listeners like what they hear, they may accept our ideas and suggestions. Often this acceptance is only on a trial basis, as receivers sometimes need time to evaluate or try out our ideas. Nevertheless, we do have some impact upon them, at least for a while.

5. Promotion. If we are really successful, either through skill, luck, or divine intervention, this is the result we will achieve. Our receivers will not only accept what we say, they will become disciples who scurry about trying to get other people to accept it as well. You can see this sort of thing happen all the time: the religious convert who becomes an active minister, the former smoker who now drives other smokers berserk by trying to get them to stop smoking, or the weight watcher/jogger who scrutinizes the eating habits of others and tells them stories about the joys of jogging and his last five 20-mile runs. This type of response is our ultimate goal—to communicate so effectively that our receivers themselves become advocates of our viewpoints.

But how can we accomplish this? How can we get people to accept and even promote the things we propose? The key to answering that question is supplied by Blake and Mouton (1970) and, even earlier, by Kurt Lewin (1947). All of them suggest that we must, at the very beginning of our preparations, determine four things:

1. How do we want things to be? That is, when our speech is concluded, what state of affairs should exist? Obviously, we answer that question automatically by phrasing our statement of objective.
2. How are things now? How does the present situation differ from the situation which we want to exist? In later sections of this chapter, we will examine methods for answering this question rather precisely. Still, when you phrase your objective statement, you should do so with the knowledge that currently things are different from what you want them to be. Otherwise, why try to accomplish your objective in the first place?
3. What forces oppose or resist your desired state of affairs? For example, what things might keep the audience from learning the information you have to offer, or what things might keep them from doing the things you request? You need to determine what you are up against—what obstacles you must

overcome—if you are to succeed. In fact, you need to go a step further and decide how strong each of those obstacles is. After all, you ultimately will have to set some priorities as you prepare to present your viewpoints, and those priorities should reflect the relative strength of the opposing forces: the strongest force should get the most attention, the second strongest the second most, and so on.

4. What forces favor or drive toward your desired state of affairs? What things might help the audience learn your information or accept your suggestions? Certainly, you need to know what things exist which might work to your advantage.

Figure 2-1 illustrates all four of these things—the present situation, the desired situation, driving forces, and resisting forces. When the combined strength of the driving forces and of the resisting forces are equal, the present situation will remain the same. Therefore, to achieve the desired state of affairs (and, hence, to achieve our objective), we must either increase the number or strength of the driving forces, or we must decrease the number of strength of the resisting forces. The middle and lower charts in Figure 2-1 illustrate these principles.

We arrive, then, at this realization: in order to achieve our objective, we must analyze thoroughly the audience we will face so that we can adapt to the driving and resisting forces they hold. But as we consider audience analysis here, note one important thing: the purpose of audience analysis is not to enable you to find out what they want to hear so that you then can give it to them. Some politicians do precisely that. They conduct opinion polls to find out what you like, and then, hoping that ultimately you'll like and vote for them, they tell you that they like it too. Well, let the politicians sell out; we're not in that business. Rather, our use of audience analysis is to discover the driving and resisting forces relevant to our objective—to determine the things we can appeal to and the things we have to work against if we are to convince the audience to change. With this in mind, then, we turn to our consideration of the nature of audiences.

WHAT ARE WE LOOKING FOR?

Before you begin analyzing an audience, it helps to know what you are looking for when you analyze them. Although later in this chapter we will see a host of audience characteristics that concern us, the whole process of audience analysis really boils down to determining six things about the audience: their interests, their beliefs, their attitudes, their values, their needs, and the interrelationships among these things. Let's examine each of those factors for a moment.

Interests

Your first concern must be the question, What things, in general, do my listeners find interesting? Answering this question correctly is crucial. If you misjudge their interests, you may well deliver a speech they find incredibly irrelevant and boring. And if that happens, then no matter how well organized, carefully prepared, and dynamically delivered it is, the speech will fail.

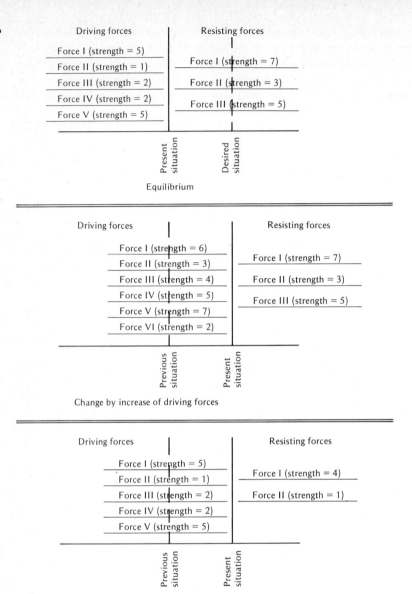

Figure 2-1: Analyzing Audience Change Forces

We can divide audience interests into three categories. Central interests are those things with which audience are actively involved–things related to their profession, their home life, their community activities, and so on. In essence, these are things which are very important to the audience because they directly affect their personal lives. If you can discover these central interests, you have a powerful tool for maintaining the attention of the audience. If you cannot locate central interests, how-

ever, then you must look for *peripheral interests,* or things that are still important to
the audience but do not impact their lives directly. Many forms of entertainment fall
into this category: people are interested in movies and football games, even though
they do not actually act or play the game. Granted, their interest in these matters is
less powerful than their concern for their jobs, their physical well-being, and other
types of central interests, but they still will devote their attention to a discussion of
these peripheral matters.

If central and peripheral interests cannot be discovered in a particular audience,
perhaps because the people comprising that audience are extremely diverse, we have
to resort to a third interest type, *momentary interests.* What things might be on your
audience members' minds at the moment? What devices (figures of speech, visual
aids, stories, jokes, and so on) can you introduce to get their attention? What reasons
brought your audience here in the first place? What events affecting your audience
occurred during the past 24 hours? All of these things are only of temporary
importance or interest to your audience, probably, but they still serve to maintain audience attention while you talk. In a later chapter, we will look in detail
at some devices you can use to maintain audience attention by creating momentary
interests.

Beliefs

Beliefs are held by everyone. For example, we may believe that the world is round,
that the sun will rise tomorrow, that the South will rise again, and that the 1962 Mets
were the greatest baseball team ever. As these examples illustrate, beliefs primarily
are judgments about matters of fact—of truth or falsity. One judges the existence or
nonexistence of something, the relationship among two or more things, or the characteristics of something. Thus, such objectively verifiable statements as "A man is
standing in front of me," "He is holding a gun," "He is pointing it at me," "He wants
my money," and "This is a stick-up" are all belief statements, but so are statements of
"fact" which are much less verifiable: "Life exists on other planets," "The future of
the stock market lies in sow belly futures," "An earthquake will soon make Reno,
Nevada, an oceanside resort," and so on.

Rokeach (1968) and Bem (1970) suggest that beliefs may be put into three
general categories. *Central* beliefs, which are of extreme strength and importance to
the individual, are in the first category. We learn most of these beliefs early in life,
although we continue to validate them throughout our existence. Rokeach also points
out that these beliefs may be generally accepted ("The world is round" or "What
goes up must come down") or relatively individualistic ("God controls my life" or
"Walking under ladders brings bad luck"). In either case, the belief is central to the
individual's belief system.

Beliefs connected with some *authority* comprise the second category. Generally, we learn that certain people are trustworthy, while certain others should not be
trusted. Thus, when our boss (whom we have come to trust completely) tells us that
there is a wage freeze in effect so that no one will get a raise for the next six months,
we believe her. And when the person in the office next to ours tells us that the
president's son-in-law just received a large salary increase, we naturally do not
believe him. Such beliefs, although held less firmly and persistently than central
beliefs, are important to us and resistant to attempts by other people to change them.

The least powerful set of beliefs are those which are *peripheral*. Our feeling that the 1962 Mets were the greatest team ever might be one such belief, as would be the belief that men look best with short hair or that the best entertainment is Saturday morning cartoon shows. Sometimes, these beliefs stem from our central beliefs, as when our feeling that smoking is bad grows from our belief that doing anything to harm our bodies is immoral. Often, however, peripheral beliefs seem simply to be a matter of taste not based on any central or authority belief.

Our division of beliefs into these three types allows the formulation of some general principles relevant to public speaking by objectives. First, the more central a belief is, the more difficult it is to change. Thus, we probably would have greater success trying to change a peripheral belief rather than a central or authority-based one. Second, beliefs based on central beliefs are more difficult to change than are those which exist in isolation. This principle, in turn, is related to a third, that the more central a belief is, the more widespread changes in the entire belief structure will be when the original belief is changed. Changes of isolated peripheral beliefs thus are easily accomplished but confined in their effects, while changes of central beliefs are more difficult to achieve but more wide sweeping in their effects. Finally, as we already have seen, beliefs usually are interrelated, so that changes in one often are accompanied by changes, intended or unintended, in others. This becomes a problem when we are concerned with persuasion: we might, by changing some belief, produce secondary changes which may be detrimental to our main objective. We must therefore take care when we select the audience beliefs about which we will speak.

Beliefs also impact behavior. As we shall see later in this section, our beliefs cause us to anticipate certain consequences based upon our behaviors; that is, if we do *X*, we can expect *Y* to occur. To a large degree, this sort of reasoning forms the basis of all motivational strategies we might use when speaking. We must make our listeners believe that if they listen to, remember, and act upon the information we give them, they will be able to obtain certain desirable consequences. Thus, we again see the importance of determining initial audience beliefs before beginning to plan our primary and secondary speaking objectives and strategies.

Attitudes

It is difficult to define specifically what attitudes are, as can be seen when we examine some of the more prominent definitions which theorists have offered. Allport (1935) suggested that an attitude is "A mental and neural state of readiness, organized through experience, exerting a directive or dynamic influence upon the individual's response to all objects and situations with which it is related." Krech and Crutchfield (1948) don't help matters much when they define attitudes as "an enduring organization of motivational, emotional, perceptual, and cognitive processes with respect to some aspect of the individual's world." Basically, they all are saying that an attitude is how we feel about something—whether we are for it or against it, like it or dislike it, and so on. Thus, our attitude system may be such that we like (have a positive attitude toward) baseball, apple pie, motherhood, highway safety, and the flag and dislike (have a negative attitude toward) communists, perverts, left-wing radicals, and the New York Yankees.

We Need to Know Listeners' Attitudes Toward Each Other

Allport and Krech and Crutchfield list several important characteristics of at-titudes. First, they have an object. That is, they are tied to something we know about. We feel positively toward something, probably because of a set of beliefs we have about it (for example, we like to play tennis because we believe it keeps us in shape), or we dislike something because we have a different set of beliefs about it (we don't like smoking because we believe it causes cancer). For our purposes, there are three attitude objects we need to be concerned with: attitudes toward us as speakers, attitudes toward our topic or point of view, and attitudes toward the audience them-selves. If the audience dislike us, we have to find ways of changing that attitude; if they like us, we need to capitalize on that feeling. If they like our topic or favor our viewpoint, we can concentrate on getting them to do something about it; if they dislike or disagree with our topic or viewpoint, we first have to change their minds. And finally, while their attitudes toward themselves probably are positive, we still must take them into account in constructing our message.

Second, attitudes have direction, degree, and commitment. Direction indicates whether the attitude is positive or negative; degree considers *how* positive or negative the attitude is; commitment determines how firm the attitude is, or how likely it is to change. Obviously, we need to consider all three of these things when analyzing the audience, because they determine the amount of time and effort we need to spend in dealing with their attitudes toward us, our topic, or themselves.

Third, attitudes, like beliefs, are learned. We are not born with attitudes toward motherhood, highway safety, or the Yankees; rather, we acquire them through direct or indirect experience with the objects of our attitudes. If, on repeated occasions, we are bitten by small dogs, we will develop a negative attitude toward them. Or, if a friend repeatedly is bitten and tells us about it, we again will probably develop a negative attitude toward small dogs. Or, if we read in the newspaper that all members of the Yankees were bitten by small dogs, we might decide that dogs aren't so bad, after all. Our communication with other people, then, serves to provide us with many of the attitudes we presently hold. And by the same token, our messages to other people can create or change attitudes within them.

Values

Another general audience characteristic we need to consider is the audience's value system. According to Minnick (1957), a value is an "explicit or implicit concept of acceptable behavior by which an individual chooses from available means and ends of action." Our value system, then, tells us what is moral, right, just, or desirable.

Rokeach (1968) suggests that we have three types of values. First, *core values* are those so central to our belief system that to change one of them would amount to a fundamental alteration of our very self-concept. Most people in our culture, for example, hold human life dear, value good over evil, and think that the democratic form of government is the most desirable of all available alternatives. Change in these values, particularly the first two, would be extremely difficult. *Authority values*, secondly, are based upon the reference groups and individuals who influence us. American businesses value the free-enterprise system, profits, and progress; teenage gang members value proficiency in fighting, avoiding arrest, and taking risks. Such values are considerably easier to change than are core values. Third, *peripheral values* are more or less incidental beliefs that we happen to hold at the moment. Americans typically believe that bigger is better, that things sounding scientific are desirable, and that it's nice to be generous. But in a specific situation, these values can be set aside or changed rather easily. Our task in audience analysis, then, is to locate and work within core values of the audience and to specify so that we can either adapt to or change their authority and peripheral values.

German scholar Eduard Spranger developed a theory of human behavior in which he maintained that there are six primary types of people, and he labeled these types according to their dominant values (Spranger, 1928). Using his system, we can construct a value system that, although by no means complete, seems to represent the sorts of values to which many Americans adhere. Note that my purpose here is not to provide you with the definitive picture of the American value system; rather, it is to show you the sorts of things that comprise the values people hold.

1. Thought-related values
   a. Americans respect the scientific method and things labeled scientific.
   b. Americans want to be reasonable and rational and to get all the facts.
   c. Americans prefer quantitative rather than qualitative methods of evaluation.
   d. Americans respect common sense.
2. Economic values
   a. Americans measure success primarily by economic standards.
   b. Americans value efficiency—anything that does more in less time with less effort.
   c. Americans think one should be thrifty and save in order to get ahead.
   d. Americans believe competition is basic to economic life.
   e. Americans distrust big business in general.

3. Aesthetic values
   a. Americans prefer the useful arts: landscaping, automobile design, and so on.
   b. Americans prefer physical activities to art, music, or literature.
   c. Americans value neatness and cleanliness.
   d. Americans stress good grooming and appearance.
4. Social values
   a. Americans value honesty, sincerity, kindness, friendliness, and generosity.
   b. Americans admire fairness and justice.
   c. Americans admire dependability, ambition, and people who treat others as equals.
   d. Americans admire the wisdom of the common man.
5. Political values
   a. Americans prize loyalty to community, state, and nation.
   b. Americans believe democracy to be the best possible form of government.
   c. Americans value the individual above the state.
   d. Americans believe that government ownership generally is undesirable.
   e. Americans dislike political corruption but think it inevitable.
6. Religious values
   a. Americans value Christianity above other religions.
   b. Americans think there is life after death.
   c. Americans believe there is a God who created and watches after the universe.
   d. Americans think one should belong to and support a church.

It is true, of course, that not all Americans adhere to all of these values and that all of us hold a multitude of values not present in this list. Also, this system is culture bound; other cultures and peoples have very different value systems. Nevertheless, generally these values are representative of the "Great American Value System," and they illustrate the sorts of things which you should examine in your audiences.

Needs

A somewhat different component of our listeners is the set of needs each of them has. These needs, also called motives or drives, are internal forces which produce external behaviors designed to satisfy, or at least to reduce, them. Typically, needs are divided into two types: *primary* or physiological needs and *secondary* or sociopsychological needs. Primary needs involve things necessary for survival, including the needs for water, food, air, sleep, and proper temperature. These needs are universal although they vary from person to person in intensity. Secondary needs are more difficult to specify, and we will consider them in more detail below. At this point, we will note only that they are learned through interaction with others, vary widely across people and situations, operate in interacting sets rather than individually, involve vague feelings rather than physical sensations, and often remain below our level of con-

Figure 2-2: Maslow's Hierarchy of Needs

sciousness. They affect our behavior profoundly, however, and thus must be understood to some degree if we are to communicate successfully with others.

While a great number of need-related theories exist, one of the most widely accepted is the one developed by Abraham Maslow (1943; 1954). In his opinion, we have five basic needs: (1) physiological, (2) safety and security, (3) social, (4) esteem, and (5) self-actualization. Moreover, these needs are arranged in a hierarchy so that only when the needs at one level are satisfied do our needs at the next level become activated. Figure 2-2 illustrates Maslow's need hierarchy.

At the base of the hierarchy lie physiological needs, which correspond to the primary or survival needs we described above. As their position in the hierarchy indicates, these needs are our first concern: only when our drives for food, water, air, proper temperature, and so on are satisfied will we become concerned about needs on the next level. On the second level, our needs for safety and security cause us to see that our physical well-being not be threatened and that the future be relatively predictable. Health insurance companies, the Social Security administration, and unemployment programs all exist in response to (and perhaps capitalize upon) our safety and security needs. When we feel safe and secure, our next concern becomes our social needs. On this third level, we seek inclusion by others, affection from them, and some degree of control or dominance over them. Again, these needs vary from one person to the next. Some of us have relatively little need to control other people, for example, while others feel their need is satisfied only when they have become little (or in some cases, big) dictators. Nevertheless, all of us have these needs to some degree, and all of us strive to satisfy them before moving up to the next need level. On level four, we confront our need for esteem. Actually, this need can be divided into two subneeds: the need for esteem from others and the need to think well of ourselves. Certainly, these two are related. We think well of ourselves only if we get positive responses from others, and we are better able to get esteem from others if we first think well of ourselves. Finally, when all four of the preceding levels have been satisfied, we move to the fifth and highest level, self-actualization. This need is the desire to become all we are capable of becoming—to fulfill our potential. Since we usually are kept busy trying to satisfy needs on lower levels, we rarely encounter this

fifth need. Nevertheless, such behaviors as serving others more than self, completing
some task simply for the satisfaction it provides, or reading just to improve ourselves
are manifestations of this level of motivation.

The important aspect of our internal needs is that they cause us to behave. We
actively try to satisfy those internal needs which continually drive us on. So our needs
serve to make us do something. *What* we do, however, seems to be a function of our
beliefs, attitudes, and values. We know that we must do something to make our
drives quiet down, and in deciding what to do we consult those other three systems.
For example, imagine our need for food was acting up so that we felt hunger. Our
beliefs tell us that eating something will make hunger go away, if only temporarily.
Our attitudes tell us that we would rather eat some things than others. And our values
tell us that we should acquire our own food rather than steal, borrow, or beg for it.
Thus, we stagger into the nearest McDonald's (where, we believe, food might be
found), order a burger and fries (which we prefer over a fish sandwich), pay for it
(which is consistent with our value system), and then gobble it in the parking lot
(because we have no beliefs, attitudes, or values concerning table manners). Our
needs, beliefs, attitudes, and values thus serve to stimulate and steer the behaviors in
which we engage.

Interrelationships

Although a belief, attitude, value, or need may exist in isolation, independent of all
other components of one's psychological system, usually it is part of a complex
system of interrelated beliefs, attitudes, and so on. In our McDonald's example, for
instance, our choices and behaviors would be determined by a whole set of beliefs
(concerning where we can get what foods, which foods are good for us, and so on),
attitudes (concerning McDonald's as a company, the prices they charge, everything
on their menu, and so on), and values (concerning whether we should eat or try to
diet and meet society's "slimness" ideal or whether we should spend money on this
food or save it and make our own hamburgers). Similarly, virtually every situation
involves many interconnected cognitive components. Thus, our understanding of the
characteristics of the people in our audiences would be incomplete if we did not
consider the interrelationships among those cognitive elements.

A great number of theories have been developed to describe and explain these
interrelationships. Termed *cognitive consistency* theories, they include the "Balance"
theory (Heider, 1946), "Symmetry" theory (Newcomb, 1953), "Congruity" theory
(Osgood, Suci, and Tannenbaum, 1957), and "Cognitive Dissonance" theory (Festinger, 1957). In their various forms, however, all these theories operate on one basic
assumption: that we strive to maintain consistency among our beliefs, attitudes, values, and behaviors (McGuire, 1966). From this assumption grow two additional
principles: (1) if we discover inconsistency, we experience psychological discomfort,
and (2) this discomfort motivates us to reestablish consistency. Although we will
consider in more detail the utility of these principles, at this point we simply should
note that, because they influence audience behaviors, these interrelationships are
important elements of audience psychology which we should consider as we analyze
our listeners.

We have noted that, in analyzing our audience, we are studying their interests, beliefs, attitudes, needs, and values, and the interrelationships among these factors. We also have a general idea of why we study these things: so that we can determine what must be accomplished in order to achieve our main objective. But we need to become more specific and to isolate the things which we should adjust in our speeches based on what we discover about our listeners. Basically, those things include the following:

1. The Topic.   Perhaps you already have selected your topic since it is easier to formulate a main objective statement when you have a topic in mind. But perhaps you have not, or perhaps you still need to identify specific subtopics which will comprise your message. Since the audience should be a central consideration in your topic choice, you should have delayed formulating a topic until now.

When you speak, you either will have a choice of what to talk about, or you will be assigned a topic. But even in the latter situation, you will have some latitude in deciding what specific things you are going to say. When you are making your selections, you should consider three things.

First and foremost, consider yourself—your interests, motives, knowledge, attitudes, and values. Your topics and subtopics *must* fit these things if you are to communicate ethically and successfully. But this should be no problem, right? After all, who knows better than you the things you are interested in, motivated toward, knowledgeable about, concerned about, or devoted to? Still, people often have a difficult time choosing a general speech topic. Thus, in Table 2-1 are listed a variety of topic areas that may serve as actual speech topics or may simply stimulate your thinking as you search for a topic. Be sure, though, that you choose something you want to talk about. Then worry about the next couple of considerations.

The second thing you should keep in mind when choosing your topic is the audience. Usually, it is best to choose a topic in which they are interested and about which they already know something but would like to learn more. Again, you should not "sell out" to the audience by choosing a topic which you know they will like (even though it is unimportant or distasteful to you) or in which you can tell them what you think they want to hear (regardless of your own attitudes). But it should be as appropriate as possible to the five audience characteristics we considered earlier.

Third, your topic should fit all elements of the setting. It should fit *audience expectations,* or at least take them into account in some way. It should fit any *time limits* which have been imposed ("The History of Western Philosophy" would hardly be an appropriate five-minute speech). It should fit *your purpose* in speaking as expressed by your objective statement. It should fit the *occasion* if some special occasion has brought this audience and you together. And it should fit the *setting* if the speech occurs in some special place (for example, the topic you discuss in a church might differ from the topic you cover in a business boardroom).

In effect, we have isolated the criteria for a good speech topic. It is *appropriate* to the speaker, audience, and setting. It is *significant* as we saw when we considered

TABLE 2-1   POTENTIAL SPEECH TOPIC AREAS

POLITICS

Who should (should not) have the right to vote?
Who is (are) the best candidate(s) for the next election?
How should the electoral process be changed?
What powers of the president (Congress) should be curtailed?
What was the strangest election in history?

THE LAW

What are the strangest laws on the books?
What laws should be changed?
What tax breaks are legally available to everyone?
How might the crime rate be reduced?
How has the role of the policeman changed through history?

EDUCATION

How should elementary (secondary, college) education be improved?
What are the drawbacks of being a teacher?
How can public support for education be increased?
How has education in America changed in history?
What are the drawbacks of being a student?

RELIGION

What relationship should exist between church and state?
What do the world's major religions have in common?
What religious beliefs do you hold, and why?
Is religion really the "opiate of the masses"?
Are religious "cults" good, bad, or neutral?

ENTERTAINMENT

Which movie is this year's best?
Is television having a positive (negative) impact upon viewers?
How does one play a particular game or sport?
Are the Olympics a good, bad, or neutral event?
Are sports cruel to animals?

ECONOMICS

What might be done to curb inflation?
What might be done to reduce unemployment?
How should the national (state, local) tax structure be changed?
Does America still have a "class" system?
What careers offer the best potential for future employment?

objective statements in the preceding chapter; that is, it is something worth talking about in the first place. And, if possible, it should lead to some measurable *results* or changes in the audience.

2. The Amount of Material.   To a large degree, the audience dictate the amount of information you will need in your speech. If, for example, they have a low opinion of you as a source, you'll need a great deal of information to prove to them you are competent and trustworthy. If they know a lot about the topic, you'll have to know even more. If they disagree with your viewpoint, you'll have to include a lot of evidence to prove your arguments; if they agree with you, you can spend more time appealing to their emotions and directing their behaviors. Again, almost all of this is dictated by the nature of your audience.

3. *The Type of Appeals.* As we will see in later chapters, the sorts of strategies you employ are dictated by the nature of your audience. Fear appeals, for example, are effective only if the audience have a high opinion of you as a source. Logical appeals are necessary for audiences who initially disagree with you; emotional appeals work best for audiences who share your views. And the sorts of arguments you use must be consistent with audience values and motives.

4. *The Organization of the Message.* The way in which you structure the entire speech also must fit the audience. If they disagree with your ultimate point (that is, the thing you want them to accept and act upon), then that point should be kept hidden until the end of the speech, presented only after you have offered the audience all the evidence and reasoning you can muster. Conversely, if they probably agree with your point, then start with it and spend the rest of the speech strengthening their commitment and telling them how to act on it.

5. *The Language You Use.* In every sense, your language should fit your audience. It should be neither too simple nor too complex for their level of knowledge. It should fit within their value systems (for example, the kind of language you use speaking to an audience of nuns might differ from the language you use speaking to a group of your drinking buddies). It should also fit the occasion (humor is a little out of place in a funeral oration, perhaps) and you, the speaker (Billy Graham probably would lose some of his effectiveness if he suddenly became obscene).

In summary, then, you analyze your audience so that you can adjust your topic, amount of material, type of appeals, organizational pattern, and language to them. This enables you not to tell them what they want to hear, but to make your message more acceptable to your audience so that they are more willing to perform the behavior you have specified in your objective statement.

WHERE DO WE LOOK FOR IT?

We know what we're looking for and why; now we need to determine where. Basically, there are three sources of information you can use. First, you can employ what knowledge you have about your audience's general characteristics to infer their interests, motives, and so on. Second, if and when circumstances allow, you can actually measure the five characteristics we are concerned about. Such circumstances are rare, but when they present themselves, you should use the opportunity to its utmost effect. And third, you can observe the audience's actual reactions to your speech and infer their characteristics from those. In this section, we will examine the inferential and measurement methods; we will defer consideration of audience responses until a later chapter.

Inferences

Often, this method of audience analysis is the only one available to you. It consists of learning all you can about your audience, and then inferring from this knowledge their interests, motives, knowledge, attitudes, and values. Really, it involves a lot of guesswork, but at least it's educated guesswork. Researchers in communication and

research findings, we can reach some conclusions about what we should do when we
confront certain types of audiences. Let's consider some of those characteristics now.

General Audience Characteristics

Types of Audiences.   H. L. Hollingworth (1935) developed a concept he called
polarization and used it to define five types of audiences. Briefly, polarization considers the commonality of the audience—the extent to which they direct their attention to a common object. Without some degree of polarization, a crowd is just a
crowd. Shoppers who line New York's Fifth Avenue just before Christmas are not an
audience; they have no common focus. But suppose one of those shoppers happens
to notice a man threatening to jump from a twentieth-story ledge. The shopper yells
"Look at that!" and everyone's attention turns upward. The crowd have become an
audience.

According to Hollingworth's scheme, five degrees of polarization, and hence
five types of audiences, can be identified. *Casual audiences* are least polarized. Our
Fifth Avenue shoppers would be such an audience: they were just milling around
when their attention happened to be arrested by some object. Streetcorner speakers
and department store product demonstrators face the same sort of audience. More
polarized are *passive audiences*. Most often, these are composed of captive listeners,
such as the listeners one typically finds in college classrooms or ceremonial dinners.
Selected audiences are composed of people who have gathered for some common
and known purpose; thus, they are more polarized still. Often, the individuals in such
audiences have been specifically invited to attend, as in some business meetings or
conventions; hence, the term *selected*. *Concerted audiences,* have active purposes
and united goals but no clear division of labor or rigid organization of authority.
Examples include specialized training groups, political meetings, and religious revi-
vals. Finally, *organized audiences* are most polarized of all. Like military units and
football teams, they have a clear, unitary purpose, a high degree of dedication, and
clearly designated responsibilities and authorities.

But why should we care about how polarized audiences are? The reason is that
different types of audiences require different strategies from us. Hollingworth offers
the following table of responsibilities corresponding to each audience type:

Casual Audiences	Passive Audiences	Selected Audiences	Concerted Audiences	Organized Audiences
Attention				
Interest	Interest			
Impression	Impression	Impression		
Conviction	Conviction	Conviction	Conviction	
Direction	Direction	Direction	Direction	Direction

Thus, with casual audiences you must obtain their attention, interest them in your
topic, impress upon them the need for change, convince them that the change you
advocate is best, and direct them in how to actually accomplish that change. As

Casual or Passive Audiences Require the Most Work by a Speaker

audiences become more polarized, the number of things you need to do lessens until ultimately with organized audiences you need only to tell them what to do and how, when, and where to do it. Since this text takes a similar step-by-step approach to speaking, it is important at the outset to know what type of audience you will be facing.

Audience Homogeneity. We need also to consider how similar, or homogeneous, audience members are to each other. Such similarity may be in terms of many characteristics: sex, age, background, economic status, education, religion, occupation, politics, knowledge, attitudes, intelligence, and so on. If members of the audience are very similar in most of these respects, your task is much easier—you can tailor your message specifically to meet those audience characteristics. Too often, however, you will face a very heterogeneous audience. That's when things get challenging. You have to construct very general appeals that will be persuasive to almost everyone, and you will have to have a variety of appeals to ensure that, at least once, you will strike upon something persuasive to each audience member. Obviously, you need some idea of the homogeneity of your audience in order to determine the sorts of appeals you will employ.

Audience Size and Density. Both the number of people in the audience and the degree to which they are crowded together have an impact upon our planning although they are of less importance than are audience type and homogeneity. Large audiences tend to be more frightening so that we have to take greater pains to compensate for stagefright; more heterogeneous, so that we have to construct more appeals and more general appeals; and more psychologically distant from the speaker, so that we have to try harder to establish a sense of commonality or identification with them. Certainly, it is easier to cope with smaller audiences.

As for density, Minnick (1968) claims that audiences tightly packed together are more suggestible and responsive than audiences which are spread out. As he puts it:

"A communicator who wishes to attain maximum suggestibility and strong emotional response often tries to seat his audience elbow to elbow and to fill clusters of vacant seats or vacant rows between the audience and the rostrum. Since a person's emotional responses are heightened and facilitated by awareness of the responses of others, a communicator who assures crowded seating provides a condition of maximum effectiveness" (p. 70). Note something important: crowding serves to intensify audience feelings. If those feelings are for you, fine. But if those feelings are likely to be against you, the last thing you want is to stir them up. So we arrive at a two-part conclusion: (1) if audience sentiment is for you and your topic, crowd audience members together and appeal to their emotions; (2) if audience sentiment is against you and your topic, try to spread them out and to keep them calm and rational.

Members' Demographic Characteristics

Age.   Research conducted over the past several decades has determined that there are some reasonably consistent differences among various age groups. Interests vary with age: younger people generally are more isolationist in their political views than older people; those in their forties and fifties are particularly concerned with taxes, business, and the economy; and older people are more interested in pensions, Medicare, and social services for the aged. Middle-age people generally are less self-centered than either younger or older people, who are particularly susceptible to appeals directed to their personal well-being, satisfaction, and security. As people grow older, they tend to become more cautious and conservative—less willing to accept major changes in their lives or surroundings. And finally, young people tend to be optimistic and idealistic while older people tend toward pessimism and practicality. According to your audience's overall age group, then, you need to adjust your topic to fit their interests, your appeals to fit their self-centeredness, cautiousness, conservatism, optimism or pessimism, and idealism or practicality, and perhaps your objective to fit their willingness to undertake major changes.

Sex.   While sex roles are rapidly changing so that much of past research findings may no longer hold true, it still is worthwhile to examine some of the differences which have been discovered between males and females. Incidentally, the differences referred to here are psychological; the rest you can work out for yourself. Generally, the interests of males and females seem to parallel the social roles they play. Women have been found to be more interested in children, fashions, and the home, while men are more interested in the economy, business, politics, and sports. In addition, women seem to be more humanitarian than men—more favorably disposed to social programs such as aid for dependent children, unemployment, old-age assistance, Medicare, and the like—and men seem more concerned with things, such as cars, money, physical activity, and so on. And finally, there is some evidence that women are more persuasible and more susceptible than men to group pressure for conformity. The topics you consider and the appeals you use therefore should be adjusted to the sexual composition of your audience.

At this point, however, we must note something important about audience analysis. Our society is changing, perhaps more quickly than it has changed in the past. With that change come changes in the roles played by society's members. Certainly, the roles of men and women are changing, and most of the traditional sex role stereotypes are being dramatically revised. It would be dangerous, then, for us to draw conclusions about our audience based upon their sexual composition and upon dated research findings about psychological differences between men and women. Indeed, it may be dangerous to draw conclusions about an audience based upon *any* set of stereotypes which we might hold. People are individuals, and their reactions to speeches are determined largely by their individual characteristics. So my point is this: consider all aspects of your audiences as you prepare but beware of stereotypical judgments that ignore individual differences.

Education.   Several differences have been found between well-educated and poorly educated audience members. First, well-educated audiences respond best to logical appeals and arguments, while less educated people are most susceptible to emotional appeals. Second, the opinions of well-educated people are more stable and hence harder to change than are the opinions of the poorly educated. Moreover, when educated people do change their minds, it usually is in response to new information, while uneducated people defer more often to expert judgment, authority figures, or group pressure. And finally, educated people are more anxious to keep up with current events and are more optimistic than the uneducated. Again, then, you must adjust your strategies and appeals in order to adapt to the general education level of your audience.

Socioeconomic Status.   Because socioeconomic status and educational background are closely related, the differences found between high and not-so-high income groups parallel the findings between educated and uneducated audiences. Generally, higher-income groups are more motivated to achieve, more responsive to logical rather than emotional appeals, more concerned with current events, more optimistic, and more concerned with humanitarian causes and volunteer work than are low-income groups.

Occupation.   If you are speaking to an audience consisting of people who do much the same sort of work for a living, you are lucky: there are a whole host of things you can infer about your audience. You can judge their interests; people naturally are interested in things related to their jobs. Similarly, you can judge to some degree the things they probably know about based on what they do. You might be able to judge their motivations. For example, business people often seek money, power, and status; social workers and religious leaders seek to help people; and college professors strive for knowledge—for themselves and their students. Of course these are stereotypes to some degree, but they still often are accurate indicators of the forces that motivate these occupational groups. Finally, you can even judge their attitudes and values: business people tend to oppose government regulation and value free enterprise, educators often favor state support for education and value knowledge for its own sake, and so on. Indeed, if your audience is homogeneous in terms of occupation, you can adjust almost every element of your message to fit them.

Much of the research concerning audience personality characteristics is virtually worthless when you try to apply it. Consider the findings, for example, that dogmatic people are difficult to persuade and respond best to authority-based arguments, that authoritarian personalities also respond best to authority figures, or that people with low self-confidence are more easily persuaded than highly confident people. All of this is interesting, but rarely do audience members wear little tags saying, "Hello, there. I'm a dogmatic authoritarian personality who lacks self-confidence." And without such tags, how do you locate those people in the first place? They all look alike to me. So let's look at some characteristics you can at least infer about your audience and then use to adjust the message you send them.

Intelligence can be inferred to some degree from education and occupation, and some characteristics of intelligent people have been isolated. Research studies have determined that intelligent people tend to be critical listeners and respond best to logical appeals and well-supported arguments. Less intelligent people are not so critical, and emotional appeals are more effective with them. *Group identification* also is an important consideration: with what larger groups do the members of this audience identify? Such larger groups may be ethnic, racial, religious, political, social (such as fraternities or sororities), or any of a multitude of other group types. Knowing the audience's psychological reference groups may assist you in inferring their interests, motives, attitudes, knowledge, or values. And third, if you can learn or guess *audience goals,* or their reasons for being in the setting in the first place, you also may be able to infer their interests, motives, and so on. There are reasons why people attend classes (for grades, knowledge, social contacts, and so forth) or church services (for salvation, out of civic responsibility, or for social contacts), for example. Determine those reasons, and you have the key to determining their other characteristics as well. But beyond intelligence, group identification, and audience goals, there is little about audience personality and psychology characteristics that we can use.

Measurements

In the preceding section, we relied on educated guesswork. In this section, however, we turn to something considerably more accurate: actually measuring the audience characteristics with which we are concerned. Again, the occasions in which you will actually be able to measure audience characteristics are likely to be rare, but when they arise, you should be able to take advantage of them. Thus, we will consider first the types of measures you can use, and then we will examine the step-by-step procedures for putting each type into play.

Types of Measures

Dichotomous Scales. As its name implies, this measure gives the person filling it out (whom we shall call the respondent) two choices: *Yes* or *No.* Consider these examples:

Should prostitution be legalized? (circle one)	Yes	No
Is prostitution immoral?	Yes	No
Have you read much about prostitution?	Yes	No

Assuming that your topic is the legalization of prostitution (something you are favoring), you can learn several things by having the audience complete these scales. You can assess their attitudes toward your topic, you can learn how prostitution fits with their value system, and you can discover how much they are likely to know about the topic. But note one important thing: these scales show you only one characteristic of audience attitudes—direction. They tell you whether the audience favor or oppose legalization of prostitution, but they do not tell you *how favorable or unfavorable* they are. That is, you do not learn the intensity of their attitudes. Still, Yes-No scales do give you some information about your audience.

Dichotomous scales can use alternative answers other than *Yes-No.* For example:

Prostitution is (circle one)   Moral   Immoral
How much do you know about prostitution?   A lot   A little

Thus, to use a dichotomous scale you present the respondent with a question or statement and then offer two responses from which to choose. Be sure, incidentally, to instruct the respondent how to indicate a choice—"circle one," "underline one," "check one," or whatever.

Rank/Order Scales.   These scales provide a very different sort of information. Basically, they consist of two parts: some criterion for judgment and then a list of things which the respondent is told to rank/order according to that criterion. For example:

Below are listed five common objections to prostitution. Rank/order them according to how important to you each of them is. (Give the most important objection a 1, the second most important a 2, and so on.)
_____ Prostitution is immoral.
_____ Prostitution encourages other types of crime.
_____ Prostitution spreads disease.
_____ Prostitution degrades women.
_____ Prostitutes on the street spoil the neighborhood.

Similarly, you could have the respondent rank/order a list of topics according to interest or knowledge about each, and so on. The key thing is, provide him or her with a clear standard or criterion for ranking the items and indicate how to rank them ("the most important gets a 1, the second most important a 2"); otherwise, you won't know what a 1 or a 5 means. Note, too, that you can use any number of objects to be ranked (provided it's more than one, of course). But the more things to be ranked, the more difficult and confusing the job becomes; thus, it is usually best to keep the number of items under ten.

Rank/order scales tell you the relationships among the objects you have listed: how important they are relative to each other, how interesting they are relative to each other, and so on. We might be able to conclude from our scales on prostitution, for example, that immorality is the most important objection, that crime is the second

most important, or that disease is least important. When writing our prolegalization of prostitution speech, then, we would be sure to include arguments concerning morality and crime, but we probably would not include material about disease. But what rank/order scales *do not* tell us is the absolute value of the objects which have been ranked. Is the morality issue really important to the audience? Well, we know it's more important than the other issues, but what does that mean? Maybe none of them is really important to the audience, but morality is less trivial than the others. So rank/order scales tell us the relative importance, interest, and so on of the objects which are ranked, but they do not tell us how important, interesting, and so on each of those objects is to the audience.

Likert Scales. Named after their creator, Rensis Likert, these scales provide the respondent with a statement and then ask him or her to indicate the extent to which he or she agrees or disagrees with that statement. For example:

Prostitution should be legalized. (Put an *X* in the space which best reflects your feelings.)

_____	_____	_____	_____	_____
Strongly agree	Agree	Neutral	Disagree	Strongly disagree

Prostitution is immoral.

_____	_____	_____	_____	_____
Strongly agree	Agree	Neutral	Disagree	Strongly disagree

Prostitution is an important social issue.

_____	_____	_____	_____	_____
Strongly agree	Agree	Neutral	Disagree	Strongly disagree

With scales like these, then, we can assess just about anything we want to know about our audience.

Again, we need to take note of a couple of things. As with the earlier scales, be sure to tell the respondent how to complete the Likert scales ("Put an *X* in the space which best reflects your feelings," "Check the appropriate space," and so on). Probably you will need to do this only with the first scale; from then on the respondent should be able to remember how things work. Notice also that the Likert scales gives two dimensions of attitudes: direction and intensity. We not only know whether he or she agrees or disagrees, we also know how strongly he or she feels about each statement. Thus, these scales have a distinct advantage over dichotomous scales. And finally, if we want to determine the rank/order of the statements, we have only to compare the responses given to each. That is, if we gave the five statements we saw under the rank/order scales section and had the respondent agree or disagree, we could compare the five ratings to see which of them he or she agreed most strongly with, which was second, and so on. So with a little ingenuity, we can accomplish everything that the dichotomous and rank/order scales do, and learn also how intense the respondent's feelings are.

Semantic Differential Scales.   Developed by Osgood, Suci, and Tannenbaum (1957) and by Smith (1961; 1962), these scales probably are the most versatile of the audience measures we have available. The semantic differential presents some concept or object to the respondent, and then asks him or her to rate that object on a list of scales, with each scale having opposite adjectives at either end. For example:

On the scales below, place an X in the space which best reflects your own feelings about the thing named at the top of the scales.

Prostitution

Important ⟋ ⟋ ⟋ ⟋ ⟋ ⟋ ⟋ ⟋ Trivial
Neutral

Moral ⟋ ⟋ ⟋ ⟋ ⟋ ⟋ ⟋ ⟋ Immoral
Neutral

Good ⟋ ⟋ ⟋ ⟋ ⟋ ⟋ ⟋ ⟋ Evil
Neutral

Legalizing prostitution

Positive ⟋ ⟋ ⟋ ⟋ ⟋ ⟋ ⟋ ⟋ Negative
Neutral

Desirable ⟋ ⟋ ⟋ ⟋ ⟋ ⟋ ⟋ ⟋ Undesirable
Neutral

Important ⟋ ⟋ ⟋ ⟋ ⟋ ⟋ ⟋ ⟋ Trivial
Neutral

Obviously, you can obtain a lot of information about your audience very quickly through the use of semantic differential scales. You have only to decide what concept you want rated, the adjectives you want applied to that concept, and the way in which you want the scales marked (placing an X in the appropriate space is the most common way), and you are ready to assess audience attitudes. And as with the Likert scales, you measure both direction and intensity of attitude; however, you also measure several attitudes, not just agreement-disagreement. In many respects, then, the semantic differential is the most desirable measure of audience characteristics we can use.

Having seen some of the types of measures available to us, we turn now to the step-by-step process for actually using them. For each scale, the steps you take are these:

Step 1. Decide What You Want to Know

    a. *Objects to be evaluated.* Decide what questions you want answered (dichotomous scales), what objects you want ordered (rank/order scales), what statements you want evaluated (Likert scales), or what concepts you want rated (semantic differential).

    b. *Types of responses desired.* Decide whether you want questions answered, objects ranked, statements agreed or disagreed with, or concepts rated.

    c. *Content of responses desired.* With dichotomous scales, decide if you want *Yes-No* responses or some other choice of response (*A lot–A little, Important–Not important, Good-Bad,* and so on); with semantic differential scales, choose the adjectives you want applied to the concepts—ones that provide you with information useful to you.

Step 2. Develop the Measuring Instrument or Questionnaire

Write up your scales, including the objects (questions, objects, statements, or concepts) to be evaluated, the scales with which to evaluate them (Yes-No, list to be ranked, Agree-Disagree, or opposite-adjective semantic differential), and instructions on how the scales are to be completed ("circle one," "fill in number," "place X in space," and so on). If possible, try to keep the whole thing short—one page, if you can.

Step 3. Administer the Questionnaire

How you actually do this will depend on the situation. Basically, it involves handing out the questionnaires, having respondents fill them out, and then collecting them. This might be done by mail prior to the speaking situation, by having the audience complete them during some earlier meeting of the group, or by some other method. Remember, though, that you need to do all of this far enough in advance for you to analyze their responses and adjust your speech accordingly.

Step 4. Analyze the Responses

In this step, you convert the respondents' answers into numbers, and then you combine those numbers to produce averages for each scale. To illustrate, consider each scale type.

    Dichotomous Scale. This scale is easy to analyze. Simply count the number of Yes and No answers to determine how many audience members feel each way. If you want to get really exotic, calculate the percentage of people giving you each response by dividing the total number of respondents into the number of Yes answers and number of No answers, respectively. That is,

$$\text{Percent who said Yes} = \frac{\text{Number of Yes answers}}{\text{Total number of answers}}$$

$$\text{Percent who said No} = \frac{\text{Number of No Answers}}{\text{Total number of answers}}$$

Obviously, it is easy to analyze responses to dichotomous scales—that's one of the advantages to using this scale type.

Rank/Order Scale.   Here you want to calculate the average ranking of each item you listed for the respondents to rank. It's easy to do. You just take the first item on the list (the one at the top), add up all the rankings it was given, and divide by the total number of rankings. For example, suppose we had 20 people fill out our ranking scale on prostitution. For the first item, "Prostitution is immoral," 10 people gave it a 1, 5 gave it a 2, 3 gave it a 3, 1 gave it a 2, and 1 gave it a 1. You would add all of these rankings (10 + 10 + 9 + 2 + 1 = 32) and divide by the total number of rankings (20, one for each person completing the questionnaire) to produce the result: 1.6. Do this for the remaining items in the list and you can determine the average ranking for each item and thus determine which is most important, second most important, and so on.

Likert Scale.   This scale is a little more complicated. First, you have to assign a number to each space. Typically, we use 5 for *Strongly agree,* 4 for *Agree,* 3 for *Neutral,* 2 for *Disagree,* and 1 for *Strongly disagree.* Then, taking one scale at a time, count the number of people who marked each space. For example:

~~THH~~	~~THH I~~	~~THH~~	~~III~~	~~I~~
Strongly agree	Agree	Neutral	Disagree	Strongly disagree

Next, multiply each space's value by the number of times it was chosen:

Strongly agree	5 × 5 =	25
Agree	4 × 6 =	24
Neutral	3 × 5 =	15
Disagree	2 × 3 =	6
Strongly disagree	1 × 1 =	1

Then add these numbers: 71
And divide by the total number of responses: 71 ÷ 20 = 3.61
On this scale, then, people on the average tended to agree with the statement, although not strongly.

Semantic Differential Scale.   These scales are analyzed in the same way as Likert scales. First, you assign numbers to each space, but this time they run from 1 to 7, with 7 at the end where the "good" adjective is located (for example, *Important, Moral,* or *Good*) and 1 at the end where the "bad" adjective is (*Trivial, Immoral,* or

Evil). Again, you count the number of times each space was marked, multiply by the value of each space, add the seven numbers which result, and divide by the total number of ratings you received. For example:

Important /IIII/THII/III / III / II / I / I /Trivial
       (7)   (6)   (5)   Neutral   (3)   (2)   (1)
                          (4)

$$7 \times 4 = 28$$
$$6 \times 6 = 36$$
$$5 \times 3 = 15$$
$$4 \times 3 = 12$$
$$3 \times 2 = 6$$
$$2 \times 1 = 2$$
$$1 \times 1 = 1$$
$$100 \quad 100 \div 20 = 5$$

For this scale, then, people on the average felt the object was important, but not very important (the average of 5 was just one step above the neutral point of 4).

Step 5. Interpret the Results

Now you must decide what the numbers mean. Are most audience members in agreement with you? Disagreement? Are they evenly divided in their feelings? What items were ranked highest? Did people generally give the same rankings, or are there a wide variety of feelings existing in your audience? Generally, what you are looking for is three things: direction of attitude (positive or negative), strength of attitude (very positive or just slightly positive; very negative or just a little bit so), and homogeneity of attitude (do members of the audience tend to respond in the same way, or do they give you a wide variety of responses?).

Step 6. Adapt to the Results

You have the information; you have a powerful tool which you can use to make your message more effective. In effect, you have conducted the type of analysis we saw at the beginning of this chapter, determining what factors are in your favor and what things must be overcome. Thus, it falls to you to construct a message which maximizes your advantages and minimizes or overcomes your disadvantages. In subsequent chapters, we will discuss methods of constructing such messages.

SETTING PRIMARY OBJECTIVES

The purpose of all we have done in this chapter is to enable us to answer one basic question: "What must I accomplish with my audience to achieve my main objective?" Taken into account by this question are several subquestions:

"Must I interest my audience in my topic, or are they already interested?"
"Must I motivate them to listen to me, or are they already motivated?"

"Must I give them a great deal of information about the topic, or are they already sufficiently knowledgeable?"

"Must I change their attitudes toward me, my topic, or themselves, or are their attitudes already what I would like them to be?"

"Must I adapt to or change their value systems, or are their values consistent with or unimportant to my objective?"

When we answer these questions, we have established for ourselves the *primary objectives* that we must accomplish in our speech. We may discover that all of these objectives must be achieved, or we may discover that only one must be accomplished to reach our main objective. However, if our audience analysis indicates that none of these primary objectives needs achievement, then we need to rethink our main objective: the state of affairs we desire may already exist, or the objective may be either unachievable or not worth achieving in the first place.

Audience analysis not only establishes our primary objectives, it also provides the key for our selection of secondary objectives and objective-directed strategies. The objectives and strategies we use to achieve our main and primary objectives will be determined by the nature of our audience, as we shall see in subsequent chapters.

SUMMARY

The most effective speeches, and hence the speeches which are most likely to achieve the speaker's objective, are adapted to the characteristics of the audience who hear them. But to adapt our speeches, we first must know something about the people we are adapting to. Thus, our objective in this chapter was to examine the concept of situational analysis, a process whereby we examine the characteristics of the setting with particular attention to the audience.

After examining the initial analysis, in which one tries to identify forces favoring and resisting change, we discussed two general methods of audience analysis that can be used to assess members' interests, motives, knowledge, attitudes, and values so that we can adjust our topic, material, appeals, organization, and language to them. The first method involved drawing inferences about the audience based upon their general characteristics (type of audience, homogeneity, and size and density), their demographic characteristics (age, sex, education, socioeconomic status, and occupation), and their personality characteristics (intelligence, group identification, and goals). The second method was more scientific, involving measurement of audience characteristics through the use of dichotomous scales, ranking scales, Likert scales, or semantic differential scales. Finally, we observed that the end product of audience analysis should be a set of goals that need to be accomplished if our objective is to be met and an understanding of the audience that will help us select strategies for achieving those goals. In the next several chapters, we will examine specific strategies which can be employed in achieving the goals we have set.

Allport, G. W. "Attitudes," in *Handbook of Social Psychology,* ed. C. Murchison, pp. 798–884. Worchester, Mass.: Clark University Press, 1935.

Bem, D. *Beliefs, Attitudes and Human Affairs.* Belmont, Calif.: Brooks/Cole, 1970.

Blake, R. and J. Mouton. "Change by Design, Not by Default," *Advanced Management Journal* 16(1970):29–34.

Festinger, L. *A Theory of Cognitive Dissonance.* Evanston, Ill.: Row, Peterson, 1957.

Heider, F. "Attitudes and Cognitive Organization," *Journal of Psychology* 21(1946):107–112.

Hollingworth, H. L. *The Psychology of the Audience.* New York: American Book, 1935.

Krech, D. and R. Crutchfield. *Theory and Problems in Social Psychology.* New York: McGraw-Hill, 1948.

Lewin, K. "Frontiers in Group Dynamics," *Human Relations* 1(1947):5–41.

McGuire, W. "The Current Status of Cognitive Consistency Theories," in *Cognitive Consistency,* ed. S. Feldman, pp. 2–4. New York: Academic Press, 1966.

Maslow, A. "A Theory of Human Motivation," *Psychological Review* 50(1943):370–396.

———. *Motivation and Personality.* New York: Harper & Row, 1954.

Minnick, W. *The Art of Persuasion.* Boston: Houghton Mifflin, 1957.

———. *The Art of Persuasion,* 2nd ed. Boston: Houghton Mifflin, 1968.

Newcomb, T. "An Approach to the Study of Communicative Acts," *Psychological Review* 60(1953):393–404.

Osgood, C. et al. *The Measurement of Meaning.* Urbana: University of Illinois, 1957.

Rokeach, M. *Beliefs, Attitudes, and Values.* San Francisco: Jossey Bass, 1968.

Smith, R. "A Semantic Differential for Theatre Concepts," *Speech Monographs* 28(1961):1–8.

———. "A Semantic Differential for Speech Correction Concepts," *Speech Monographs* 29(1962):32–37.

Spranger, E. *Types of Men,* 5th ed. Amsterdam: Max Niemeyer Verlag, 1928.

PROJECT

THE PERSONAL EXPERIENCE SPEECH

Speeches of this type present incidents drawn from your own life experiences. Your purpose in such a speech may simply be to give your audience information, to inspire them with a dramatic event, to persuade them through your own behaviors, or to entertain them with suspense or dramatism. Whatever your purpose, you must prepare this sort of speech carefully; you should be doing more than simply relating an event in your life to a bunch of onlookers. Specifically, you should do the following:

1. Select a topic. Possible topics include:

When my life nearly ended	An interesting experiment I tried
An auto accident	My strangest relative
The big game	A religious experience
The time I was a hero	Something I built
My favorite job	My favorite movie
My favorite book	An inspirational experience

2. Establish your purpose.
3. Gather your material. Write down the things you will present to your audience during the speech.
4. Organize your material so that it follows some logical sequence.
5. Develop an introduction that gets attention, arouses interest, and shows your own involvement in the topic.
6. Develop a dramatic conclusion that makes some reference to the attention-getting statement you made in your introduction.
7. When you deliver the speech, do so naturally, in a conversational manner. Act as though you are describing an event to a group of friends.

Name _____

Date _____

Speech Type _____

Speech Outline, Project Number _____

Speech Topic: _____

Speech Objective: _____

_____

Speech Title: _____

Introduction

    Attention:

    Motivation:

    Credibility:

      Preview

      Body

      Conclusion

Instructor's Comments:

SUPPLEMENT

ANALYZING THE SPEECH AND SPEAKER

In the preceding chapter, we examined techniques for analyzing our audiences and the situations in which we confront them. But communication, remember, is two-way: there are sources who must analyze their receivers, but there are also receivers who must analyze their sources. Therefore, in this supplemental section we will discuss analytic techniques that apply when you are in the other communication role—the role of listener.

When we speak of *listening,* we really are talking about three distinct processes. The first is reception, or the taking of stimuli from the environment. When we hear some sound, we have taken that sound from the environment via our senses. But hearing is not the sole component of listening—the second process is interpreting. That is, we must make some sense of the things we hear; we must form some meaning based upon the things we have perceived. As we saw in Chapter 1, communication has occurred when we have received and interpreted some sound. Yet another stage remains: evaluation. Listening involves not only receiving and interpreting sounds, it also involves evaluating those sounds, developing judgments and conclusions concerning their qualities. The accuracy of our evaluations, of course, is determined by the accuracy of our interpretations, which in turn are influenced by our hearing. Thus, all three stages are interrelated, and the principles we shall see in the sections which follow apply to each.

The importance of good listening cannot be overemphasized. In fact, much of our success as a speaker ultimately stems from our abilities as a listener. This is true for several reasons. First, listening gives us most of the facts we know. Although we may read a great deal, most of what we know has been obtained through listening to other people, to radio, or to television. As the playwright Wilson Mizner once observed, "A good listener is not only popular everywhere, but after a while, he knows something." Second, listening allows us to analyze and evaluate facts, opinions, or ideas. By comparing the things we hear with other information obtained through listening, we can make judgments about the meaning and accuracy of the messages we are receiving now. Thus, we become better able to understand and evaluate the environment in which we exist. Third, listening also inspires us, causing us to generate new ideas and beliefs that, at some future time, we might be able to pass along to our audiences. In each of these ways, then, effective listening can lead to effective speaking. But there is one other reason for studying listening: the more you know about your own listening behavior, the more you know about your audience, for they behave in the same general ways. And of course, the more you know about your audience, the better able you will be to influence them. Thus, in this supplement we will consider two topics relevant to improving listening: the barriers which often obstruct our listening efforts and some techniques for listening more effectively.

Barriers to Effective Listening

Among the most prominent students of listening behavior was Campbell (1958), who listed several sources of systematic error that inhibit listening.

1. Message Length. The longer the message, the more we tend to simplify, shorten, and eliminate detail from the things we hear. We thus lose information and accuracy. The lengthier the message becomes, the more we lose. As listeners, then, we must make a special effort to concentrate during lengthy messages; as speakers, we must include as many attention-getting devices as possible in our longer messages.

2. Middle of the Message. Dispute continues among communication scholars as to whether listeners remember best the *first* or the *last* things they hear. But everyone agrees on one thing: listeners tend to lose information presented in the *middle* of the speech. Again, this suggests a need for concentration during the body of the speech, and a need for including attention getters throughout the speech.

3. "Rounding Off" the Message. Listeners tend to tailor messages to suit their own needs or beliefs, and thus they often distort the message's true content. This behavior is, of course, consistent with the principle of psychological comfort we saw earlier: people distort information to make it more comfortable to them. We thus must take pains to remain open minded and accepting while we are listening and to be as clear and specific as possible when we are delivering information the audience are likely to distort.

4. The Influence of the Past. Unclear or ambiguous messages must be interpreted by the listener, and part of that interpretation is accomplished in terms of the perceived positiveness or negativeness of past messages. That is, if the speaker has said positive things in the past, this message also will be perceived to be positive; if the source usually has said negative things, this message probably will be judged negative as well. Only through careful concentration can we avoid this influence of past messages, and only through clear presentation of our current point of view can we prevent our audiences from assuming that we are expressing now the same attitudes we have expressed in the past.

5. Reductive Listening. This principle is similar to the preceding. Instead of judging the speaker's attitude, however, we are in this instance judging his or her ideas. If the message is unclear, we assume that the ideas it expresses are the same as those which the speaker has expressed in the past. Concentration and clarity again overcome this obstacle.

6. Expectations. As we already know, listeners (including ourselves) often arrive with some pretty specific expectations concerning the speaker and his or her message. The more ambiguous the message is, the more likely it is that we will interpret the message in terms of those expectations, hearing what we expect to hear. It falls to us as listeners to suspend those expectations as much as possible, and as speakers to refer to and, if necessary, correct the expectations of our listeners.

7. False Agreement. This error is most common when the source is highly credible and hence someone with whom the audience very much would like to agree. If his or her point of view is ambiguous, the audience are likely to assume that he or she agrees with them, sharing their beliefs, attitudes, or values. Some politicians deliberately capitalize on this principle: they deliberately speak in vague generalities, knowing that their listeners will assume agreement even when it has not been expressed. When listening, then, it is important that we guard against this sort of self-deception and assess carefully the viewpoints (if any) which the speaker is expressing. When speaking, it also is important to take this tendency into account, for if our future behaviors are going to show the audience that, in fact, we do not agree with them, they are likely to become extremely disillusioned with us when the truth surfaces.

8. *Dichotomous Listening.* We have a tendency to polarize the world, to create dichotomies in which things are either one way or the other: right or wrong, good or bad, beautiful or ugly. Although most speakers express ideas falling somewhere between these two extremes, we tend to assign those ideas to one category or the other. We need to be conscious of this tendency when speaking or listening—to be careful not to assign ideas to categories automatically—and to point out that the views we represent should not be categorized in that way.

9. *"Filtered" Listening.* We tend to filter messages we hear through the opinions and ideas held by people with whom we identify—our reference group. Rather than make up our own minds, we let others do it for us and ask ourselves, "Now, what would they think?" or "How would so-and-so react?" Other points of view are useful, of course, but we should make the ultimate decision ourselves. Still, as speakers, we have to recognize and account for the influence of reference groups; that's why they were included in the situational analysis we conducted in the previous chapter.

Although Campbell's list of listening barriers is lengthy, it still is incomplete. There are other problems which also can interfere with an audience's listening abilities. Among them:

Ignorance. If you know nothing about the topic, you probably will not be a good listener. You may hear and understand every word the speaker says, but you still have no way of judging the accuracy, relevance, or completeness of what he or she is saying. Good listening typically requires that we be informed enough to make an intelligent judgment about what the speaker is saying. And good speaking requires that we give our listeners enough information for them to make an intelligent decision.

A Closed Mind. If you "know" what is right before the speaker ever begins, both you and the speaker are wasting each other's time. You will accept points of agreement, reject or distort points of disagreement, and leave the situation the same person you were when you came in because no communication has occurred. Although we certainly should have our own opinions, we also should be willing to suspend those opinions temporarily so that we can give the speaker's point of view a fair hearing. But if we, as speakers, face an audience likely to be closed minded, we must do two things: use as many attention-getting devices as possible to keep them involved in the

Avoid Overcritical Listening

speech and withhold our point of view until as late as possible in the speech to give ourselves a chance to make our facts and arguments heard before the audience discover that we disagree with them.

Antagonism.   It is difficult for us to listen objectively to speakers whom we dislike. In such situations, then, it is particularly important that we try to suspend our feelings so that we can accurately evaluate the ideas we hear. From the speaker's viewpoint, this is a particularly difficult situation, and in later chapters we will look for methods to cope with it.

Overcriticalness.   When our goal as a listener is to discover as many errors in grammar, organization, evidence, style, or delivery as we possibly can, we will succeed in finding them, but we will miss the ideas which the speaker is expressing. Obviously, this is a matter of priorities: our main priority in listening should be to get information not to find fault. Still, as listeners we must also be concerned with the quality of the speeches we hear. The point, then, is not to lose sight of our main purpose for listening and not to descend into a search for minor flaws in the speech.

We have seen, then, some of the problems commonly associated with listening and some of the ways in which we, as listeners and as speakers, can go about coping with them. But there are some other things you should do to achieve effective listening, and we will consider them in the next section.

Techniques for Effective Listening

Although there is no sure-fire method for listening effectively, the following techniques have been found to be effective in improving most people's listening efforts.

1. Prepare to Listen.   If you know what the topic of the speech will be, learn something about it ahead of time so that you will not be an ignorant listener. Even some careful thinking about the topic will help you listen more accurately when the speech ultimately begins.

2. Determine Your Purpose.   Just as speeches should be centered on some objective, so too should your listening efforts be objective based. Generally, there are four types of purposes you might have: to get information, to evaluate an appeal (as when you listen to a sales pitch), to be entertained, or to be inspired (as when you attend a church service or a political rally). Any of these might be your ultimate purpose in listening. The key thing is, decide what your purpose is ahead of time so that you know the goal toward which your listening efforts are directed.

3. Determine the Speaker's Purpose.   Try to determine what his or her objectives (both main and primary) for the speech are. Particularly look for hidden objectives. How do they compare with the objectives (if any) the speaker has stated? What are the implications of these hidden motives? Try to develop, both prior to the speech and during the speech itself, as complete a picture as possible of the objectives that underlie the things the speaker says.

4. Determine the Speech's Organization.   Try to list the major points of the speech, and try to determine what type of organizational pattern the speaker is using. If possible, try also to identify the subpoints that are offered as support for each main point. The more thoroughly you can analyze the organization of the speech, the more likely it is that you will comprehend and remember the speech material.

5. Project.   As the speech progresses, try occasionally to guess what is coming next. What might the next major point be? What facts is the speaker likely to offer in support of the argument? What conclusion is the speaker likely to draw? This sort of guessing game will keep you alert mentally, and it will help you to interpret the points once they actually are given.

6. Summarize.   While the speech is going on, it may be useful occasionally to summarize where the speech has been. What was the purpose the speaker gave? What main points were covered? What subpoints relevant to the main point presently being considered were mentioned? Such mental summaries help you to stay oriented to the topic and to the points the speaker is trying to make.

7. Analyze.   Listen with a critical ear. Do not accept everything you hear at face value; think about the validity of the message. Do the speaker's arguments make sense? Do the facts match what you know to be true? Are the sources of information dependable? Is the speech delivery conducive to the content of the message? Overall, how good are the content and the delivery of the message? To help you analyze the speeches you hear, the next page offers a standard form for speech criticism which asks you to rate (from 5 for *Superior* to 1 for *Poor*) the important characteristics of content and delivery. In the remainder of this book we will study specifically the ways

Speaker's name: _____ Critic's name: _____

Rate each of the characteristics listed below from 1 to 5:
   5 = Superior; 4 = Above average; 3 = Average; 2 = Fair; 1 = Poor.

I. <u>CONTENT</u>

   Introduction: gets attention _____
                   motivates audience _____
                   establishes speaker's credibility _____

   Thesis statement clear _____

   Preview: specifies points to follow _____

   Body: main points clear _____   need established _____
          organization logical _____   plan clear _____
          information accurate _____   advantages proven _____
          information complete _____   objections answered _____
          reasoning clear _____   transitions clear _____

   Review: main points summarized clearly _____

   Conclusion: effective _____

II. <u>DELIVERY</u>

   Use of voice: pitch varied _____
                   rate varied _____
                   volume varied _____
                   fluent _____

   Use of eye contact _____

   Use of facial expressions _____

   Gestures: natural _____
               varied _____
               appropriate _____

   Posture: appropriately relaxed _____
              use of movement _____

   Appearance: appropriateness _____

   Proxemics: use of podium _____
               speaks to all audience members _____

   Use of language: grammatical correctness _____
                     correctness of pronunciation _____
                     quality of word choice _____
                     clarity of speaking _____

   Use of visual aids (if applicable):
                     quality of visual aids (comment) _____
                     use of visual aids (comment) _____

OVERALL IMPRESSION LEFT BY THE SPEECH _____

   Additional comments:

in which each of these characteristics should be used. For now, however, simply note that each of these characteristics is an important element of public speaking. Not all of the content points under the "Body" heading may apply to every speech, incidentally; the points in the first column apply to all speeches, but some of the points in the second column (such as "need established," "plan clear," "advantages proven," and "objections answered") apply almost exclusively to persuasive speaking. Nevertheless, this form provides a useful guide to the characteristics of public speaking you should isolate as you evaluate the quality of a particular speech.

8. Motivate Yourself. As the preceding list should indicate, effective listening is hard work. You can't just sit back and let the speaker's ideas soak in. By thinking about the rewards of listening or the benefits you might obtain by understanding and using the speaker's message, try to motivate yourself to listen.

SUMMARY

Listening is not easy. You have to make an effort to interpret and evaluate the things people say to you. But the rewards of listening can be substantial. You can improve your knowledge, you can discover new opportunities for self-improvement, you can develop methods for influencing others—indeed, virtually every aspect of your contact with other people can be improved by improving your listening. Overcoming the barriers to effective listening and implementing the techniques listed above can do much to make you a better listener and, just as importantly, a better speaker.

REFERENCE

Campbell, D. "Systematic Error on the Part of Human Links in Communication Systems," *Information and Control* 1(1958):334–369.

PART II
PRESENTATION

Think of the worst speech you ever heard. Or, think of the worst speaker you ever heard. Perhaps you are thinking of a certain professor's lectures, or of a certain coworker's reports, or of a certain politician's campaign address, or of a certain minister's Sunday sermon. Probably you can think of horrendous examples of each. But the real question is, Why was the speech or speaker so bad? What was it that made his or her speech so memorably miserable? Odds are good that the problem was the speaker's delivery. Probably, he or she spoke in a monotone, used no gestures, never moved from behind the speaker's stand, spoke at a slow and constant rate, or did things that distracted and annoyed the audience. Probably, too, you no longer have the foggiest idea what the topic of the speech was or what the speaker wanted you to do.

As you doubtless recognize, *what* you say in your speeches is vitally important. But no less important is *how* you say it. If the manner in which you deliver your speech to your audience is dull or distracting, your content probably will be lost regardless of its quality. If, on the other hand, your presentation is lively and supportive of your material, then even less-than-terrific content can be extremely effective. Therefore, you should plan the delivery of your message just as carefully as you prepare the message itself.

In this section, we will consider the nature of nonverbal communication, or the cues you transmit in addition to the words themselves. According to Raymond Birdwhistell (1955), a widely recognized authority on nonverbal communication, in face-to-face interactions the words we say account for less than 35 percent of the meaning our listeners form; the remaining 65 percent is elicited by your nonverbal cues. Obviously, the way you use nonverbal communication to deliver your message is important. But there is another important aspect of nonverbal communication: while you are delivering your message to your audience, they are delivering messages to you. Through their nonverbal responses, they tell you whether they understand you, agree with you, are interested in you, or are even listening to you. Since adapting to their responses is a key to successful speaking, you must learn to "read" audience feedback. In the next two chapters, then, we will consider several important topics. We will devote attention first to the problem of stagefright, as we seek ways to control both your own fear and your physical responses to that fear. Second, we will discuss methods of delivering speeches, looking at the sorts of nonverbal cues you might employ to achieve the results you desire. Finally, we will consider other elements of speech delivery, such as visual aids and the use of notes, that also impact the overall effectiveness of your speech. As an introduction to these topics, however, we will consider here the types and the functions of nonverbal communication.

TYPES OF NONVERBAL CUES

Theorists in the field of nonverbal communication (see, for example, Knapp, 1978) have suggested a variety of methods to categorize nonverbal cues. While all of these category systems are legitimate, our purposes here are best suited by a six-part system that consists of the following types:

1. Proxemics. Your location in space relative to the location of others around you is taken into account by this first category. Moreover, the locations of the people to whom you speak are considered here. Thus, such things as the distance between you and your audience while you speak and the seating arrangement of the audience members fall into this category of nonverbal communication.

2. Appearance. Your clothing, jewelry, physique, general attractiveness, and so on all comprise your physical appearance, and these things communicate certain messages to your audience. Moreover, their general appearance may communicate things to you which cause you to modify your message as you speak to them. In either case, despite social injunctions not to "judge a book by its cover"—not to judge people by their looks—we and our audiences reach conclusions about one another based upon physical appearance.

3. Bodily Posture. Both you and your audience communicate through general bodily movements: the way you stand, the way they sit, the way you move about the platform while you talk, and so on.

4. Gestures. This category also consists of bodily movements, but on a more specific level. Here we encounter hand gestures, arm and wrist movements, head movements, and other specific changes in bodily positioning. Obviously, the gestures you use while speaking are important, but so are the gestural movements made by your audiences, as we shall see shortly.

5. Eye and Face Behaviors. The most expressive form of nonverbal communication stems from this category. Our facial expressions and our eye behaviors reveal much about our attitudes and emotions. As speakers, we must be aware both of the things our own behaviors are revealing to our audiences, and of the things audience members' behaviors probably reveal about them. This category is a difficult

Appearance Communicates Things to the Audience

one to deal with because facial expressions and eye movements are extremely subtle and difficult to interpret; nevertheless, it is important that we draw at least some general conclusions about the behaviors this category comprises.

6. Vocal Behaviors. The vocal characteristics that accompany spoken words fall into this category. Such things as voice pitch, volume, articulation, and rate of speaking have communicative value, and it is important that we use them to best advantage as we deliver our speeches.

From this list, it should be clear that nonverbal communication is a complex and varied area of study. Yet even this list does not provide a complete view of the things people term nonverbal. For example, theorists have argued that such things as the use of time, the physical environment (including such matters as climate, urban versus suburban location, room color, or furniture placement), touch, and culture also fall under the umbrella of nonverbal communication. However, those things are beyond our immediate concern; here, our purpose is to deal with things that you can control and use to enhance your speaking effectiveness. Thus, we will limit our consideration of nonverbal communication to the six categories just described.

FUNCTIONS OF NONVERBAL CUES

Now that we have seen some types of nonverbal cues, let's turn to some of the things nonverbal cues do—to their functions in human communication. These functions are defined in terms of the relationships between nonverbal cues and the words they accompany (or substitute). First, nonverbal cues can take the place of words—the *substituting* function. For example, the "V for victory" gesture using the index and middle finger stands for words typically left unsaid, just as the "OK" gesture with thumb and index finger forming a circle substitutes for the statement that things are all right. At the University of Texas, people run around giving the "hook 'em horns" gesture, which consists of a fist with the index and pinky fingers extended. And at universities everywhere, a variety of gestures are used to substitute for a variety of words that cannot be printed here. Similarly, crying nonverbally expresses extreme sadness (or happiness), running away substitutes for statements concerning great fear, and turning your back on someone substitutes for the words "I don't want to talk to you."

Nonverbal behaviors secondly can perform the *repeating* function, serving simply to restate the message delivered verbally. A speaker who says "There is just *one* way to do this" while holding aloft an extended index finger uses gestures to repeat the thought she has spoken. Or the friendly policeman who helps you when you are lost by saying "Go down to the light, turn left, then go one block and turn right" while pointing straight, then left, and then right also uses gestures to repeat the words. Through this function, then, nonverbal cues make messages more clear and more memorable to listeners by telling them visually what they are receiving verbally.

Third, nonverbal cues can add information to that provided by words, performing an *elaborating* function. Your facial expressions, for example, show your listeners the emotions that underlie the things you say, and your tone of voice or rate of speech tell them how the spoken message is to be interpreted; that is, whether you are sincere, sarcastic, and so on. By the same token, the little boy who says "Mommy, I love you *this* much!" while holding his hands far apart is using gestures to add information to what he is saying.

A fourth function of nonverbal cues is that of *accenting* spoken words—drawing attention to specific parts of the verbal message through vocal or physical actions. If, for example, you talk softly throughout most of your speech but SCREAM one or two key words, you will attract the attention of the audience and direct it toward the words you screamed. Or if, as you speak, you pound the podium at certain times during the speech, this action also will accent or emphasize the words you are saying. In effect, then, nonverbal cues are used here to draw attention to the words you particularly want your audience to hear and remember.

Fifth, nonverbal cues serve to control interaction between people, *regulating* their conversations. This function is seen most clearly in face-to-face conversations. As one person begins speaking, she probably will be looking into the eyes of the other person. As she continues, however, she will look away awhile but then, as she concludes her statement, look back into the eyes of the other. This signals the listener that the speaker is about to finish her comments and that he had better be ready for his turn. In this and other ways, then, nonverbal cues control the interaction between people. Of course, this has little application in public speaking (except when people raise their hands to ask a question), because the speaker typically does all the talking. Nevertheless, nonverbal cues also can signal movement in thought or a transition from one main point of the speech to the next. In a sense, then, they serve as markers during the speech, showing the audience that the speech is progressing. Although this is not regulating interaction in the strictest sense, it still is a part of the function of controlling the flow of communication.

Lastly, nonverbal cues can perform the function of *contradicting* the words. Inept liars have problems with this function: when they tell falsehoods to other people, they are betrayed by their nonverbal behaviors. For example, if you cannot look someone in the eye while talking to him or her, you may be judged as insincere or dishonest in what you are saying. Or if you profess verbally to be upset but seem calm and composed in your nonverbal actions, your words will have been contradicted. And the opposite is true, of course: if you profess to be cool and calm while you are shaking, sweating, and convulsing with fear, people probably will doubt the validity of your words. Which brings up an important point. When your words and nonverbal cues conflict, which will your listeners believe? Think back to Birdwhistell's formula concerning meaning: nearly two-thirds of meaning is produced by nonverbal cues, while only about one-third is elicited by words. Thus, people are more likely to believe what they see you doing rather than what they hear you saying. Actions speak louder than words.

Before leaving these six functions of nonverbal cues, one last idea must be stressed. Later in this part we will see that nonverbal cues used in the delivery of speeches should be *purposeful*—they should perform some useful function in making the speech more effective. The list of six we have just reviewed provides a key by which you can judge the purposefulness of your own and others' nonverbal actions. In assessing your own speaking gestures, for example, ask yourself which of the six functions those gestures perform. If the answer is "none of the above," then those gestures constitute only random movements that add nothing to the meaning of the speech and may even distract from it. When planning and practicing the delivery of your speeches, then, you should use these six functions as a guide, deciding first what primary objectives leading to your main objective you want to achieve, and then developing secondary objectives and strategies for nonverbal actions geared toward those functions. Through this sort of deliberate, objectives-oriented planning, you will be more likely to employ a style of delivery that facilitates rather than hinders achievement of your overall speech objective.

REFERENCES

Birdwhistell, R. "Background to Kinesics," *ETC* 13(1955):10–18.
Knapp, M. *Nonverbal Communication in Human Interaction,* 2nd ed. New York: Holt, Rinehart and Winston, 1978.

CHAPTER 3
COPING WITH STAGEFRIGHT

PRIMARY (PRESENTATIONAL) OBJECTIVE:
To gain control of your own stagefright

Secondary Objectives	Corresponding Strategies
To control the fear drive	Physical exercise Objectification Goal setting Distraction Systematic desensitization
To develop desirable habits	Practice Develop sense of humor Protect memory

CHAPTER OBJECTIVES
After studying this chapter, you should be able to:

- List the symptoms of stagefright
- List and describe the causes of fear in public speaking settings
- Implement strategies for controlling fear in public speaking
- Describe the role of habit in public speaking
- Implement strategies for developing desirable public speaking habits

INTRODUCTION

Of the problems faced by people preparing and delivering speeches, none is more difficult to overcome than severe stagefright. Research conducted both formally and informally by Ross (1977) and Baird and Knower (1968) indicates that more than three-fourths of all beginning public speakers typically express concern about coping with stagefright, and about one-third of that group considers stagefright to be a serious problem. Indeed, questionnaires distributed to public speaking students at the University of Michigan during the 1977–1978 school year demonstrated that over 95 percent of those students felt that reducing stagefright was one of their primary goals in taking the course. Without question, then, the phenomenon of stagefright is a critical factor in people's minds as they prepare to speak.

It may interest you to learn that a great deal of controversy surrounds the nature of stagefright. Several scholars have become embroiled in a war of words concerning what this thing should be called: "Communication-Bound Anxiety" (McCroskey, 1970)? "Communication Apprehension" (McCroskey, 1972)? "Verbal Reticence" (Lustig, 1974)? Frankly, when stark fear has me convulsing prior to delivering a speech, I find it difficult to feel very concerned about what to call it. In a similar vein, other researchers have sought to determine whether this thing, whatever it is called, is a *trait* (that is, a characteristic which is a part of the individual regardless of the situation) or a *state* (something the individual experiences as a function of the situation, but which is not an enduring characteristic of his or her personality). Although recent evidence (Beatty, Behnke, and McCallum, 1978) supports the state school of thought, the issue is by no means resolved. But the problem we face is not what to call this thing or whether it is a basic part of our nature, it is: what the heck do we do when we are about to speak and find ourselves scared senseless? This chapter should provide some workable answers. But first, a word about cockroaches.

OF COCKROACHES AND COMMUNICATORS

Yes, cockroaches.

The story you are about to read is completely, absolutely true. For the most part.

If you have had any experience with cockroaches at all, you probably have observed one very important cockroach characteristic: cockroaches do not like light. Late some night, go out into the kitchen and switch on the light. All the cockroaches on the floor will immediately leave, probably annoyed because you interrupted their little cockroach cocktail party. They're not leaving because they fear being squished (in fact, being squished seems never to enter a cockroach's mind until it's too late); they're leaving because they don't like the light.

This dislike of light was actually put to use in a series of experiments conducted on cockroaches at the University of Michigan. The researchers went all around Ann Arbor and collected the biggest and best cockroaches they could find in that city's apartment buildings and dormitories. They then transported the captive cockroaches (in little cockroach buses, I suppose) to a laboratory, where they had constructed some apparati, represented in Figure 3-1.

The drawing on the left represents a plexiglass tray filled with water. At the top end is a box with a hole cut in it at water level. At the bottom end is a diving platform. Along the sides are also platforms whose function will be explained momentarily. The center drawing shows a cut-away view of the tray.

Behind the diving platform was a light bulb. When the experiment began, a

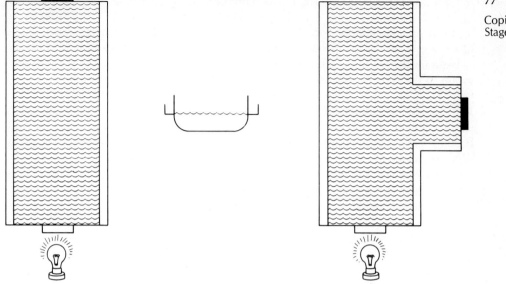

Figure 3-1: Cockroach Swimming Pools

cockroach was placed on the diving platform, wished the best of luck, and left to its (as it's difficult for noncockroaches to tell her from him) own devices. Then the light was turned on. The experimenters, knowing as you now do that cockroaches do not like light, expected the little devil to try to get away from the light. And they were not disappointed. As soon as the light was switched on behind the cockroach, it plunged into the water, freestyled its way down to the other end just like a little Mark Spitz, climbed into the box, and escaped the light. The experimenters, scientists all, stood back and timed the performance. They did this repeatedly, finding that it takes your average cockroach about 30 seconds to backflip into the water, swim to the other end, and climb into the box (note: the times here are only approximations used for purposes of comparison—somewhat like E.P.A. mileage estimates for your car).

Having established a cockroach swimming baseline, the experimenter moved to the second phase of the experiment. All along the sides of the plexiglass tray, on the platforms we saw in Figure 3-1, they placed a little cockroach cheering section. The cheering cockroaches could see the swimmer, of course, because the tray was made of plexiglass, but they were shielded from the light so they wouldn't try to leave. The light was switched on, the cockroach did a half-gainer into the water, the cheering section screamed their little heads off, and the cockroach plowed its way to the other end while the experimenters timed it. But something remarkable happened. While it had taken the cockroach 30 seconds to swim the tray unobserved, this time it completed the trip in an average of 20 seconds. In other words, having an audience improved the performance significantly.

But the experiment was still not over. The researchers next decided to play a trick on the cockroaches. They created a new plexiglass tray, but this one had a right turn (see the right-hand drawing in Figure 3-1). The cockroach thus had to swim halfway down the tray, turn right, and swim to the box at the end of the turn in order to escape the light.

The bulb was turned on, the cockroach dove in and swam straight down to the other end. And bashed its head against the wall. After a few more bashes, it finally worked the whole thing out, backed up to the middle of the tray, turned right, and swam to the box. All of this bashing and swimming took about one minute.

Then, as before, the experimenters provided a cockroach cheering section. The light lit, the cockroach dove, the cheerleaders cheered, and the cockroach swam straight ahead. And bashed its face against the far wall. And kept bashing. And bashing. A lot of cockroaches drowned during this part of the experiment; those that didn't, however, took an average of two minutes to get to the box.

Now, observe what has happened here. In the straight-ahead situation, the presence of a cheering section improved the swimmer's performance, cutting its time from 30 to 20 seconds. In the right-turn situation, however, the presence of the cheering section destroyed its performance, doubling time from one minute to two minutes. Why this opposite effect? Glad you asked. The answer, provided by Zajonc (1965), is:

$$D \times H = B$$

The formula means "Drive times habit equals behavior." In other words, the things we do in a given situation are the products of two factors: the amount of physical energy we experience in that situation and the behavioral habits we have formed through the years. According to this formula, the higher drive becomes, the more powerful and influential habits become.

Let's apply this principle to our cockroaches. Their habitual behavior is to swim straight ahead; turning right requires them to deviate from their habits. The presence of a cheering section increases their drive: no cockroach wants to look like a jerk in front of its peers, so it is motivated to try harder when other cockroaches are present. In the first situation, then, performance improved because the cockroach's habits were appropriate to the task: the cheering section increased its drive, its habitual behavior of swimming straight ahead improved, and its time decreased. But in the second situation, the cockroach's habits were inappropriate to the task. It had to break its straight-ahead habit in order to turn right. Alone, it could do this with just a little difficulty; with a cheering section increasing its drive, it had a great deal of trouble overcoming its habits.

But what have cockroaches to do with communication? Surprisingly, a lot. The $D \times H = B$ formula applies to people every bit as much as it does to cockroaches. When we have to deliver a speech, our drive (because of nervousness or fear) increases. Thus, our habitual ways of behaving tend to take over. Unfortunately, for most of us the habitual response to fear is not to deliver a speech; rather, it is something considerably more practical, like running away. Thus, when called upon to give a speech we find ourselves in a situation similar to that faced by the drowning cockroaches: we must overcome our own habits in order to perform the task successfully.

In the remainder of this chapter, we will consider separately the two elements of the $D \times H = B$ equation. First, we will examine the nature of the fear drive, list some of the factors that produce fear, and offer some methods by which you might control that drive. Then, second, we will turn to the concept of habit and analyze some ways in which you might develop the sorts of habits you would want to take over when stagefright strikes. And all of this will be based upon the knowledge we have gained from cockroaches.

DRIVE

The drive with which we are concerned here, of course, is fear (or apprehension, anxiety, reticence—whatever you want to call it). Although most of us recognize when we experience fear, we nevertheless will consider first some common fear symptoms, and then we will turn to some causes of fear and some methods by which the fear drive might be controlled.

Symptoms of Fear

We can obtain three lists of symptoms that typify stagefright: those supplied by speakers, those suggested by observers, and those detected by mechanical devices. If a speaker were describing her own experiences, she probably would mention such things as a tightened throat, strained or quivering voice, dry mouth, or shortened breath. She might also report a raised pulse rate, flushed face, and perspiring face, forehead, neck, or underarms. Further, she could talk about weak knees, cold and shaking hands, a "sinking" feeling in the pit of her stomach, or faintness. On a psychological level, she might mention that the audience was a "blur," that she was unable to focus on any one person in the audience, that she felt confused or disorganized, that she lost all sense of time, and that her mind went "blank." And, underneath all of these symptoms, she might confess to a strong fear of forgetting, of adverse audience responses, or of failing to do a good job. Sound familiar?

Observers, on the other hand, might report somewhat different symptoms. They may note unclear articulation or slurred speech, slips of the tongue or frequent nonfluencies (such things as "uh," "um," "you know," or "I mean"), a lack of volume, pitch, and physical variety, a strikingly limited vocabulary, and a lack of eye contact with the audience. They also might comment on the speaker's irregular breathing, frequent swallowing or licking of lips, awkward posture and movements, aimless gesturing or pacing, and abnormally fast or slow rate of speech. Or, if they are close enough to the speaker to observe such things, they might report that she fidgeted with inanimate objects (such as a pencil or notecards), that her hands were shaking, or that her face and neck were flushed. And, like the speaker, they might state that the speech was confused or disorganized.

Mechanical devices would detect other stagefright symptoms. Scholars of communication have measured increases in pulse rate and blood pressure, increased glandular secretions, and reduced digestive processes. Additionally, they have observed increases in perspiration and have detected irregular breathing patterns.

Taken together, then, these lists constitute a rather formidable array of symptoms, none of which is particularly conducive to effective public speaking. But note something important: most of these symptoms point to a common principle—that stagefright produces an increase in your physical energy. Potentially, this is some-thing good. If you could only find a way to control and channel that energy, you could use it to your advantage, directing it toward more effective delivery of your message. Later, we will search for some methods by which you might be able to do precisely that.

Causes of Fear

Stagefright seems to stem from three sources: the audience, the message, and you, the speaker. Let's look at each category, noting specific causes within each.

The Audience

1. Evaluative Apprehension.   Perhaps this is the single most potent cause of stagefright. When discussing the cockroaches, we saw how the presence of other cockroaches seemed to increase the swimmer's drive. In speaking, the presence of the audience produces fear, but the reason for that fear goes beyond the mere pres-ence of others. For example, before you go to watch a football game you probably do not become terribly nervous and think to yourself, "Wow, I sure hope I do a good job of cheering. And maybe I better practice my drinking just to be sure I can do it all right." Even though tens of thousands of people might be surrounding you at the game, you probably will not experience stagefright. The reason: no one will be paying attention to you. We become anxious only when we know that the audience will be watching us and evaluating our performance.

The reason we become apprehensive when we are evaluated lies with one of our basic social needs: the need for esteem, from others and from ourselves. Whenever we are evaluated, we run the risk that the evaluation will be negative—that our performance will be judged inadequate and that our esteem will be dam-aged. Public speaking thus is a threatening experience as we expose ourselves to the judgments of others and, in so doing, risk damage to our public and self-esteem.

2. Size.   This source of fear stems directly from the preceding one. The larger the audience, the greater the fear you are likely to experience. The reason is simple: more people means more judgments to be made of you. More judgments means greater likelihood that at least some people will find your performance lacking. Thus, the threat to your self-esteem is increased. Of course, there must be some point at which increasing audience size has no impact. When you are speaking to a crowd of 10,000, for example, having one more person wander into the setting probably will not distress you greatly. But until that saturation point is reached, the principle holds: more people in the audience means more fright in the speaker.

3. Fate Control.   There are situations in which an audience of one can be pretty frightening: job interviews, conferences with the boss, and the like. Such audiences provoke fear because of the control they exercise over your fate. The interviewer controls whether you get that job you want; the boss determines whether you get promoted or fired. In effect, important future events rest in the hands of these individuals. Your performance for these people thus assumes significance even beyond your esteem needs—these people exert control over your ability to satisfy a variety of your desires and needs. Confronting them therefore is extremely threatening, and extreme stagefright often is a result.

4. Status. Aside from fate control, the status of the audience members influences your stage fright. Suppose, for example, you are about to be introduced to the president of the United States. He exerts no control over your fate; he can neither hire nor fire you. Still, you will be nervous prior to meeting him simply because he holds such high status in our society. Similarly, any audience consisting of people holding status higher than your own will produce stagefright, while audiences of equal or lower status tend to elicit lesser fear reactions.

5. Familiarity. The degree to which the speaker is acquainted with the members of the audience also has an impact upon stagefright. While some people prefer to speak to total strangers, most of us experience the least fear when we confront people with whom we are well acquainted. But familiarity goes beyond acquaintance to include the concept of similarity: for the most part, we feel relatively secure speaking to people who are like us and least secure speaking to people who are extremely different. Students tend to be most comfortable talking to students, executives to executives, athletes to athletes, and so on. Being able to identify with the audience members, either through acquaintance or similarity, seems therefore to be an important key in reducing stagefright.

6. Agreeableness. The attitudes of the audience toward the speaker and his topic comprise the final audience-related source of stagefright. If the speaker perceives that the audience dislike him or disagree strongly with his views, he probably will fear the prospect of facing them. However, if he feels that they like both him and his views, he may even be eager to speak to them. Thus, our own attitudes toward speaking are strongly influenced by our perceptions of the audience's attitudes toward us.

The Message

1. Familiarity. Like unfamiliar audiences, unfamiliar speeches strike terror into the hearts of those who deliver them. And well they should. The less well you know your speech materials, the greater the risk that you will forget them or misrepresent them when the big moment arrives. However, this source of fear should exist only when you have an unfamiliar topic assigned to you at the last minute. Otherwise, you should select a topic which you know something about, and you should thoroughly familiarize yourself with your speech materials before you speak. Failure to do either of these will produce stagefright, and it will be your own fault.

2. Complexity. Material difficult to comprehend (and thus difficult to explain) causes fear in the people who must deliver it. The sheer difficulty of presenting that information to your audience increases the likelihood of failure, so that the riskiness of the situation increases. Only through careful and thorough preparation can we ensure success and thus minimize fear.

3. Interestingness. Occasionally, we will have to present information that is uninteresting. Suppose, for example, we are asked to present the quarterly budget report to company personnel managers. The information is dull to us, and it almost certainly will be dull to the audience. Again, the likelihood of failure increases, and with it, fear. But there are steps we can take to counter this problem. By incorporating interest-arousing materials, such as stories, jokes, visual aids, and illustrations, we can accomplish three things: make the speech more interesting to our audience, make it more interesting to ourselves, and reduce the threat (and hence the fear) which presenting the material might create.

4. Significance. If we feel that the audience will perceive our topic to be important, we will be eager (or at least willing) to present it to them. If, however, we expect that the audience will think the subject trivial, our fear of presenting it to them will increase. Again, fear of failure is the root cause: it is difficult to succeed with a speech topic the audience believe to be unimportant. Two remedies are available: choose a topic which you know the audience will perceive to be important and demonstrate the importance of your topic in the beginning of your speech.

The Speaker

1. Self-expectations. It is a good thing to demand a lot of yourself—to set high standards of achievement, which you have to work to reach. But you can overdo this business of standard setting, establishing goals or standards for yourself that are completely unrealistic and unattainable. It seems silly to do that, of course, but a great many public speakers commit exactly this mistake. When preparing for their speaking engagements, they set for themselves (often unconsciously) goals that are completely out of reach: "I am not going to forget anything, make any mistakes, use any 'you knows' or 'I means,' or show any sign of nervousness. I am going to use smooth gestures, perfect postures, and impeccable language. In fact, I am going to deliver the greatest speech in the history of the Western world." A speaker striving to achieve such goals will be frightened out of his wits, and he should be: there is no way that he will succeed. On the other hand, the speaker who decides that "I will give a speech that is at least coherent and understandable to my audience" stands a far better chance of succeeding and thus feels significantly less fear.

2. Unpleasant Experiences. If, sometime in the dim and distant past, you have delivered a speech and, in your own mind, "blown it," you probably will fear repeating that experience in the next speech you present. In effect, you now lack confidence in your ability as a speaker and suffer stagefright as a result. Like the tightrope walker who has fallen, the key to recovering your speaking confidence is to "get up there again." You might want to do it in stages of increasing difficulty, speaking first to small audiences of friends and progressing to larger audiences of strangers, but you should force yourself to continue speaking rather than let one setback end your speaking career. We all suffer our little disasters; the main thing is that we do not let those disasters defeat us.

3. Lack of Experience. People unfamiliar with the public speaking situation typically experience the greatest fear. Happily, however, the longer and more often you present speeches, the less your fear becomes (although, from my own experience, it never seems to disappear completely). By giving many speeches over time, and by receiving training in speaking methods, you can acquire the experience and the confidence you need to perform well and to minimize stagefright.

4. Fear Behaviors. Imagine this scene: You are giving a speech, talking smoothly and confidently, and everything is going well. You look down at the notes you are holding in your hand and discover . . . "Uh oh. My hand is shaking. I must be scared. I wonder if the audience can see it?" The discovery of this fear behavior serves to scare you further, which increases your fear behaviors, which scare you even more, and so on—a vicious circle that ultimately leaves you lying on the stage, a little puddle of protoplasm. Or you feel your knees shake, your stomach tighten, your voice quiver—any of the symptoms we saw earlier. This awareness only serves to remind you that you are nervous and to make you wonder whether the audience are aware of these symptoms as well. In effect, then, you scare yourself.

Controlling Stagefright

Clearly, there are a whole host of factors contributing to your feelings of stagefright. No wonder stagefright is one of the most commonly felt emotions. What we must do now is seek some method by which these factors can be counteracted so that the degree of fear we experience is minimized. Thus, we turn to some methods of controlling stagefright.

Note one important thing at the outset. What we are considering here are "controls" of fear, not "eliminators" of stagefright. There are two reasons for this emphasis on control. First, eliminating fear probably is impossible; no matter what measures you take to protect yourself from stagefright, you still are likely to experience some of the symptoms we examined earlier. But second, eliminating fear also is undesirable. The energy that a little bit of nervousness generates can actually help you to improve your performance, just as a little stagefright seemed to help the cockroaches we discussed earlier. Rather than to eliminate fear, then, our task is to keep it at a manageable level so that we can use the energy it produces to our advantage.

One other point needs to be made here. Recall the state versus trait controversy described at the beginning of this chapter. To this point, we have implicitly taken the state viewpoint—describing those characteristics of the speaking situation that seem to produce stagefright and omitting the psychological traits that are related to that phenomenon. However, the controls listed below are applicable to either school of thought; they will help you to control your anxiety regardless of its situational or personal nature. And they apply to situations other than public speaking. You will find them helpful for reducing tension prior to job interviews, tests, important meetings, or any other anxiety-arousing situation. With this orientation in mind, then, let's examine some of the controls you might employ.

Physical Exercise

The fear behaviors and symptoms that result from stagefright have a common core: excess energy. Our hands shake, knees tremble, voices quaver, and so on when we have more energy than we can control. Particularly troublesome is adrenalin, one of those glandular secretions that occur when we are frightened. When it is released, our energy level skyrockets for a very brief time and then drops to a level substantially below our normal level of operation. No matter when adrenalin kicks in, it is detrimental. Often, it happens while you are waiting to speak. You are sitting there, waiting your turn, when suddenly you are overcome with a tremendous surge of energy. You freak out, ripping up your notes, destroying your chair, mangling everything within reach, and suddenly your name is announced. As you sprint toward the speaker's stand, wham! Your energy level drops to a tremendous low. You barely have enough energy to stay awake, let alone to deliver a dynamic speech.

Or adrenalin may begin to flow while you talk. That is when your movements become frequent and random flailings; your hands, knees, and voice tremble; your stomach tightens; and so on. Again, your speech suffers as a result. The key, then is to prevent the flow of adrenalin and to control excess energy. The method is physical exercise.

The sort of physical exertion suggested here is not the long-term, get in shape type (although such exercise certainly would not hurt). Rather, it consists of mild physical effort designed to expend just enough energy to keep your actions under control. For example, walking a long distance on your way to speak, or briskly climbing a flight of stairs on your way to the room will serve this purpose. You might be a bit winded when you arrive, but that will quickly pass. Another useful sort of exercise is isometrics: the unobtrusive use of pressure against pressure to expend energy. While waiting to speak, you might press your feet down against the floor, or pull up on the table or desk top (being careful not to tip it over or tear it loose), or push your hands against each other, or in some other way exercise yourself mildly. In any case, the point is this: through mild exercise immediately before you speak, and through purposeful movement while you speak, you can expend just enough energy to keep your physical responses and behaviors under control. In so doing, you can reduce both some symptoms and a cause of stagefright.

Objectification

A second strategy for controlling stagefright involves the use of rational thinking as a means of reducing the unthinking, abstract fear that anticipation of speaking can produce. When we deal with speaking on a purely abstract, emotional level, it is frightening. When your thinking goes no further than "Oh my gosh, I've got to give a speech to a bunch of people!" you allow your emotions to take over and fear to dominate. Thus, in order to avoid this pitfall, you should use the technique called *objectification,* in which you rationally, intellectually analyze all elements of the speaking situation. Think, for example, about the audience. Who will actually be there? How frightening are they, really? Or think about the consequences of the

Physical Exercise Helps to Control Fear

speech: how awful or permanent would failure really be? Or think about yourself: does your self-worth really rest upon this one speech? Through thought processes such as these, in which you dissect piece by piece the situation in which you will be speaking, you probably will be able to take the situation out of its abstract, emotional state and put it into a reasoned, rational, mental framework you can handle.

Goal Setting

As we saw earlier, unrealistic, unachievable goals increase stagefright by increasing the likelihood that our speech will fail. Hence, to avoid this problem you need to consider carefully what goals you hope to accomplish with this particular speech. Using the speaking by objectives approach we have followed throughout this text will help a little by forcing you to focus on your audience rather than on yourself. But you still must take care not to expect too much of yourself. A good, coherent, influential speech, yes. A perfect one, probably not.

Distraction

Consider what Jane Fonda has to say about acting (Battelle, 1961):

> It's really not fun, acting. Always that tremendous fear. . . . Do you know that before a performance sometimes Laurence Olivier goes back to the foyer and, to release his tension, swears at the audience? Some actors even stick pins in themselves.

What she is talking about here is two forms of yet another stagefright reduction method: distraction. One of the forms, physical distraction achieved by inflicting pain on yourself, I don't particularly recommend, but do whatever turns you on. The other method, emotional distraction, can be accomplished just as effectively and with considerably less bloodshed. This method is based upon a theory, developed more than 50 years ago, that holds that it is impossible for us to experience more than one strong emotion at any one moment (James and Lange, 1922). When we feel fear, that is all we feel. When we experience anger, that is our only emotion. Or when we are extremely happy, that happiness blocks out all other feelings. To achieve emotional distraction, then, we need to do what Laurence Olivier does: substitute some strong emotion for the fear you normally would feel. Become angry, for example—at your audience or at some object with which you want your audience to be angry as well. Or think about things that make you happy or about your commitment to your speech topic. In essence, conjure up any emotion you can to replace the fear.

Yet another type of distraction occurs at the intellectual level. Here you distract yourself by concentrating on something else. One particularly good thing to think about is the speech itself. After all, it isn't the speech that is scaring you, it's the audience or the situation or both. By mentally rehearsing your speech, you gain a double benefit: distracting your thoughts from the elements that are frightening and fixing the speech more firmly in your mind.

Systematic Desensitization

While the first four methods suggested above can be used relatively easily, this method requires a great deal of time and discipline, perhaps aided by the help of a trained therapist. It involves two basic steps, repeated over and over until an association is built in your mind between relaxation and the thing used to scare you. First, find some place that is quiet, where you can relax completely without being disturbed. After getting yourself situated, concentrate first on completely relaxing. Starting with your toes and working upward, think about relaxing every muscle in your body. Take each muscle one at a time and concentrate on it until it is completely relaxed. Then move to the next muscle, and so on, until your entire body is free from tension. Then move to the second step: think about the thing that scares you—the speech, test, or interview. Immediately, you will feel your body tense up. As soon as that happens, go back to step one, concentrating on relaxing each muscle. When you are relaxed, repeat step two and think again about the frightening stimulus. Again you will tense up, and again you will revert back to step one. After repeating this process several times, however, you will notice something interesting: you can think about the thing for increasingly longer periods of time before becoming tense. The reason is that you have begun to associate relaxation with the frightening thought. Eventually, you will be able to think continually about the speech or interview without becoming tense or nervous.

The difficulty with systematic desensitization is that it takes a great deal of time. Literally for hours you must repeat over and over the process described above. But the technique works if you have the willpower to use it. And for people who suffer from extreme stagefright, it often is the only technique that works.

There are, of course, other methods of controlling stagefright. Self-hypnosis, for example, or yoga can be useful. But for quick, fairly simple reduction of stagefright, the methods outlined above seem the best. Try them; I guarantee that at least one of them will help.

HABIT

We come now to the second half of the $D \times H = B$ equation explaining stagefright. We know already that our habitual responses to fear, even controlled fear, do not include delivering eloquent speeches. Thus, in this section our task is to discover ways of developing habitual behaviors that take over automatically when we become frightened in front of an audience. To build such habits, you should do three things:

1. Practice. "Sure," you think "what would you expect a speech text to say?" Well, you are right; this speech text is telling you to practice. And for a very good reason, the same reason that football teams, basketball teams, actors, and singers practice: in order to make the desired behaviors habitual so that, when stagefright occurs, those behaviors also occur. But practice will do something else, too. By familiarizing you with your speech, practice also will make you more confident and, in so doing, lessen your stagefright in the first place. So what do you have to lose?

2. Develop a Sense of Humor. By sense of humor, I don't mean memorizing the *Henny Youngman Book of Party Jokes*. Rather, you should develop a sense of humor in your outlook on life and yourself. If everything, including speaking, is dead serious to you, then you will certainly suffer stagefright. And ulcers, high blood pressure, and other tension-related complaints. So relax. Laugh at yourself. A bad speech isn't the end of the world, and besides—if you prepare carefully, chances are your speech will be good, anyway. So as your habitual way of looking at life, have a sense of humor.

3. Protect Your Memory. When you are frightened, you do not automatically remember everything you have learned since infancy. Quite the contrary. Your mind tends instead to empty itself, with all of your energies being channeled instead to your physiological functions. So you should, as a matter of course, use techniques designed to help you remember your speech materials even in the most nerve-racking situations. Some of those techniques include:

Logical Organization. If your speech is sensibly organized so that one point flows naturally into the next, you will find it much easier to keep track of your progress and remember upcoming points as you deliver your message. And of course, your audience will find it easier to follow the sequence of your speech, too.

Notes. In the next chapter, we will discuss the use of notes during public speeches. For now, simply this: whenever you can, use notes of some sort. If you lose your place, you have them to consult. But even if you don't use those notes, it still is comforting to have them there—they make a terrific security blanket. You don't want those notes to become a crutch, of course; you should be able to deliver your speech smoothly without them. But you should have them, just in case.

Visual Aids.   Another topic to be considered in the next chapter is the use of visual aids, such as graphs, charts, maps, and diagrams. These aids, as we already know, increase audience interest in your speech, but they also serve to jog your memory. In effect, they are also speech notes, but ones which the audience can see, too. So, like clear organization, visual aids are useful to both you and your listeners.

Summaries.   In a sense, the summary should be your parachute. Whenever you lose your place in your speech, whenever you forget what is supposed to come next, whenever you find yourself in trouble and need to bail out—summarize. Naturally, this technique is not very effective at the beginning of your speech: "Good morning, ladies and gentlemen. Uh, now let me summarize that . . ." is not the most rousing beginning you could use. But later in the speech, if you forget your place, the summary can be extremely helpful. It serves to jog your memory by getting you back "into the flow" of the speech and should develop momentum to carry you on to the next point you momentarily had forgotten. And, as with clear organization, summaries are helpful in keeping your audience oriented, too. So, as a matter of habit, resort to the summary whenever your memory fails.

Mneumonic Devices.   As we will see in a later chapter, mneumonic devices are techniques that, through similarity or association, improve our ability to remember lists of names, ideas, speech subpoints, and so on. For example, having your major ideas consist of single words having the same number of letters or beginning with the same letter might enable you both to stimulate your own memory and to enhance that of your audience.

The key to using the habit half of the formula, then, is two-pronged: you must develop habitual behaviors that you want to occur when stagefright strikes, and you must protect yourself from undesirable behaviors that tend to occur naturally in response to fear. The techniques described above will help you to accomplish these things.

SUMMARY

Virtually everyone experiences the unpleasant sensations associated with stagefright when he or she faces the prospect of delivering a speech. That bit of knowledge, however, probably is small comfort to you when you are suffering from severe nausea while preparing your speech. Thus, in this chapter, we sought some practical methods to minimize the symptoms of stagefright. First, we examined the concept of drive, or the fear response that stems from the speaking situation. We noted three sources of fear—the audience, the message, and the speaker—and then considered some techniques to counter those sources and control the fear drive. Then, second, we turned to the concept of habit and observed some methods by which desirable habits might be developed and undesirable ones avoided. By using these techniques in combination, then, you can learn to overcome stagefright and use the energy that a little fear produces to deliver a more dynamic, influential speech.

Baird, A. and F. Knower. *Essentials of General Speech.* New York: McGraw-Hill, 1968.

Battelle, P. "Stars Give Their Views on Acting as a Career," *The Detroit News,* December 6, 1961.

Beatty, M., R. Behnke, and K. McCallum. "Situational Determinants of Communication Apprehension," *Communication Monographs* 45 (1978):187–191.

James, W. and C. Lange. *The Emotions.* Baltimore: Williams and Wilkins, 1922.

Lustig, M. "Verbal Reticence: A Reconceptualization and Preliminary Scale Development." Paper presented at the Speech Communication Association, Chicago, 1974.

McCroskey, J. "Measures of Communication-Bound Anxiety," *Speech Monographs* 37(1970):269–277.

———. "The Implementation of a Large Scale Program of Systematic Desensitization for Communication Apprehension," *Speech Teacher* 21 (1972):255–264.

Ross, R. *Speech Communication: Fundamentals and Practice.* Englewood Cliffs, N.J.: Prentice-Hall, 1977.

Zajonc, R. "Social Facilitation," *Science* 149(1965):269–274.

PROJECT

THE PET PEEVE SPEECH

This type of speech presents one thing (or person or idea or group) that really irritates you. Your purpose in such a speech may simply be to inform the audience about the causes of your irritation or to convince them to be irritated as well or to persuade them to act against the irritation source or to entertain them with the nature of the irritant. Information about the topic will come to some degree from your own feelings (that is, why you are irritated), but you may also need some factual material to support claims you make about the nature of the irritant. While the pet peeve speech allows you to present and support your personal feelings, you still should prepare the speech carefully by completing these steps:

1. Select a topic. Possible pet peeves include:

My roommate's bizarre behaviors	Professor's behaviors
How people act while shopping	Politician's behaviors
The way some people drive	Groups which ask for money
Poor sportsmanship while playing	Fanatics of any sort
People's disgusting habits	Inconsiderate smokers
Students' actions during class	Aggressive nonsmokers

2. Establish your purpose.
3. Gather your material. Write down all the reasons you are peeved and find the facts you need to support the claims you make.
4. Organize your material. Divide and subdivide the material into main and supporting ideas—three or four main ideas at most.
5. Develop an introduction that gets attention, motivates interest, and shows your familiarity with the topic.
6. Develop a conclusion that ends with a dramatic statement about the source of your irritation.
7. Deliver the speech as actively and dramatically as you can.

Name _____

Date _____

Speech Type _____

Speech Outline, Project Number _____

Speech Topic: _____

Speech Objective: _____

_____

Speech Title: _____

Introduction

    Attention:

    Motivation:

    Credibility:

      Preview

       Body

      Conclusion

Instructor's Comments:

CHAPTER 4
DELIVERING THE SPEECH

PRIMARY (PRESENTATIONAL) OBJECTIVE:
To use nonverbal speaking cues that add to the impact of your words

Secondary Objectives	Corresponding Strategies
To use proxemics effectively	Using personal space Using seating arrangements Using furniture
To use appearance effectively	Using physical attractiveness Using clothing
To use bodily postures effectively	Using purposeful movement Using appropriate movement
To use gestures effectively	Using natural gestures Using varied gestures Using appropriate gestures
To use eye and face behaviors effectively	Using natural facial expressions Using eye contact
To use vocal behaviors effectively	Using intelligible vocal cues Using varied vocal cues Using fluent vocal cues Using pleasant vocal cues
To use visual aids effectively	Preparing good visual aids Presenting visual aids appropriately

To use notes effectively

Using impromptu speaking
Using extemporaneous speaking
Using manuscript speaking
Using memorized speaking

To adapt to audience feedback
effectively

Interpreting audience feedback
Adjusting to audience feedback

CHAPTER OBJECTIVES
After studying this chapter, you should be able to:

- Implement strategies for using proxemics to achieve desired effects
- Implement strategies for using appearance to achieve desired effects
- Implement strategies for using postures to achieve desired effects
- Implement strategies for using gestures to achieve desired effects
- Implement strategies for using eye and face behaviors to achieve desired effects
- Implement strategies for using vocal behaviors to achieve desired effects
- Implement strategies for using visual aids to achieve desired effects
- Deliver an impromptu speech
- Deliver an extemporaneous speech
- Interpret and adapt to audience feedback

INTRODUCTION

The concept of *delivery* takes into account the way you present your ideas to the audience: your use of gestures, postures, voice, eyes, visual aids, and so on. And, as we already know, your speech delivery is of vital importance in determining the success of the speeches you give. But there is something else about delivery you should realize: delivery is much like an umpire in baseball or a referee in football or basketball. The best referees and umpires are those whom you do not notice during a game; the best delivery does not call attention to itself during a speech. In this chapter, we will be seeking delivery techniques that are not flamboyant but subtly add impact to the words they accompany.

Most of this chapter will be descriptive rather than prescriptive. That is, I generally will not tell you what to do or how to do it. Instead, as we review the types and techniques of nonverbal communication, my purpose will be to tell you, "If you want this effect, try these behaviors." By planning your objectives, you should yourself determine which of the strategies discussed in this chapter you want to employ. With these these things in mind, then, let's consider some objectives and strategies relevant to our delivery of public speeches.

USING NONVERBAL CUES

At the beginning of this part, we saw the types of nonverbal cues and the functions they perform. As we consider the secondary objectives necessary for achievement of our primary presentational objective, we will again explore those nonverbal categories.

Using Proxemics Effectively

When we consider the nature of spatial relationships in public speaking, three topic areas assume importance. Those three are: personal space, audience seating arrangements, and the use of furniture. Let's consider each in turn.

Personal Space

According to Hall (1966), people are like all animals in that they claim as their own certain areas or territories in their environments. Such territories include the objects, such as purses, briefcases, or books, we carry around with us, the objects we frequently use and thus come to consider "ours" (such as a desk or an office or a particular chair around a conference table), and even larger areas, such as houses or cars, to which we have both a personal and a legal claim. When someone else invades or uses these territories without our permission, we typically become rather annoyed. Imagine, for example, that you are at work and have to leave your office for a short time. When you return, some stranger is sitting in your chair at your desk, rummaging through your briefcase while wearing your glasses and smoking your pipe. Probably your response would be something stronger than, "Pardon me. Could I use those when you're done?" We tend to be upset when people invade our territories, and we usually will take steps to defend those territories (unless, of course, the invader is your boss, in which case you might offer her your clothing and children as well).

One particularly interesting sort of territory we claim and defend is the space that surrounds our bodies. As Figure 4-1 illustrates, each of us claims an egg-shaped sphere around our bodies which extends about arm's length in front of us and a few inches to the side and behind us. When someone "invades" that territory by standing too close while talking or by putting an uninvited hand on our shoulder, we tend to become uncomfortable and usually will try to reestablish our territory by taking a step backwards. However, as Sommer's (1969) experiments demonstrated, if we cannot reestablish our territories (either because of physical restrictions or social norms), we probably will exhibit a variety of nervous behaviors as we psychologically try to cope with this unsettling situation. Note, however, that there are circumstances in which territorial invasions do not pose a problem: close physical environments (such as a crowded elevator), close interpersonal relationships, and varying cultural norms all change our environmental claims. Still, for the most part we become unsettled when our space is violated and, if we cannot reestablish that space, we become psychologically vulnerable.

Salespersons know this principle all too well. One reason that most used-car and insurance salespersons are considered "pushy" is that, when they talk to us, they invade our space. They stand too close, breathing on our glasses, while they try to sell us their products. We, on the other hand, do not want to seem impolite so, rather than turn away or back up, we stand there and take it. But the situation is such that we are thown off balance psychologically; we are disconcerted by the salesperson's actions and, as a consequence, we are less able to deal critically with the things he or she is

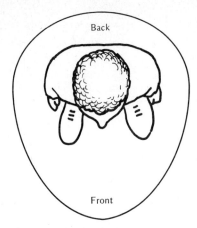

Figure 4-1: Individual Personal Space Claim

saying. Thus, we become more persuasible and more likely to give in to his or her appeals. This "pushy" salesperson has used personal space as a tool to make us more susceptible to his or her message.

But what has all this to do with public speaking? Oddly enough, the principles of personal space described above also operate in the public speaking situation. There is an "audience space" and a "speaker space" as Figure 4-2 illustrates. We are comfortable when the audience are on their side of the invisible boundary line and the speaker is on his or hers. When a violation of that boundary occurs, as when a speaker comes down from the platform and wanders about the audience while talking, it unsettles the audience a little bit; their territory is being invaded. Thus, while no experimental evidence exists to prove this conclusion, it seems highly likely that the audience become less resistant to persuasion when the speaker invades their space during the speech. They are thrown slightly off balance and therefore are less able to construct mental arguments against the speaker's views.

Before leaving this matter of personal space, however, we must understand two points. First, while the principle sounds good, it is sometimes difficult to put into practice. Invading the audience's space can be unsettling to you as a speaker, too. Your space is the area in front of the audience, and leaving that space to enter theirs means abandoning the security which your own space provides. Thus it can be as unnerving for you as it is for them to enact this sort of territorial invasion. Nevertheless, if you can bring yourself to do it a few times, you eventually will become accustomed to it and, like many evangelists who wander about the auditorium while they exhort their listeners, you ultimately will be able to use the strategy to maximum effect.

The second point, is not so easily dispensed with. Given the purpose of this territory-violation maneuver—to interfere with the audience's reasoning capabilities by upsetting them—we must question the ethics of using this strategy. Understand at the outset that many points of view exist concerning the nature of ethics. Some people feel that the end justifies the means—that if we are trying to achieve something honorable or just, any means necessary to achieving that end are ethical. Others

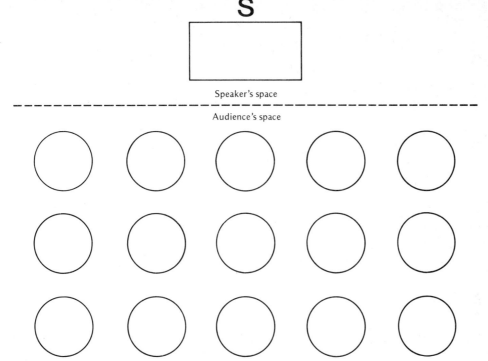

Figure 4-2: Personal Space in Public Speaking

feel that something is ethical if it does the greatest good for the greatest number. Thus, while you may mislead or distract an audience, if you are doing it for their own good (or at least the good of the majority), you are behaving ethically. My own standard, which you may take or leave, is somewhat different from these two, however. My belief is that the thing that makes people uniquely human is their capacity to reason, and that we should judge the ethics of public speaking in terms of the impact of our words and actions upon an audience's reasoning capabilities. Thus, things that enhance their ability to reason (such as accurate information or logical arguments) are ethical, while things that debilitate the reasoning capacity (such as false information, misleading arguments, or distracting behaviors) are unethical. Clearly, then, the territory-violation strategy would be considered unethical; it is designed specifically to interfere with our listeners' abilities to analyze and criticize the things we are saying. Nevertheless, as I prefer not to impose my own ethical standards upon you or anyone else, I will offer only two suggestions here: (1) recognize the impact of this strategy so that, when someone tries to use it on you, you can better defend yourself against it; (2) consider your own ethical standards and, if this strategy is in violation of those standards, do not use it.

Audience Seating Arrangements
Generally, this element of nonverbal communication will be beyond your control. Audience members will sit where they want within the environment available to you

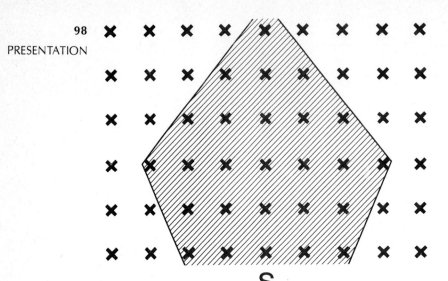

Figure 4-3: Adapting to Audience Seating: Normal Speaker Attention Areas

and them. You might try to influence their seating choices (as when a minister asks the members of the congregation, all of whom are packed into the back pews, to move forward into the empty front pews), but for the most part you will have to work with the situation as the audience construct it. But in any situation, you must be able to adapt to the audience's seating choices, and it is here that your use of nonverbal communication becomes important.

Figure 4-3 illustrates an audience and a speaker. The shaded area extending from the speaker to the audience indicates something interesting: the typical pattern of a speaker's eye behavior. While speaking, we tend to look most at the people seated directly in front of us and, moving back, at the people seated in the middle of the room. People seated in the front and rear corners tend to be neglected. Obviously, in most situations all audience members are important and to neglect any of them during our speech would be a mistake. Thus, we must take pains to devote attention to all audience members and to establish eye contact with each of them, regardless of their location, while we talk.

Furniture Usage

To understand the communicative impact of furniture, consider for a moment the arrangement of furniture in an office. Figure 4-4 illustrates two possible situations: one in which the office occupant confronts a visitor across a desk, and another in which occupant and visitor converse with no desk interposed. Surprisingly, two quite different impressions are created in the visitor's mind by these two arrangement patterns. White (1953), for example, studied communication in doctors' offices and found that, when a desk separated doctor and patient, only 10 percent of the patients seemed "at ease," while removal of the desk produced a situation in which 55 percent of the patients seemed relaxed. Zweigenhaft (1976) studied students' reac-

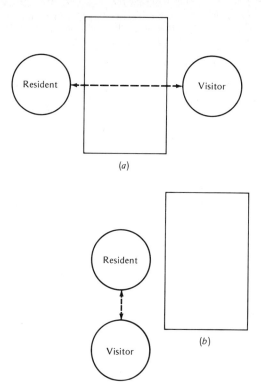

(a)

(b)

Figure 4-4: Office Furniture Arrangements

tions to professors who did and did not interpose a desk between themselves and their visitors and found that the unseparated professors were rated by students as more willing to "encourage the development of different viewpoints by students," as ready to give "individual attention to students who need it," and as less likely to show "undue favoritism." In both the professors' and the doctors' office settings, then, use of furniture created quite different effects.

In many public speaking settings, you may have to choose the way you will use a podium. You can stay behind it, perhaps clinging to it for dear life (as far too many speakers do), or you can step around it, facing your audience directly with no interposing furniture. The choice you make will create a very definite impression. Staying behind the podium will establish a formal, distant relationship between you and your audience. Standing next to or in front of the podium, conversely, will establish a more informal, conversational situation. But note that neither atmosphere is inherently better than the other. Your choice of strategy should be determined by your overall objective and by the impression you want to create in achieving that objective. If, for example, you seek to provide your audience with information and you perceive that your credibility is rather low, you might want to stay behind the podium, using it to create a more formal, authoritative, impressive mood. On the other hand, if your purpose is to persuade and you want to achieve it by establishing a casual, friendly atmosphere, you might choose to come out from behind the podium to address your audience. In any case, the impact of the podium must be taken into consideration as you devise your communication strategies.

Appearance

As we will see later in our consideration of source credibility, physical appearance influences our listeners' evaluations of the messages we send them. Specifically, our general attractiveness seems to influence listeners' credibility judgments (increased perceived attractiveness is associated with increased perceptions of credibility), as does our pattern of dress (high-status outfits seen to enhance credibility). Yet our choices of clothing transmit messages other than our status to our audience. For example, group identification is indicated by clothing, allowing the audience to determine which groups of people we seem to perceive ourselves as a part of. Suppose we delivered a speech wearing a black leather jacket with "Hell's Angels" embroidered across the back. Our group identification would be fairly clear. Or if we were dressed as a nun, again our affiliation would be pretty obvious. Of course, if we were dressed as a nun with "Hell's Angels" embroidered across the back, our audience would be confused. In most instances, these sorts of judgments are rather general: "He looks like a student," "She looks like an executive," and so on. Nevertheless, audiences still categorize you according to your clothing so that you need to consider what their judgment is likely to be when selecting the outfit in which you will speak.

Your self-concept also is shown by your clothing. Advertisers long have believed that our clothing choices represent our "idealized" selves—that we choose clothes that project the sort of image we would like to have. If this principle is true, and one suspects that it is, then we can judge a person's self-concept by observing his or her clothing choices. For example, consider two college professors: one always wears three-piece suits in which to teach and the other wears more casual clothing. Probably, these clothing patterns are indicative of a variety of other attitudinal patterns: conservatism versus liberalism, formal versus informal, and so on. But the point is really this: even if there is no true relationship between clothing and self-concept—even if the professor in cut-offs and sneakers is as conservative as they come—audience members assume that the clothing–self-concept relationship exists and draw inferences about the speaker accordingly. So again, you must make a choice: what self-concept do you want your audience to think you have?

Finally, clothing also may have an impact upon the person who wears it; that is, it may truly influence your own feelings, moods, self-confidence, and so on. Barnlund (1968), for example, suggests that our clothing may affect our mood—that if we get up one morning terribly depressed or listless, we might perk ourselves up by wearing a bright-colored outfit. Similarly, our self-confidence may be destroyed by a poor selection of clothing. Imagine attending what you thought was a come-as-you-are party dressed in your one-piece, footed pajamas only to discover that everyone else is wearing tuxedos and gowns. You probably would not be able to leave fast enough. Conversely, you may have outfits in which you feel particularly good. This enhancement of your self-confidence probably will also enhance your speaking performance.

In this section, then, we have seen the impact clothing can have on your audience and on yourself. But let me emphasize something important here: my purpose in this section was not to tell you to "sell out" or to dress in ways dictated by others. Do what you want. Dress however you choose. But realize that your selection of clothing has a definite impact, positive or negative, upon your audience's perceptions of you. They have valued forms of dress, and they have dress patterns they dislike or disrespect. If you dress in a way they value, your credibility and effectiveness probably will increase; if you dress in a way they dislike, your credibility and impact probably will drop. So dress however you please when you speak, but realize that your success in achieving your speaking objective will be significantly influenced by the clothing choices you make.

Bodily Posture

The general postures and movements of your body while you speak have an important impact upon your communicative effectiveness. More precisely, two characteristics of your overall bodily movement are particularly useful: general bodily tension and bodily movement.

The impact of bodily tension is best illustrated by two extremes: very relaxed posture and very tense. The speaker who is too relaxed, who props himself up on the podium or casually stands with one leg crossed over the other while he talks, creates an impression of indifference or unconcern about his speech. This impression can lead to two conclusions in the mind of the audience: either the speaker truly does not care about the speech, or he really does care and is nervous but is trying too hard to hide it. Either way, the speaker loses. Indifference and deception both are antithetical to high source credibility, and if your posture transmits impressions of either, your effectiveness will be severely hampered. On the other hand, the speaker whose posture is too tense—knees locked, arms pressed to the sides, and body stiff—creates an impression of lacking self-confidence. After all, if she were confident she would not be quivering in fear. And if she is not confident, what does that imply about her competence? Obviously she doubts it, and so will the audience. Again, bodily posture has betrayed the speaker.

The key to effective speaking posture is to find a midpoint between extreme relaxation and extreme tension. You should stand straight, with your weight evenly distributed on both feet, but you should not look like inspection time at the Marine Corps. You should move in a casual, relaxed manner, but the audience should not perceive a danger of your falling asleep. In essence, you should avoid going to either extreme in exhibiting bodily tension. One useful method for achieving this "golden mean" is employing deliberate bodily movement—our second important element of bodily posture.

Rather than stand in one spot while you talk, you occasionally should move around during your speech. Such movement produces several desirable effects. First, it helps maintain audience attention. We have a natural tendency to give attention to moving objects in our environment. If, for example, while you are reading or watching television you catch, in the corner of your eye, a glimpse of something moving, you probably shift your attention immediately to that thing. The reason: we tend to look at things that move and to stop looking at things that stand still. When giving a speech, of course, you want your audience to watch you. Your moving occasionally from one spot to another will help keep their eyes fixed on you.

Too Relaxed or . . .

Too Tense

Movement can serve a second function: providing a visual transition to accompany the spoken transitions you give as your speech moves from one main idea to the next. As you conclude one thought and provide a transition into the next, such as "Let's move now to my second argument," you might take a step or two to one side or the other, indicating physically the psychological movement of your speech. Of course, you do not want to be too obvious in doing this or the whole thing becomes a ludicrous pantomime. But a shift in posture or position at the right time can be a useful transitional device.

While movement helps your audience maintain attention and follow the flow of your speech, it also can help you. For example, moving about while you talk is a useful means of releasing the excess energy stagefright often produces; thus, movement helps you better control your physical activities during the speech. But the possibility also exists that physical movement aids your own psychological movement. Books and magazines on jogging are full of claims by joggers that their best ideas come while they are running. Perhaps the stereotypical picture of the scientist pacing back and forth deep in thought has some basis in fact: physical movement may truly promote our thought processes. While speaking, then, you should make an effort to move occasionally from your present spot to another one—it will help your listeners, and it will help you.

It is important to note, however, that random movement is not the sort that we want. Probably you have seen this sort of movement as well—a speaker who rocks back and forth while talking or a professor who paces back and forth in front of the classroom while lecturing. In such cases, the movement is a distractor not an attention getter. It serves no useful purpose and takes the listeners' minds off the speech and focuses their attention on the bizarre behavior. To avoid this pitfall, there are two principles of effective movement you always should keep in mind while speaking:

1. Movement should be purposeful. Like all other elements of speaking, your movements should be designed to accomplish some specific purpose.
2. Movement should be appropriate. The movements you exhibit should fit and enhance the meanings of the words you say.

If you adhere to these two criteria, your movements will be a powerful element of your overall presentation.

Gestures

For centuries theorists in public speaking were very much concerned with the "proper" use of gestures. Tremendous amounts of time and study were devoted to the development of systems of "elocution" that told speakers the right sorts of gestures to use at the right times. Indeed, less than a century ago people were using a system of notation, similar to musical notation, that indicated on a speech manuscript the exact point in the speech at which to perform a certain gesture. The result of all of this, of course, was a lot of artificial gesturing and a lot of silly-looking speeches.

Surprisingly, some rather recent texts in public speaking have offered similar sorts of advice. For example, one text suggested that you "stand with the feet about 6 inches apart, with one foot placed slightly behind the other," that you "keep one hand on the podium at all times," and that when gesturing, you should "let the wrist lead, with the hand following at first and gradually catching up by the time the stroke is completed." Try it; you will feel silly, too.

In this text, you will not find specific prescriptions for gesturing. Rather, I will simply offer three principles you ought to keep in mind as you deliver your speeches:

1. *Be natural.* When you gesture, you should do so because you feel like it. In addition, you should perform the gesture you feel like performing. You should not use preplanned gestures, nor should you try to use gestures that looked terrific when you saw some other speaker use them. When gesturing, do what comes naturally.
2. *Be varied.* When the same gesture is repeated over and over, it becomes a distractor. Thus, it is important that you use a variety of gestures while you speak. But here we might have to violate the "naturalness" rule. It may be that you have one and only one natural gesture and that you use it repeatedly while talking. If that is the case, then you will have to bend the naturalness principle just a little and try to work some variety into your movements.
3. *Be appropriate.* The gestures you use should fit the words you say. They should add meaning to the words: repeat them nonverbally, elaborate on

them, or emphasize them. They should not be random flailings, which you do because you are nervous or because you think you should have some sort of gestures in your speech. You should use gestures, but they ought to fit the meanings of the words.

Natural, varied, and appropriate gestures add a great deal to the spoken message. They maintain audience interest by providing physical movement; they add meaning to the words by performing the functions of nonverbal cues which we discussed at the beginning of this section; they provide you with a release of pent-up energy. Thus, even though it may be natural for you to stand absolutely still while you speak, you should make up your mind to use gestures while you speak and then, while actually speaking, you should use gestures which are natural, varied, and appropriate.

Eye and Face Behaviors

Of all the nonverbal cues we control, the most expressive are our facial expressions and our eye behaviors. By observing our facial and eye movements, audiences infer our entire emotional state—how we feel about our topic, ourselves, and our listeners. Since it is crucial that we convey the proper emotions to our audience, we need to know the sorts of face and eye behaviors that portray particular feelings to others.

The enormous complexity of facial expressions has posed a continuing problem to researchers: since a wide variety of emotions are conveyed by almost undetectable changes in facial expression, no one yet has been able to establish direct correlations between specific expressions and exact emotional states. However, Ekman (1971) has managed to isolate certain areas of the face that seem to express better than other areas some general emotional states. His studies indicate that happiness is shown most in the lower face and eyes; that sadness is seen in the eyes; that surprise is shown in the eyes and lower face; that anger is exhibited in the lower face and brows/forehead; that disgust can be observed in the lower face; and that fear is shown most in the eyes. While these findings are mildly interesting, however, they have little practical applicability for us as public speakers. We can hardly decide that "I want them to think I'm angry at this point in the speech, so I'll flop my eyebrows and stick out my lower face." Instead, our main concern must be one of consistency. Our facial expressions must fit the moods we try to create and the words we speak. If you smirk or grin (even out of nervousness) while giving a serious message, if you are calm and impassive while delivering a highly emotional message, or if you are frowning and gloomy while describing a particularly enjoyable event, your audience is going to wonder about your sincerity and perhaps your sanity.

The ironic element of facial expressions is that, when engaged in normal conversation, we all generally are quite expressive. Our facial movements exhibit clearly the emotions we are experiencing, and they add a great deal of meaning to the words we transmit. When confronted with an audience, however, we seem to find it difficult to relax and let our face act as it normally would. Yet the key to effective facial expressions is precisely that: relax and let your face behave normally. The suggestions we considered in the preceding chapter for handling stagefright will help promote good facial expressions and so, too, will concentration upon the content of the speech. If you become "wrapped up" in what you are saying, you will be so personally involved in the speech that facial expressions will occur naturally and will add considerable meaning to your words.

Probably you already know the "bottom line" of eye behavior: maintain eye contact with your audience. But you may not know the reasons behind that injunction, and those reasons are important. Research summarized by Knapp (1978) has identified the situations in which we seek eye contact and the situations in which we avoid it, and other research has determined the impressions we convey to others through our eye behavior. Briefly, the findings of these research studies can be summarized in this manner:

We Seek Eye Contact When	**We Avoid Eye Contact When**
We want to communicate	We do not want to communicate
We are physically distant	We are physically close
We are friendly toward the other	We are unfriendly toward the other
We want feedback from the other	We fear feedback from the other

Probably you have seen these principles in action yourself. For example, imagine that you are sitting in your local Howard Johnson's restaurant starving to death while waiting for service. What do you do to flag down a waitress? Probably, you try to establish eye contact with her, because eye contact is a signal that communication is desired. And probably the waitress studiously avoids eye contact with you because she has 50 other tables to handle. Similarly, as you are sitting there eating the cold spaghetti you finally received, you might notice someone you utterly despise walking in the door. The last thing you want to do is communicate with that person (particularly while you are trying to eat), so you avoid eye contact at all costs, staring down at your spaghetti or counting the spots of spaghetti sauce that are all over your front. Through eye contact, then, we seek or avoid interaction with others.

Eye contact serves a second function. When we are physically distant from someone to whom we are talking, we tend to have a good deal of eye contact with them. Conversely, when we are physically close, eye contact seems to decrease. Consider what happens, for example, when you and a friend enter a crowded elevator. Before getting into the elevator, you probably are maintaining a great deal of eye contact while you talk. But what happens when you enter the elevator? If you ever have watched people in an elevator, you have observed how virtually no eye contact occurs: everyone carefully studies the flashing floor numbers or the graffiti on the walls, but no one looks into another's eyes. It seems, then, that eye contact serves to decrease the psychological distance between people who are physically distant, and that eye contact becomes less important in this regard as the conversing parties move closer.

Still other messages are transmitted by eye contact. Imagine that you are back at Howard Johnson's eating spaghetti, and that the despised individual you wanted to avoid has spotted you and taken a seat in your booth. As the two of you talk, you probably will have little eye contact with him. The reason: your eye behaviors mirror your personal feelings. If you are attracted to someone, so are your eyes, so that you tend to look more at that person. If you are repulsed, your eyes also show it, as they tend to look away from the individual. Indeed, eye behaviors are usually reliable indicators of how one person feels about another. But eye contact shows one other thing: a desire to obtain or avoid feedback. Suppose your companion asks, "Well, aren't you glad to see me?" Polite person that you are, you might answer, "Of course—I'm delighted." Probably you would find it difficult to look him in the eye while delivering this falsehood. In fact, any time we lie to someone we probably find it difficult to look at him or her. The reason is that we fear the feedback which we might receive. Whenever we lie, there always is the chance that we will be caught— that the other person's response will be one of disbelief. Only the most accomplished liars can look other people directly in the eye and spew out their tales. Conversely, if we want to see how the other person is responding, we will try to maintain eye contact with him or her.

The importance of eye contact in public speaking thus should be obvious. We want to open communication channels with our audience, we want to close the psychological distance between them and us, we want them to know that we like them, and we want to obtain their feedback. For all of these reasons, then, we should maintain eye contact with them. If eye contact is missing, our audience are likely to assume that we don't want to communicate with them, that we are unconcerned about our physical distance from them, that we do not particularly like them, or that we are not interested in their responses. Any one of these assumptions could be extremely damaging. So again we arrive at this conclusion: look at your audience while you talk to them.

One final point needs to be made. Perhaps you have heard some of the "helpful hints" often given concerning the use of eye contact: "look over the audience's heads while speaking;" "talk to the back wall;" "look at your listener's foreheads or noses;" and other useless pieces of advice. The audience can tell where you are looking. If you look over their heads, they will wonder about the acuity of your eyesight; if you look at the back wall, they will turn around to see what about that wall is so fascinating; if you look at their foreheads or noses, they will take out mirrors and start checking for warts. "Eye contact" is precisely that: contact between your eyes and theirs. When speaking, look into the eyes of audience members at some point during the speech. Period.

Vocal Behaviors

The way we use our voices can make the difference between a rousing success and utter failure. Doubtless we all have heard speakers who spoke in a lifeless monotone or who talked so fast we could hardly understand them or who spoke so softly we had to strain to hear them. Doubtless, too, we do not count these speakers among the greats whom we have encountered. The best speakers are those whose vocal behaviors have four characteristics: intelligibility, variety, fluency, and pleasantness. They achieve these characteristics through their specific vocalic behaviors, including pronunciation, articulation, pitch, volume, rate, and quality. Let's examine each of the four desirable vocal characteristics and determine the behaviors that contribute to their development.

Intelligibility

If you are to be effective, you must be understood by your audience. Thus, your speech must be intelligible. Several aspects of your vocal cues contribute to your intelligibility. Pronunciation is one: you must pronounce words properly if your

audience are to understand them. Sometimes this can become a problem, as pronunciations change from one geographical region to the next. If you are in France, for example, you would pronounce *Pierre* as *pea-air;* if you are in South Dakota, you would pronounce the state capital "peer." Similarly, *Versailles* is *vare-sigh* in France and *ver-sayles* in Kentucky, and while *Prague* rhymes with *frog* in Europe, it rhymes with *plague* in Oklahoma. Perhaps the only consistent rule concerning pronunciation that one should follow is this: in a particular region, pronounce words in the same manner that educated people in that region pronounce them. By following that rule, you probably will deliver speeches that are understandable to your audience.

Intelligibility also springs from articulation, or the precision and clarity with which you say the words. Common articulation faults include slurring sounds or words together, adding unneeded sounds (*ath-a-lete* instead of *athlete* or *idear* instead of *idea*), omitting sounds (*fim* rather than *film* or *goverment* instead of *government*), substituting sounds (*minny* rather than *many* or *git* rather than *get*), and transposing or reversing sounds (*hunderd* rather than *hundred* or *nuculer* rather than *nuclear*). Again, if you do not speak clearly or if you misarticulate words, your audience will find it difficult to understand what you are saying.

Two other vocal characteristics related to intelligibility are volume (or how loudly you speak) and rate (or how rapidly you speak). The principles here are simple: speak loudly enough for all members of the audience to hear you and slowly enough for all members of the audience to understand you. By watching the responses of your audience (something we will consider a bit later in this chapter), you will be able to judge whether they can hear and understand you. If they seem to be straining to hear or concentrating to understand, you may need to turn up your volume or slow down your speed.

Variety

As we already know, change attracts attention. Certainly, this principle applies to your vocal behaviors: by changing your vocal cues, you can do much to maintain audience interest. The vocal cues that should be varied include: rate (speed up at some points and slow down at others), pitch (avoid a monotone by changing how high or how low your voice is while you talk), and volume (speak loudly at some points and softly at others). Unfortunately, achieving variety in these cues can be difficult—we all have our own "normal" rate, pitch, and volume of speech. Thus, you must make a conscious effort to change these characteristics while you talk, and only through practice will you become proficient at using your voice in this way. But the effort is worth it: the best speakers are those whose vocal cues add interest to the speech by adding variety to the delivery.

Fluency

To speak fluently, you must have both a rhythm in your speaking and an absence of nonfluencies in your words. Rhythm has to do with the regularity or irregularity of accenting and phrasing with which you present your words. Consider, for example, the accenting and phrasing of everyone's favorite poem:

MA-ry HAD a LIT-tle LAMB
its FLEECE was WHITE as SNOW;
and EV-ery WHERE that MA-ry WENT
the LAMB was SURE to GO.

The rhythm of the passage is achieved by the pauses at the end of every line and by the accenting of every other syllable in the words. To see the impact of irregular rhythm, try reading the poem with pauses and accents misplaced:

ma-RY HAD a lit-TLE (*pause*)
LAMB ITS fleece was WHITE (*pause*)
AS snow and ev-ERY where THAT ma-RY (*pause*)
WENT the lamb (*pause*)
WAS sure to GO.

In order for the poem to make sense, pauses must come after completed phrases and accents must add meaning to the words. So it is with your speech. You should pause for a breath at the appropriate places in your sentences, and you should use vocal variety to provide accents in regular, meaningful ways.

Nonfluencies are meaningless sounds and phrases such as "um," "uh," "I mean," "Ya know," and the other useless noises that litter our speech. The rule here is simple: avoid them. The presence of nonfluencies in your speech hurts you in two ways: it makes your speech more difficult to understand and it lowers your credibility. While the effect upon understandability is obvious, the effect upon credibility deserves some explanation. Typically, nonfluencies are interpreted by listeners as being indicative of two things: nervousness or inexperience. Either interpretation is detrimental to you as a source. However, if your speech is fluent (that is, free from nonfluencies), the audience will interpret that fluency as the mark of a confident, experienced speaker. Your credibility thus rises. It is important to your success, then, that you speak in a manner that is both rhythmic and free from disfluencies.

Pleasantness

Virtually all characteristics of your voice contribute to the pleasantness of your speech. If you speak too rapidly, too loudly, at too high or too constant a pitch, inarticulately, or with poor pronunciation, your audience probably will not enjoy listening to you. But one other element of pleasantness exists that we have not yet considered: vocal quality. Perhaps the best way to define good vocal quality is in terms of what it is not: a good voice is not harsh, husky, hoarse, breathy, nasal, shrill, or screechy. The causes of unpleasant vocal qualities are numerous, ranging from momentary illnesses to permanent impairments to poor speaking habits. The cures for unpleasantness are equally numerous and many of them require the assistance of a professional therapist. Still, some suggestions for improving vocal quality can be offered:

1. Listen to yourself on tape. This will allow you to hear yourself as others hear you, and it will provide you with keys for improving your vocal quality.

2. Speak at a comfortable volume and pitch. When you strain your voice, you usually will lose whatever pleasant qualities you normally have.

3. Maintain adequate breath support. Take deep breaths while you speak and tighten your stomach muscles in order to maintain a strong flow of air through your vocal mechanisms as you talk. This will help you maintain a normal vocal quality while achieving the volume level you need to reach everyone in the audience.

Overall Nonverbal Strategies

In this section, we have observed several techniques for using each type of nonverbal behavior. When you look at all of the techniques we have considered and break them down to their most basic elements, however, you arrive at two basic strategies for effective delivery.

1. Plan your general nonverbal cues. In the preparatory phases of your speaking, decide what objectives in the use of nonverbal behaviors you want to accomplish. You might decide, for example, that you are going to use gestures, that you are going to move about as you talk, that you are going to appear a particular way, that you are going to maintain eye contact, and that you are going to incorporate the four desirable vocal characteristics we discussed above. Thus, you make up your mind at the outset that you are going to employ nonverbal cues throughout your speech.

2. Let specific nonverbal cues occur naturally. For example, while you decide to use gestures while you speak, you should not decide which gestures you are going to exhibit. Rather, you should let your gestures flow naturally from your words. Similarly, your movements, expressions, vocal inflections, and so on all should occur naturally and not because you have mapped them out ahead of time.

If you follow those two strategies, you probably will deliver your speeches in an interesting, effective manner. In so doing, you will greatly enhance your chances for achieving the objectives toward which your speeches are directed.

USING VISUAL AIDS

In the preceding section, we saw how you can use your own appearance and actions to add visual interest and impact to the words comprising your speech. But there are other devices you can employ to give further visual appeal to your message, and these devices commonly are referred to as visual aids.

Several types of visual aids are available: the actual object being talked about (as when you use a real pistol to demonstrate and illustrate how firearms work), a model of the object if the real thing is too big (such as a model airplane in a speech about principles of flight), slides or movies, charts, graphs, maps, and diagrams. Used correctly, these things serve several useful functions. They add interest to the speech by giving the audience something to watch while you talk to them. They clarify the things you are saying by providing a visual illustration of the points you make. They even serve to jog your memory as you talk and act as a set of "notes" that can be seen by both you and your audience. Indeed, every speech you give should, if possible, incorporate some visual aid in the presentation.

Visual Aids Act as Notes Visible to You and Your Audience

When using visual aids, there are two sets of rules you should follow to be maximally effective: rules for preparing visual aids and rules for presenting them. Both lists of rules are presented below.

Rules for Preparing Visual Aids

1. Make them visible. They should be large enough for everyone to see, and their parts should be distinguishable. The use of dark lines and contrasting colors helps audience members determine what the visual aid is all about.
2. Make them simple. They should not have too much detail, or they will become confusing or difficult to sort out. Figure 4-5, which was used in a speech about poor flight patterns, illustrates the need for simplicity in visual aids.
3. Make them complete. While visual aids must be kept simple, they also should present all the needed visual information; important parts should not be left out.
4. Make them appropriate. Good visual aids fit the purpose, tone, and content of the speech.
5. Make them communicative. Good visual aids add something to the speech. You should use them because they have some purpose or objective and not just to be using a visual aid.

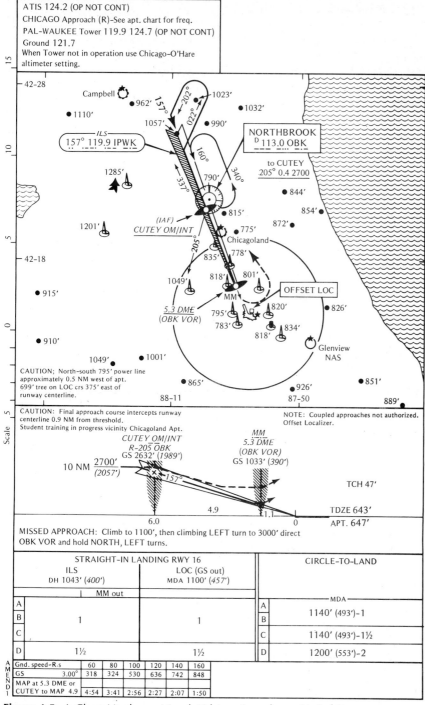

ATIS 124.2 (OP NOT CONT)
CHICAGO Approach (R)—See apt. chart for freq.
PAL-WAUKEE Tower 119.9 124.7 (OP NOT CONT)
Ground 121.7
When Tower not in operation use Chicago-O'Hare
altimeter setting.

NORTHBROOK
D 113.0 OBK

ILS
157° 119.9 IPWK

to CUTEY
205° 0.4 2700

(IAF)
CUTEY OM/INT

Chicagoland

OFFSET LOC

MM

5.3 DME
(OBK VOR)

Glenview
NAS

CAUTION; North-south 795' power line
approximately 0.5 NM west of apt.
699' tree on LOC crs 375' east of
runway centerline.

CAUTION: Final approach course intercepts runway
centerline 0.9 NM from threshold.
Student training in progress vicinity Chicagoland Apt.

NOTE: Coupled approaches not authorized.
Offset Localizer.

CUTEY OM/INT
R-205 OBK
GS 2632' (1989')

MM
5.3 DME
(OBK VOR)
GS 1033' (390')

10 NM   2700'
        (2057')

157°

TCH 47'

4.9

1.1

TDZE 643'

6.0   0   APT. 647'

MISSED APPROACH: Climb to 1100', then climbing LEFT turn to 3000' direct
OBK VOR and hold NORTH, LEFT turns.

STRAIGHT-IN LANDING RWY 16				CIRCLE-TO-LAND	
ILS DH 1043' (400')		LOC (GS out) MDA 1100' (457')			
MM out					
A			A	MDA	
B	1	1	B	1140' (493')-1	
C			C	1140' (493')-1½	
D	1½	1½	D	1200' (553')-2	

Gnd. speed-R.s	60	80	100	120	140	160
GS 3.00°	318	324	530	636	742	848
MAP at 5.3 DME or CUTEY to MAP 4.9	4:54	3:41	2:56	2:27	2:07	1:50

Figure 4-5: A Chart Used as a Visual Aid in a Speech on Air Safety.
What Principles of Preparing Visual Aids Does It Violate?

Rules for Presenting Visual Aids

1. Do not stand in front of the visual aid while you talk about it. This seems obvious, but it is a rule I have seen violated dozens of times. Needless to say, the visual aid loses its impact when this occurs.
2. Speak to the audience not to the aid. Continue to look at your audience as much as possible, even while you describe the visual aid you have placed in front of them.
3. Know your visual aid well. If you have to study the visual aid while you talk about it, you will both lose eye contact with your audience and seem rather badly prepared. Know your visual aid well enough that you can talk about it without constantly looking at it.
4. Point to the part of the visual aid you are discussing. Help your audience to follow your description of the visual aid by pointing to the portion of the aid under consideration. With particularly large visual aids, some sort of long pointer might be useful; otherwise, simply point with your finger.
5. Reveal it when ready; conceal it when done. If your audience are studying your visual aid while you are talking about something else, the aid is acting as a distractor rather than as an aid. Thus, you should hide the aid during the early part of your speech, reveal it only when you are ready to talk about it, and then conceal it again when you are ready to talk about something else. This same principle applies, incidentally, to the use of handouts. If possible, do not hand the material out until you are ready to discuss it, and when that discussion is finished ask your audience to put it away.

If you follow all ten of these rules, your visual aids will add tremendously to the appeal and impact of your speech. Again, if it is at all possible to do so, use some form of visual aid in every speech you give.

USING NOTES

Another aspect of the delivery of public speeches (one which certainly has already crossed your mind) is the use of notes by you, the speaker. Often people ask whether they should use an outline, a word-for-word manuscript, or no notes at all when they speak. To answer that question, we need first to consider four things: (1) preparation—your notes should reflect a desirable amount of preparation; (2) flexibility—your notes should allow you to modify your message as you speak; (3) directness—your notes should promote maximum direct contact between you and your audience; and (4) security—your notes should provide you with some recourse should you lose your place, and knowing that you have that recourse available to you should make you feel more secure. With those four criteria in mind, then, let's look at some of the notation systems available to you.

Impromptu Speaking. This sort of speaking occurs when you are called upon to speak with no forewarning. While sitting in a meeting, for example, you might suddenly be asked to report on some project in which you are involved, to describe some process with which you are familiar, or to deliver some other sort of off-the-cuff message. In such situations, you obviously have no notes (except those which you might be able to scribble on the nearest available piece of paper just before you have to stumble to the front of the room). Thus, this situation allows minimum preparation, maximum flexibility (after all, you make the speech up as you go), maximum directness (you have no notes to distract you from your audience), and absolutely no source of security. Because of the lack of preparation and security involved in this sort of speaking, you should avoid it whenever possible; deliver impromptu speeches only when absolutely necessary. Still, occasions such as these will arise, and when they do you should handle them through this four-step process:

1. State your main idea. That is, begin with the main point you want to make.
2. List your major supporting ideas. Through some quick mental dividing and organizing, develop three or four major supporting points and list them for your audience. If you have a piece of paper, you might jot these points down.
3. Develop each major supporting idea in sequence (just as you would in any speech).
4. Review your supporting points and restate your main idea. Then sit down.

Extemporaneous Speaking. This sort of speaking is the type we will be discussing throughout this book. It involves thorough preparation of content and thorough consideration of delivery, but during the speech it involves only a skeleton of the speech to be used as notes. This skeleton can take two forms. The key word outline discussed in Chapter 6 is the most common form although complete-sentence outlines also may be used. With either outline, the notes consist of main points and subpoints listed to serve as a reminder to you while you speak. The notes do *not* consist of a word-by-word manuscript of the speech; the only completely written out materials you should use are direct quotations. Thus, outlines for extemporaneous speeches provide preparation, flexibility to a degree (you can change the specific wording you use or even revise the outline as you speak), directness (provided you do not stare at your outline while you speak), and security.

The second form of extemporaneous notes you can use is pictures. Consider the chart in Figure 4-6. Each square in the chart represents one note card. On each card is a cartoon—one which you have drawn. The first cartoon represents the idea you will use; the second represents your motivational devices; the third represents your credibility statement; the next few represent the main ideas you will develop; the last represents your concluding remarks. But why use cartoons rather than an outline? Two reasons. First, the very process of preparing the cartoons will impress the speech on your mind. After all, it takes a great deal of creativity and some hard thinking to devise the cartoons in the first place so that the process will make the materials they represent extremely memorable. Second, if you use cartoons you will not be tempted to read your notes to your audience. The pictorial-extemporaneous approach to speaking thus maximizes your ability to succeed according to all four of the criteria we have established.

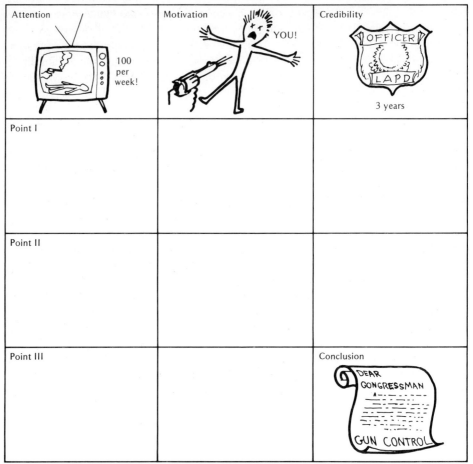

Figure 4-6: Cartoon-Notes for Speech on "Gun Control"

Manuscript Speaking. With this form of speaking, you write your speech word for word and then deliver your manuscript (without reading it) to your audience. While this sort of speaking provides maximum preparation and security, it also minimizes directness and flexibility. Indeed, when you have a manuscript in front of you the tendency to read it is almost insurmountable. Thus, you should speak from manuscript only when exact wording is absolutely crucial. That is why, for example, influential political figures typically use manuscripts—one slip of the tongue and their careers could be lost, wars started, or a whole series of undesirable events triggered. Few of your speeches will have that sort of impact; thus, you should rarely if ever speak from manuscript.

Memorized Speaking. If you really want to give yourself a nervous breakdown, try this form of speaking. Write out your entire speech and then memorize it word for word. Then try to deliver it and sound natural in the process. While this form of speaking maximizes (indeed, overdoes) preparation, it fails on every other count. It allows no flexibility; it allows little direct contact (usually the speaker's eyes are glazed over as he or she tries to remember the words that come next); it provides almost no security (in fact, it does the opposite: fear of forgetting will frighten you far more than will the audience). And above all, it leads to mechanical, feelingless speaking. Never use memorized speeches. They are tickets to failure.

Of the forms of notes we have seen in this section, then, the best (at least in my own estimation) is the pictoral notes used in the cartoon version of extemporaneous speaking. They maximize all of the four delivery criteria we established at the outset and, while they require some time for preparation, they typically produce the most effectively delivered speeches.

ADAPTING TO AUDIENCE FEEDBACK

To this point, we have considered nonverbal communication only from the point of view of the speaker. But as we saw in the first chapter of this book, communication is a circular process: all participants in the communicative act are continually sending messages to the other participants. This same principle applies to public speaking, of course. While you are speaking to your audience, they are sending messages to you. If you are able to observe and interpret those messages, you can use them to adapt your speech as you deliver it so that it more effectively appeals to your audience's current attitudes and moods. In this section, then, we will consider the sorts of nonverbal audience feedback cues you should observe while you speak, the sorts of conclusions you can draw from those cues, and the sorts of strategies you should use to adapt to your audience.

Interpreting Audience Feedback

When you are delivering a speech, there are three things you want to know about your audience: (1) Are they interested? (2) Do they understand? (3) Do they believe or agree? If the answers to all of these questions are Yes, then everything is fine; proceed as planned. But if the answer to one or more of these questions is No, then remedial action is needed. Thus, your choices of speech strategy are (or at least should be) dictated by the responses you receive from your audience. In order to make the right choice, you should observe the feedback coming to you through three nonverbal cues.

1. Eye Contact and Facial Expression. Just as your face and eyes are the most expressive parts of your body, so too are the audience reactions seen most clearly in their facial and eye behaviors. Specifically, eye contact (or the lack of it) can indicate interest, agreement, and understanding. When your audience are looking at you, it probably means that they are listening to you, that they understand you, and that they are at least to a degree in agreement with you. If, however, most of them are looking away from you for a prolonged period, this lack of eye contact may signal boredom, confusion, or disagreement. Again, action to rectify those situations will be needed. Similarly, facial expressions can be telling. If most of the audience are smiling or have pleasant expressions, things probably are all right. But if most of them are frowning, it may mean that they are having difficulty understanding you (and thus are concentrating hard to figure out what you are saying), or it may mean that they are disagreeing. Either reaction is a problem that must be handled. Absolutely blank expressions, finally, may mean that no one is listening any more, and you will need to recapture interest. By reading the listeners' face and eye behaviors, then, you can determine how well things are proceeding and decide whether new speech strategies are needed.

*2. **Head Nods or Head Shakes.*** If members of the audience are nodding their heads up and down while you speak, it usually is a good sign: they probably are listening, understanding, and agreeing. Or they may be nodding off to sleep—check their eye contact. But if the listeners are shaking their heads from side to side, you may have a problem. Probably they are listening (otherwise, why would they be reacting negatively?), but they may be having difficulty understanding or agreeing with the speech. You probably will need to take steps to correct that problem.

*3. **Posture.*** Although this is the least reliable indicator of audience members' feelings, their general bodily postures still may tell you something. If most of the listeners are sitting up in their chairs and leaning forward, they probably are interested in what you are saying. However, if they are slumped back in their chairs, leaning away from you, they may well be bored by what you are saying, confused by your speech, or in disagreement with your viewpoint. On the other hand, they might also be sitting back relaxed, enjoying the speech, and having the time of their lives. It is both difficult and unreliable, then, to draw concrete conclusions about listeners' feelings based upon their postural behaviors. Nevertheless, when considered in combination with the eye, face, and head cues we saw above, postural cues can provide insight into the interest, understanding, and attitudes of audience members.

Adapting to Audience Feedback

We have determined that we want to assess our listeners' interest, understanding, and agreement, and we have discovered that we can judge these things by observing their eye, face, head, and postural behaviors. But what do we do next? How do we adapt to audience feedback? The decision chart presented in Figure 4-7 illustrates the ways in which we should adapt to our listeners' feedback. Let's review those adaptive strategies briefly.

If the audience seem not to be interested in or listening to what you are saying, you might use some of the attention-getting or motivation-arousing strategies we discuss in later chapters. Specifically, you might:

Give a quotation
Tell a story
Ask rhetorical questions
Tell a joke
Use silence
Appeal to their curiosity
Show the utility of your information for fulfilling their needs

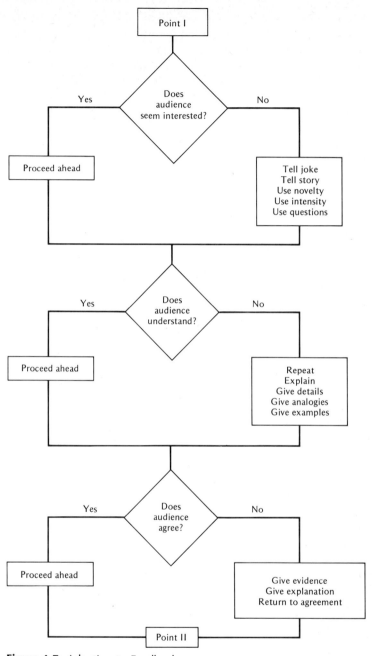

Figure 4-7: Adapting to Feedback

Or you may use any of the other dozen or so techniques we already have discussed. The point is, you should do something. You ought not simply hope that they will start listening again in a while or that they will find your next subpoint fascinating.

If the audience seem confused or unable to understand something you have said, there are a couple of things you should do. First, simply repeat the point. They may not have heard what you said, or they may not have understood the words you uttered. But if repetition does not solve the problem—if the frowns and head shakes still persist—then you will need to use some techniques for clarifying your information. Specifically, you could:

Provide an explanation of the point
Give additional details
Give examples
Provide definitions
Use an analogy
Use a contract
Use numbers to quantify the point
Get them to visualize the thing being considered

Obviously, the specific strategy you choose will be determined by the sort of point about which your audience seem confused. Nevertheless, one of the above strategies should serve to resolve the confusion. Again, it is important that you take some sort of action if you perceive that the audience do not understand you. Simply letting them stay confused will serve only to frustrate them, and it may cause them to lose interest in the speech altogether.

Finally, if your listeners seem to disagree with you, there are steps you should take in an effort to gain their assent. First, you should explain your position. Perhaps by showing the listeners your chain of thought, your reasoning and your assumptions, you can demonstrate to them the correctness of your conclusions. Second, you should use evidence to prove your position if simple explanation does not gain their agreement. The sorts of proof we discuss in later chapters, such as examples, statistics, presumptions, or quotations from recognized authorities, should be entered into the speech at this point. Third, you might return to an earlier point in your speech with which the audience had agreed. This is an important principle. When you hit upon something with which the audience agree, your natural tendency is to continue talking about that thing—to flail away at the point for all you are worth. The reason is simple: we all like to get positive responses from our audiences, and when we do, our natural instinct is to stay on the well-received point, continuing the positive feedback. In fact, we should do precisely the opposite. When it is clear that our audience agree with us, we should move almost immediately to the next point. After all, we have succeeded; why continue to beat away at a point already won? But we also should keep this point in the back of our minds for future use; we should make a mental note that this point went over well. Then, if later in the speech we encounter disagreement, we might be able to refer back to this point and use it as evidence for the new one. In effect, we would say "Look, you agreed with this point earlier. Now see how the present issue naturally grows out of the earlier one." We thus use the principle of

. consistency, showing our audience that, since they agreed with the earlier point, it is consistent for them also to agree with this one. If you can use it, this device is a very powerful form of proof, for it uses the beliefs of the audience as evidence to support the argument presently being considered.

When audience feedback indicates that things are not going very well—that the audience members are bored, confused, or in disagreement—you should take some sort of corrective action. The suggestions offered in this final section will be useful tools in adapting to and capitalizing upon the responses of your listeners.

SUMMARY

Our attention was devoted in this chapter to the actual presentation of your speech, and our objective was to discover strategies by which you can present your thoughts in the most effective way. First, we studied the ways in which nonverbal cues can be applied in public speaking. We considered the utility of proxemics, appearance, bodily posture, gestures, eye and face behaviors, and vocal behaviors, and we tried to isolate the impact which each set of nonverbal cues can have when used in certain ways during a speech. Then we noted two global principles for using nonverbal cues: plan their use in general ahead of time but let them occur naturally as you speak. In the final sections of this chapter, we discussed the construction and use of visual aids, the use of notes, and methods by which we can read and interpret audience feedback. All of this should give you greater insight into the nature of nonverbal cues as they operate in human communication processes and enable you to present more effectively the ideas you will use to achieve your speech objective.

REFERENCES

Barnlund, D. *Interpersonal Communication: Survey and Studies.* Boston: Houghton Mifflin, 1968.

Ekman, P., et al. *The Face and Emotion.* New York: Pergamon, 1971.

Hall, E. *The Hidden Dimension.* Garden City, N.Y.: Doubleday, 1966.

Knapp, M. *Nonverbal Communication in Human Interaction,* 2nd ed. New York: Holt, Rinehart and Winston, 1978.

Sommer, R. *Personal Space.* Englewood Cliffs, N.J.: Prentice-Hall, 1969.

White, A. "The Patient Sits Down: A Clinical Note," *Psychosomatic Medicine* 15(1953):256–257.

Zweigenhaft, R. "Personal Space in the Faculty Office: Desk Placement and Student-Faculty Interaction," *Journal of Applied Psychology* 61(1976):529–532.

PROJECT

THE PHYSICAL DEMONSTRATION SPEECH

Speeches of this type use the speaker's physical behaviors to demonstrate some activity to the audience. Typically, such speeches are informative in purpose, seeking to teach the activity to the audience; however, these speeches occasionally may be designed to entertain, as when the speaker uses bodily behaviors (often in pantomime) to make the audience laugh. The content of the speech consists of the sequence of actions the speaker demonstrates physically and describes verbally. Since the success of the speech rests upon the meaningfulness of the speaker's actions and the clarity of the accompanying description, careful preparation is important. Specifically, you should:

1. Select a topic. Possible topics for demonstration include:

    How to swing a golf club   How to do a particular dance
    How to hit a tennis backhand   How to do magic tricks
    How to pitch a baseball   How to cook something
    How to prevent someone from   How to shoot a bow and arrow
      choking   How to change a diaper
    Artificial respiration

2. Establish your purpose.
3. Develop your material. That is, plan the verbal description of the process you will present, using your own knowledge supplemented by any necessary research.
4. Organize your material. Plan the sequence of steps you will describe.
5. Rehearse your physical behaviors. Use a mirror to watch your actions and determine whether they truly communicate the process to your audience. Deliver the speech to a friend without using any words; ask the friend whether the meaning of the gestures is clear.
6. Develop an introduction that gets the audience member's attention, makes them want to know about your topic, and shows them why you are an expert with that topic and why you have chosen to tell them about it.
7. Develop a conclusion that motivates the audience to try this process (if your purpose is to persuade) or which makes reference to the reasons the audience should know about the topic (the reasons you presented in your introduction).
8. Deliver the speech using any visual aids (objects, drawings, charts, graphs, and so forth) you choose, but use no notes whatsoever. Let your visual aids be your notes.

Name _____

Date _____

Speech Type _____

Speech Outline, Project Number _____

Speech Topic: _____

Speech Objective: _____

_____

Speech Title: _____

Introduction

    Attention:

    Motivation:

    Credibility:

     Preview

      Body

      Conclusion

Instructor's Comments:

SUPPLEMENT

THE TECHNOLOGY OF PUBLIC SPEAKING

In the preceding chapter, we considered ten general rules about the preparation and use of visual aids. Although those rules apply to visual aids of almost any sort, each type of visual aid requires certain procedures in preparation and presentation in order for that type to be maximally effective. Thus, on the following pages are presented hints for using the most common types of visual aids: physical aids (that is, models of the things described or the actual objects themselves, handouts, and demonstrations; chalkboards or flip-pads; charts; slides; and overhead projectors). Using these hints should assist you in deriving the maximum impact from the visual aids you employ as you speak.

Hints for Using Physical Aids, Handouts, and Demonstrations

1. Where you demonstrate the *working* of equipment or a gadget, practice thoroughly. If you can't make your point quickly and faultlessly, abandon demonstration as a technique for this point.
2. Mishaps steal prestige. But don't despair. You can minimize such damage, even convert it to advantage, using the ancient gambit: "I planned this precisely to show you the *wrong* way." Obviously, the second attempt must be right. For these contingencies, have on hand spare equipment, parts, bulbs, and so forth.
3. If possible, engage a member of the audience to participate. It heightens interest. Be courteous, respectful, and careful. If anything embarrasses him (or her) or, worse, hurts him physically, you'll lose your audience.
4. Where your demonstration consists of a single, static, nonoperating product or sample, don't pass it around lest each recipient tune out your subsequent work. Also, by the time it has reached the rear of the room, the demonstration point will have been forgotten anyway. Simply advise the group that it's available for inspection at the next break.
5. Written reference materials should be given out *after* the points in them have been made. Working documents, questionnaires, or study exercises that accompany class discussion obviously should be distributed during the session.

Hints for Using Chalkboards or Flip-Pads

1. Know in advance what words or drawings you plan to set down. Assure quick, firm notes.
2. Write only words or phrases; use only broad-impression sketches. Single ideas are easier to grasp.
3. Print—it's easier.
4. Enumerate—numbers facilitate note taking.
5. Don't talk to the board: Tell the audience, turn and write, turn back.

6. If you must talk as you write, stand sideways, looking back at the audience. Spare the audience looking at your back for long.

7. Dress up your board work with symbols—circles, arrows, boxes, underlining, quotation marks, question marks, exclamation points. Doing so increases variety.

8. Use colored chalks or grease pencils or felt markers. Doing so provides novelty.

9. Do *not* spend long periods at the board. Change your pace.

10. Erase material of one point before going on to another. If what you have written is being taken as notes, be sure everyone has all the material before you erase it. Leave an empty board as you resume your lecture. Residual material will detract from new material.

11. Whereas slides do not lend themselves for mathematical formulas or equations, chalkboards and flip-charts do, providing you develop them logically.

Hints for Using Charts

1. Consider carefully the positioning of your charts. They should be placed so that everyone can see them; typically, the bottom edge should come no lower than 48 inches above the floor. As you stand next to the chart, your eye should be at about the middle of the material.

2. Practice using your charts—how you will reveal them, and how you will conceal them. Particularly, practice what you will do with the chart when you have finished talking about it. Will you flip it over? Set it next to the wall? Facing in? Facing out? How will you make sure that it does not fall over and get in your way? It is important that you dispose of your chart smoothly, so don't wait until your actual presentation to decide how you will handle things.

3. Use "chart whispers." These are key word reminders of essential points written lightly in pencil (blue pencil is least visible to an audience, incidentally) next to the chart material. These chart whispers can serve as notes, reminding you of the points you want to make as you discuss the chart, or they can provide you with stage directions (such as "show object to audience," or "move away from chart momentarily").

4. Keep charts hidden until you are ready to discuss them. When you have finished that discussion, conceal them again.

5. Avoid stopping at midchart. For example, if your chart presents six points, read all six first, and then return to the points that require elaboration. Resist the temptation to explain each point as you reach it—the audience will continue reading the rest of the chart, and your words will be ignored.

Hints for Using Slides

1. Plan your slide presentation so that it maintains a relatively steady pace. Avoid having a speeded-up sequence of a few slides, followed by a slowdown for the next few, and so on.

2. As a general rule, use about 15 slides maximum for each 20 minutes you speak. A greater number of slides per minute makes it difficult for the audience to comprehend fully the meaning of each slide.

3. If you must show the same slide at different points in your talk, make duplicate slides. Avoid having to back up or "fish" for a slide already passed.

4. When a new slide is flashed on the screen, give the audience a few seconds to study it before you resume talking. When the text material on the slide is simple, read it aloud. Read all of the material—otherwise, the audience will continue reading while you talk about something else.

5. Avoid turning your back to the audience and talking to the screen. Your notes should be keyed, preferably with paper duplicates of the slide materials, so that you can continue speaking without having to look at the slide.

6. If the material you want to convey is particularly complex, use slides to convey the most general concepts and distribute printed copies of the entire material later on.

Hints for Using Overhead Projectors

1. Avoid "keystoning." This is the wide-at-top, narrow-at-bottom effect the machine throws up because of the angle the light throws.

   At the machine, it means having the lens sufficiently high so that the throw involves no angle from lens to screen. This is generally difficult to achieve without obstructing audience view unless you situate the machine behind the group and apply a long-throw lens. This is not always available.

   At the screen, you can (many screen manufacturers provide attachments routinely) keep the bottom edge fastened to the stand while the top is brought six inches forward. Or, with a pendant screen hanging from a ceiling-mounted roller, you can tie the lower edge back, providing suitable correction of angle.

2. Avoid lightleaks and awkward askew positioning. These are two of the most irritating aspects of faulty overhead projector use. They stem from the same cause—improper positioning of the slide on the glass reflection table.

   As a rule, when you operate the machine, take a quick glance back at the screen to ensure you have positioned the slide evenly. Turning away from the audience, remember, is bad practice, but this is preferable to having the slide askew.

3. Stand alongside the screen while speaking. The projected information and the presenter should be integrated into a single combined impression on the audience so that they will associate him (or her), the expert, with his material, his expertise. For meetings up to 30 persons, it is preferable to use a pointer *at the screen*. Where you have immense meetings, running into hundreds, avoid using any pointer at all. It would have to be so big, it would

make you look like a pole vaulter. Also, avoid spotlight-type pointers because the wavering light beam distracts. Instead, make the chart so clear and
deftly use the colors to permit you to use a "verbal" pointer of "narrative
description". Speak to key elements like "shown here in red . . . the larger
of the two . . . the cross-hatched material shown at left . . ." and so forth.

4. Situate the machine so that its neck and lens will not intrude into the view of
the audience. For small groups, this means setting the projector on a chair or
low table so that the platform of the machine is flush with the table. Avoid
placing the machine on top of a table around which people are gathered.
The machine will surely intrude on their view somewhere.

5. Be sure to step away from the path of view of *all* attendees. A common
oversight by many presenters with this machine is to forget how easily you
can obstruct someone's view. If someone cranes his or her neck, it's a good
tip-off for you to adjust accordingly.

6. If you want to use a pointer, do not hold it over the platform of the machine.
The magnification makes the natural quivering of your hand look like you
have St. Vitus' dance.

   Instead, place your pointing device firmly to the transparency and firmly in
   contact with the platform. No shakes. Or, lay the pointer down. No shakes.
   Avoid a pencil; magnified, it looks like a cannon. Use a ball-point refill, a
   long toothpick, a straightened paper clip or other thin gadget.

7. Accomplish transfer quickly and smoothly. A widely resented irritation in
overhead projection use is the appearance of a full bath of hot, white light
between each slide.

   The presenter's eyes are accustomed to the intensity because he or she is at
   the platform. To the audience, however, it can prove so bothersome as to pit
   them psychologically against you and your material or to turn their attention
   away into their own inner thoughts. Therefore, you should make slide
   transfers as smooth and quick as possible—by positioning the new slide
   above the old and then removing the old one or by turning off the machine
   between slides.

PART III
PREPARATION FOR INFORMING

The most basic process of communication is providing information. It is something we do all of the time: we tell people what time it is, how to get from here to somewhere else, how to perform some activity or complete some process, and so on. Certainly, nothing could be easier than simply giving information to other people, right? Well, consider this true story. Former Secretary of Commerce Luther H. Hodges used to tell about a plumber who discovered that hydrochloric acid was terrific for opening clogged drains. He just poured some of that stuff in the drain, and zappo, the gunk was gone. But he wasn't quite sure if his discovery was the answer to all of the world's drainage problems, so he wrote a letter to the Bureau of Standards in Washington, D.C., describing his discovery and asking whether hydrochloric acid was a good thing to use.

A short time later, the plumber received this reply from a bureau scientist: "The efficacy of hydrochloric acid is indisputable, but the corrosive residue is incompatible with metallic permanence." "Terrific," the plumber thought. Then he wrote a letter to the bureau thanking them for their prompt response and expressing his gratification in learning that it was all right to use hydrochloric acid.

The scientist, upon receiving the plumber's letter, became concerned and took that letter to his boss. The boss wrote a second letter to the plumber saying, "We cannot assume responsibility for the production of toxic and noxious residue with hydrochloric acid and suggest that you use an alternative procedure." The plumber, surprised at receiving another letter from the bureau, assumed that he really must have something here, and he again wrote to the bureau reassuring them that the acid was working just fine, thank you.

This last letter was taken by the scientist to his boss, and this sage bureaucrat finally ended the whole process by writing this brief note: "Don't use hydrochloric acid. It eats hell out of the pipes."

As this story illustrates, communicating even the simplest information sometimes isn't simple at all. We must estimate the relevant characteristics of our audience, such as their current knowledge, attitudes, or values, and then adjust our information to those characteristics in order to maximize the chances that it will be understood. If we misjudge our audience, or if we fail to adapt to them properly, then we may succeed only in producing confusion.

In this part we will focus on situations in which our main objective is to provide information to our audience so that when our speech ends they possess new beliefs. Achievement of informative main objectives, however, requires achievement of three primary objectives:

1. Getting attention, so that the audience hears the information in the first place.
2. Promoting understanding, so that the audience can make sense of the things you say to them.
3. Promoting retention, so that the audience remembers the information you give them.

The next three chapters will consider these primary objectives, discussing the secondary objectives and strategies relevant to each. However, before turning our attention to those objectives and strategies that you will use in your speeches, we first must analyze the characteristics of people upon which those speech objectives and strategies are based. Thus, in the remainder of this section, we will consider briefly the nature of attention, understanding, and retention as they operate in the minds of the people to whom we speak.

THE NATURE OF ATTENTION

Attention really is synonymous with the concept of *receiving* we discussed in Chapter 1. It involves taking stimuli from our environment through our five senses: hearing, seeing, touching, tasting, and smelling. To understand how attention works, imagine a funnel (or look at the one shown). The top of the funnel represents all of our senses. Into the funnel are poured all of the stimuli (sights, sounds, objects, and so forth) our senses can pick up. But not all of those stimuli can get through. If we were to dump a bag of marbles into a funnel, and if the narrow end of the funnel was just wide enough to admit one marble at a time, we would have a situation very much like our attention process. Stimuli (the marbles) compete to get through the funnel, but only one can enter at one time. Thus, they pile up and are sorted out. But sometimes the marbles jam up, and none get through. This also happens with attention: if too many stimuli are available and cannot be sorted out, we will receive and interpret none of them. No, we have not "lost our marbles"; we simply are overloaded with stimuli.

The basis of attention, then, is selection. We can't take in all the available stimuli; we have to make some choices. Generally, the kinds of choices we make are

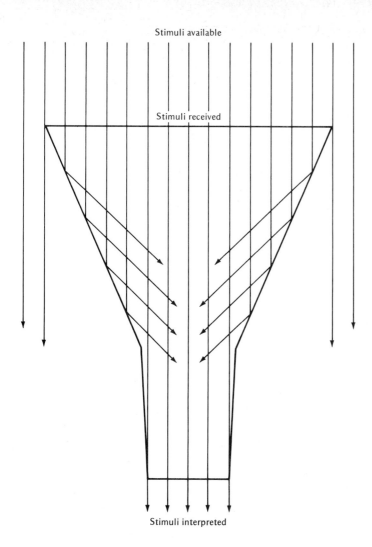

Stimuli available

Stimuli received

Stimuli interpreted

dictated by our own physiological limitations, by our psychological make-up, and by the characteristics of the stimuli themselves. In Chapter 5, we will examine each of these things, and then we will look at some strategies you can use to put these things into effect as you strive to get and maintain the attention of your listeners.

THE NATURE OF UNDERSTANDING
AND RETENTION

It is not enough simply to have people pay attention to us. If we are to achieve any of our objectives, we must be certain that our listeners both understand what we say to them and remember that information at some later time. Only by causing our listeners to understand and remember what we say can we obtain the results that will be most beneficial, both to our listeners and to ourselves.

A great deal of research has been conducted to investigate how people understand and learn things. The product of all that research, however, has been a rather simple conclusion: people learn and remember new things by relating those things to information they already know and understand. For example, in trying to learn the history of Lower Mongolia, you probably would relate events occurring at particular times in Lower Mongolia to events occurring at the same time in places with which you already are familiar; that is, you would relate the new information to information you already know. Or, if you wanted to remember the name of someone to whom you were just introduced, you might mentally relate her name (for example, "Roz") to a physical characteristic (such as her enormous "schnoz"), which you can observe upon the occasion of your next meeting, and which thus serves to stimulate your memory. Thus, to achieve understanding and retention by your listeners, you must first consider the sorts of connections or relationships you want them to make, and then devise communication strategies that bring about those relationships in their minds. Chapters 6 and 7 describe some of the techniques you can use to promote understanding and retention.

SUMMARY

In the chapters that follow, then, we will consider the most effective methods by which you can supply information to your listeners. Specifically, we will consider ways in which you can capture and maintain listeners' attention (without which your speech is doomed to failure), some techniques by which you can promote their understanding of your message, and some strategies whereby you can enhance their abilities to recall at some later time the things you have told them. Through all of this, you will be able to improve significantly your ability to achieve your informative communication objectives.

CHAPTER 5
GETTING ATTENTION

PRIMARY (PREPARATIONAL) OBJECTIVE:
To secure the attention of audience members

Secondary Objectives	Corresponding Strategies
To draw attention to the speaker	Common ground
	Self-reference
	Delivery
To draw attention to the audience	Compliment
	Involvement
	Interest appeals
	Mood recognition
	Expectation reference
To draw attention to the situation	Occasion reference
	Problem reference
	Subject reference
To draw attention to the message	Quotation
	Narrative
	Recent events
	Rhetorical questions
	Startling statement
	Humor
	Conflict
	Suspense
	Hypothetical situation
	Principle or theory
	Proximity
	Order
	Style
	Silence
	Variety

CHAPTER OBJECTIVES
After studying this chapter, you should be able to:

● Construct attention-getting statements derived from your own characteristics as a speaker
● Construct attention-getting statements derived from the characteristics of the audience
● Construct attention-getting statements derived from the characteristics of the situation
● Construct attention-getting devices which can be used throughout your message

INTRODUCTION

While you are giving a speech, your audience always are paying attention. But the question is, attention to what? Half of your audience may be paying attention to the events transpiring outside the window; one-fourth may be devoting their attention to the comic books resting in their laps; one-eighth might be attending to the couple "messing around" in the back row; one-sixteenth could be reminiscing about the great moments in their lives; one-thirty-second could be reciting to themselves the complete history of Argentina; and the other thirty-second could be listening to you. If this situation exists, you have a problem. Yet in any situation, you really have the same problem: you must cause the audience members to focus attention on you and your speech rather than on any of the millions of other stimuli available to them as they sit there in front of you.

The task of getting listeners' attention is unending. At the beginning of the speech, of course, it is crucial that you get their attention; otherwise, none of your words of wisdom will be heard. But audience members' attention spans are short—if things get just a little dull, they are likely to stop listening. Thus, throughout your speech you must work to keep their attention focused on you. As we saw earlier, this really is a matter of choice on their part: you must cause them to choose to pay attention to you rather than to something else. Thus, in this chapter we will consider the nature of the choices audience members make, and then we will analyze the sorts of strategies we can use to influence those choices.

When we are acting in the communication role of receiver, the kinds of choices we make (or the types of attention people have) can be divided into three categories. *Involuntary* attention occurs when the characteristics of certain stimuli get our attention with almost no effort on our part. A loud noise, such as a gunshot going off right next to our left ear, gets our attention. *Voluntary* attention, on the other hand, occurs when we exert some effort to receive a stimulus. We make a conscious effort to screen out all other stimuli and focus on one particular thing. While we speak, this is what we want our audience to be doing— deliberately screening out all other stimuli and focusing on our message. *Habitual* attention, finally, develops from repeated uses of voluntary attention. In essence, we get used to receiving certain stimuli so that it no longer takes conscious effort. The dedicated television watcher illustrates this attention type: he or she sits transfixed, with eyes glazed and mouth hanging open, receiving nothing except the "Gilligan's Island" rerun flickering on the set. Other stimuli, such as the fire blazing in the kitchen or the firemen hacking their way through the front door, go unattended. In a sense, then, voluntary attention has become involuntary because of repeated experiences. Obviously, this is what we as speakers would love to have happen: our audience becomes so accustomed to listening to us that automatically they screen out all other sources of distraction.

Why, then, do people pay attention to some things and not to others? What factors cause them to make the attention choices they do? A great deal of research has been devoted to discovering why people attend (voluntarily and involuntarily) some stimuli and not others, and this research has yielded the factors upon which our speech objectives and strategies should be based. Those factors fall into three categories, and we will consider each in turn.

1. Physiological Factors

Physical Location.   Where you are located serves to determine what stimuli are available to you in the first place. Thus, your location in effect chooses for you the stimuli which you are able to receive.

Physical Abilities.   Your physical capabilities also select or reject stimuli. For example, you cannot hear sounds below 20 or above 20,000 cycles per second, even though many sounds fall outside this narrow range. Similarly, sounds of very low volume may not be audible to you. Moreover, your eyes can see only about 1/70 of the light spectrum, and of the things your feeble eyes *can* see, your brain can assimilate only about 1/10,000 (suggesting that brains are even more feeble, perhaps). Indeed, it is a humbling experience to realize that our senses of smell, taste, touch, sight, and hearing are only a fraction as sensitive as those of a small schnauzer. Certainly, our physical abilities limit our attention choices.

2. Psychological Factors

Psychological Comfort.   Just as we try to be comfortable physically, so too do we choose to pay attention to things which make us psychologically comfortable (and, to some extent, to avoid things which cause us psychological discomfort). This principle applies primarily to information which agrees with our current ideas: we seek such information because it tells us that we are right and that we are (by implication) good people. Conversely, we avoid information telling us that we are wrong because such information implies that we somehow are defective. Note, however, that there are important exceptions to this second rule: we will seek out disagreeing information if we think that it might be useful to gather such information.

Interest.   Of course, we give attention to things which we find interesting. But the reasons those things are interesting deserve exploration. Perhaps *importance* is a better term; things are interesting to us because they hold some importance for us. For example, what is the one, single, most important word to you in the whole world? Think about it for a second—what is the one word that gets your attention every time you hear it? The answer? Your name. No other word is more important to you, and no other word is more effective in getting your attention. Or consider another, more sinister aspect of interest. Studies have been conducted looking at the identification of various ethnic groups. If, for example, people are shown a series of pictures showing ten people, one of whom is Italian (or Irish, or Swedish, or whatever—pick your favorite ethnic group), two groups of people consistently will be able to pick out the Italian: other Italians, because their ethnic identification is important to them, and people prejudiced against Italians because, in a sad sort of way, it is important to them to be able to identify Italians, too. So when things are important to us, for whatever reason, we tend to be interested in and pay attention to them.

Expectations.   To a degree, we perceive what we expect to perceive. For example, we expect a comedian like Johnny Carson to be funny; when we listen to him, our expectation increases the likelihood that we will laugh at what he says. Indeed, even if he delivered a serious speech, our expectations might cause us to think that he was trying to be humorous. Granted, repeated violations of our expectations would eventually change our expectations and attention behaviors, but for a long time we would act in accordance with our expectations. Therefore, it is important that we try to estimate audience expectations and, if they are contrary to what we would like them to be, that we find ways of changing those expectations so that we can achieve our objective.

Suggestion.   Our attention is influenced by those around us. In a well-known experiment, for example, an audience was told that a bottle containing a strong-smelling liquid would be opened by the speaker. They were told to raise their hands when the smell from the bottle reached them. Some people near the front raised their hands almost immediately after the bottle was opened; others near them soon raised theirs. Eventually, the audience was full of clusters of people with their hands raised. Funniest thing—the bottle was empty. The experiment demonstrated the suggestibility of some people and illustrated the importance of audience members' reactions to one another. If other people seem attentive, we are more likely to be so as well; if others seem bored, our attention also is likely to wane.

Motivation.   Related to the interest principle, motivation holds that we will pay attention to things which will provide us with rewards we want or help us avoid punishments we fear in that particular situation. When we are extremely hungry, for example, the golden arches of McDonald's attract our attention; otherwise, we may not even see them. If we are eager to pass our "Basic Needlework and Embalming" course, we will listen to the instructor's lectures no matter how dull they become. Or if we live in fear of invasion by hordes of Chinese troops, we will listen attentively to radio programs telling us what to do in case of attack. We will look in greater depth at this principle of motivation in a later chapter. For now, simply realize that motivation is another psychological determinant of attention.

3. Stimulus Characteristics

The nature of the things around us also determine the specific items to which we will attend. Generally, we will pay attention to things which have one or more of the following characteristics.

Intensity. Our attention usually is attracted to very intense stimuli: bright lights, loud noises, strong smells, and so on. To maintain attention as a speaker, then, you must be the most intense stimulus in the setting.

Change. But intensity wears off after a while. Loud noises become commonplace; bright lights become part of the environment. In essence, we become used to these things. Thus, change also is an important factor. Sudden silence after loud noise gets attention. So does a soft light following a bright one. Indeed, any change in a stimulus is likely to attract our attention.

Unity. We tend to perceive things as a whole. When we listen to a speaker, we perceive in combination his or her words, gestures, voice, and so forth. If everything fits, our attention is focused on the message. But if something is out of place, we become preoccupied with it. How often have you been distracted by certain mannerisms of,a speaker? Jingling pocket contents, drumming fingers on the podium, pacing back and forth, or nervously clearing the throat all are common mannerisms which, because they do not fit the unified whole, attract audience attention away from the message itself.

Familiarity. Things which are familiar to us (like "Gilligan's Island" reruns) attract our attention. Well-known quotations, familiar sayings, popular songs, and the like are attractive to us because we know them well and, perhaps, feel secure with them.

Novelty. The unusual, the strange, the out-of-the-ordinary also attract our attention simply because we are not used to perceiving those sorts of stimuli. A few years ago, the singer Tiny Tim sold millions of copies of his song "Tiptoe Through the Tulips" because, while the song was familiar, the voice was incredibly bizarre. So was the face. So people payed attention to Tiny Tim, and millions of television viewers tuned in to the Johnny Carson Show to watch Tim marry Miss Vickie—the televised wedding was another novelty. But after a while the novelty wore off, and Tiny Tim faded into obscurity. Similarly, you can use forms of novelty in your speaking, as we shall see. But don't beat those things to death or your fate will parallel Tiny Tim's.

Repetition. Yes, repetition. Since our attention span is relatively short and we continually are distracted by competing stimuli, it is easy for us to miss a specific sight or sound if it happens only once. But if that stimulus is repeated, it eventually will strike us during a period when our attention is directed toward that thing and we will perceive it. If a speaker has a key point which he wants the audience to get, he or she would be wise to repeat that point several times throughout the speech so that everyone in the audience is likely to hear it during one of their attention periods.

In this section, then, we have seen three categories of things which determine the things to which we pay attention. Physical factors, such as location and our capabilities, determine what stimuli we can choose among in the first place. Psychological factors, including comfort, interest, habit, expectations, suggestion, and motivation, determine to some degree the choices we make. And several characteristics of the stimuli available to us, such as intensity, change, unity, familiarity, novelty, and repetition, cause us to be attracted to some things rather than others. We turn now to the techniques with which we can put these things to use in securing and maintaining audience members' attention.

ATTENTION-GETTING DEVICES

When we think of the number of incredibly boring speakers we have endured, it comes as a surprise to discover that there are literally dozens of devices one can use to obtain and maintain audience attention. We will see about two dozen devices here; those of you who are even a little creative will find it easy to think of more. The techniques listed here fall into four categories; we will consider each category in turn.

Attention and the Speaker

These techniques all stem from you as a speaker—the things you reveal about yourself to your audience.

1. Common Ground.   We know that people listen to things which are psychologically comfortable because those things agree with their present beliefs or attitudes. Thus, we might begin our speech with the establishment of common ground. This is achieved by pointing out to the audience those beliefs, attitudes, or values which we have in common with them. A speech advocating increased taxes to support public education, for example, might begin by pointing out the value of a good education—something most audiences in our society would agree with. Or a speech favoring gun control might start with arguments about the value of human life or the dangers of crime. Again, even audience members against gun control probably would share these values with the speaker. Once this common ground between speaker and audience has been established, the speaker can move to points of disagreement with the audience and still have a good chance of maintaining their attention.

2. Self-reference.   Audiences are interested in you as a person. Really. After all, they have agreed to devote some of their time to you, haven't they? If you begin your speech by telling them something about yourself—a brief story, some of your experiences, or whatever—their interest in you will cause them to devote attention to you. Or if, when you see their attention starting to wander during your speech, you use another self-reference, you probably will be able to regain their attention. But suppose you have led a particularly dull life. Don't worry: audiences also are polite, usually. They will listen to your story about yourself just to avoid offending you. But as a rule, people are interested in people; both you and your audience fall into that category.

3. Delivery.   All elements of the way in which you present your message influence audience interest. Although we have analyzed delivery in depth in an earlier chapter, some delivery rules are worth noting here. Your delivery should be active. You should employ a lot of physical movement and vocal variety as you speak in order to capitalize on audience members' tendencies to pay attention to intense, changing stimuli. Your delivery should be part of a unified whole, directed toward emphasizing the spoken words and free of distracting mannerisms. And, of course, your delivery should fit the physical capacities and locations of all audience members. Your voice should be loud enough for all to hear, your gestures dramatic enough for all to see, your visual aids large enough for all to read, and so on.

Attention and the Audience

These techniques involve recognition of and reference to some characteristic of the audience by the speaker.

1. Compliment the Audience. There are good things to say about everyone—even that intimidating bunch of people you face as you deliver a speech. Try while preparing your speech to think of sincere compliments you can give your audience when your speech begins: good works they have done, good characteristics they have, and the like. Beginning with a compliment usually gets audience members' attention. It is psychologically comfortable to them, it is interesting to them (after all, it is about them in the first place), it is important to them (and hence, interesting). Indeed, the sincere compliment appeals to virtually every psychological characteristic the audience have. Again, the compliment must be sincere—flattery for its own sake is pleasing to no one—but done sincerely, it is an effective attention getter.

2. Involve the Audience. If you can get the audience to participate actively in the beginning of the speech, you are guaranteed their attention, at least for the time being. Ask them to indicate their response to some question by raising their hands; ask them to shout out responses to Yes or No questions; ask them to look at some object in the room. In effect, get them to *do* something. As a rule, active audiences are attentive audiences.

3. Appeal to Audience Interests. Through the situational analysis you completed in the last chapter, you should have a pretty clear idea of the topics in which your audience already are interested. Use that knowledge. If their main interest is football, start with a football story. If politics, religion, or some other controversial area is their main concern, begin with a reference to that, being careful not to offend any member's sensibilities. But remember—anything you start your speech with must ultimately be related to your topic. So be sure you can tie the two together.

4. Recognize the Mood of the Audience. Occasionally, you will face an audience that shares a common emotion: fear, anger, happiness, disappointment, or even apathy. Refer to that emotion. If you want to change the emotion, you might use the "I know you all are angry, but . . ." format to lead into your reasons why they should not be angry or should be angry at someone or something other than the present object of their hostility. If you want to use the emotion to stimulate some action, you might employ the "Of course you are angry. And you should be . . ." approach, giving them clear reasons for anger (or reviewing the reasons they already know) and telling them what to do about it. Either way, you will have the attention of

Active, Unusual Aspects of Speech Delivery Get Audience Attention

the audience simply because you have shown a recognition of their feelings, and because they probably are curious about what your response will be.

5. Refer to Audience Expectations. Often, audience members expect to hear certain things from you. Their expectations may spring from the nature of the situation, from their past associations with you, from the introduction which you were given by an earlier speaker, or some other source of information about you. You might want to begin by referring to those expectations, particularly if you intend to violate them with your speech. If you begin by saying, "I suspect you are expecting me to talk about . . . ," it will create suspense in their minds. Probably they will wonder, "Why is she telling me what I expect? What is she about to tell me?" When you tell them that you are or are not going to fulfill those expectations, they still will be looking for an explanation of why or why not. Thus, you will have their attention for at least the first few minutes of the speech.

Attention and the Situation

These techniques involve reference to things unique to the situation in which you are speaking. Since the situation is something you and your audience share, you create some of the common ground described above when you refer to it.

1. Refer to the Occasion. If some special event or occasion has drawn the audience here, you might begin by talking about it. Awards banquets, meetings, ceremonial occasions, and so on all have a purpose known to the audience. Referring to that purpose creates a common foundation upon which you and your audience can build the speech.

2. Refer to the Problem. Sometimes people meet because some problem must be resolved. Immediate reference to this problem gains prompt attention (assuming all members know what it is and think it important), whereas telling a joke, a humorous personal story, a well-known quotation, or some other introductory remark probably would only serve to make the audience impatient. If you are there to solve an urgent problem, get right to it; don't diddle around with the traditional attention-getting devices. You already have their attention.

3. Refer to the subject. If you are confident that they are interested in the topic of your speech, you might secure the audience's attention by mentioning what your topic will be. However, if your topic is not inherently interesting to your listeners, you should avoid this sort of opening. Thorough audience analysis should tell you whether or not to use this strategy.

Attention and the Message

By far the greatest number of attention-getting devices are those which are based upon the stimulus characteristics we saw a few pages ago. Again, while this list seems lengthy, it by no means exhausts all the possible message techniques for getting and keeping attention.

1. The Quotation. A thought-provoking or curiosity-arousing quotation can be an effective device for beginning a speech. The quotation should be from some source considered credible by your audience. Quoting John F. Kennedy usually makes a positive impression upon most audiences; quoting your second-grade teacher makes a very different sort of impression. The quotation also should be relevant to your topic; otherwise, the audience quickly will realize that you used the quotation just to get their attention, and they probably will become resentful. Finally, the quote should be provocative. To begin by saying, "Winston Churchill, one night over dinner, was clearly heard to say: 'Please pass the salt,' " probably would not bowl your audience over, no matter how much they admire that great British statesman. If your opening quotation meets the criteria of credibility, relevance, and provocativeness, it probably will be a good attention getter both at the beginning or in the body of the speech.

2. The Narrative. One of the most familiar methods of beginning the speech is the narrative story or illustration. Like quotations, however, narratives must meet certain criteria if they are to be effective attention getters. They must be fresh—not hackneyed, often repeated tales the audience has heard a hundred times (although these may be useful as illustrations). They should be relevant to the topic of the speech. They should be the sort of story that can be told effectively by the speaker (for example, the audience might think it odd for a speaker dressed as a monk to tell a lewd barroom story). And the story should be in good taste (one more reason for monks to avoid lewd stories).

3. Recent Events. Sometimes, we can associate the theme of our speech with recent occurrences the audience know something about. Speakers discussing infla-

Startling Statements Get Attention

tion might refer to recent increases in oil and gasoline prices; speeches about crime might cite recent crimes that have been in the newspapers. By including descriptions of recent events, we add a note of freshness and relevance to our topic, which tends to make our audience want to listen further.

4. Rhetorical Questions.   By asking a series of questions, we can cause the audience to become mentally involved in the speech. We might begin by asking, "What is reality? What is life? Is there life after death? If so, should we take a change of underwear?" Probably the audience do not know the answers to these questions—who does? But their curiosity will be aroused, and they will pay attention as they wait for you to supply answers (or at least reasons for asking). Or you might ask them questions to which they know the answers. You don't expect them to answer aloud, and they won't. But mentally they will be supplying the answers (which you should know as well) and thus will be actively involved in the situation. Either way, by creating curiosity or involvement, rhetorical questions often serve to stimulate audience interest.

5. The Startling Statement.   An apathetic audience sometimes can be jarred into attentiveness by a statement that shocks them. Consider the professor of law at the University of Michigan who is reputed to begin his first class each semester by saying to his students, "Look at the person on your left. Now look at the person on your right. By the end of this semester, only one of you will still be in this class." Needless to say, these students remain very attentive for several months. But this technique can be misused, too. When I was a graduate teaching assistant, one of my basic public speaking students began her speech by striding to the front of the room, turning and staring right in the eyes of her audience, and screaming everybody's favorite four-letter word. ZAP! There it was. The class was shocked. I was sweating profusely. She

certainly had our attention. But many members of the audience were offended by this startling statement, just as she was offended by the grade I ultimately gave her. Offensive startling statements are counterproductive and should not be used. Similarly, the criteria of relevance and appropriateness to the speaker which we saw above should be met if startling statements are to have their desired effect.

6. Humor.   As you read the first chapters in this book, did you find yourself wondering why your author included so many feeble attempts at humor? The answer is simple: humor, by virtue of its novelty, maintains audience attention. Naturally, it must be relevant, original, fresh, and entertaining in order to be effective. But note one thing: it doesn't really have to be good humor. About half of the jokes Johnny Carson tells on television are terrible. But after he tells them, he laughs (along with the audience) *at* the joke. And people pay attention. Of course, that accounts for the quality of humor in this book; laugh at it if you cannot laugh with it.

7. Conflict.   Opposing forces command attention, particularly if audience members identify with one of the opposing sides. Football games, elections, struggles by people against the forces of nature—all things like these are forms of conflict that will attract audience attention. Thus, you might begin your speech either by describing some conflict or by promising to describe it ("Today I want to tell you a story of heroism—of people taking on the forces of nature in one of the world's most forbidding places"). Again, the conflict you describe or promise to describe must be relevant to your topic and appropriate to both you and your audience.

8. Suspense.   Much of the fascination that mystery novels hold for us arises from the uncertainty about who committed the crime or, if the culprit is known, whether he or she will be caught. Perhaps, too, you have had a friend "help" you by telling you how a book you are reading or movie you are going to see comes out. Probably you protested, "Stop! You'll ruin it!" Right—the suspense would be gone, and your interest lost. You can use the appeal of suspense in the beginning of your speech. You might start by describing something, but not telling the audience what it is ("It is the biggest killer in the history of humanity. It has killed enough people to repopulate the world. Twice.") until suspense has built and you have their attention. You can point out results but leave the cause unnamed (as the preceding example does), or you can call attention to a force whose effects are uncertain. You might mention some valuable information you will divulge later ("In a moment, I will tell you how to make $1 million in one week"), after you have given them the background facts they need to understand that information. With these or any other suspense-building technique, the principle is simple: don't reveal everything. Suggest that something important will be revealed later and then develop your points as you lead up to the revelation. Make sure, too, that the suspense you build is important enough to the audience so that the suspense matters. Uncertainty about trivial matters rarely gets attention. And, as always, be sure that the suspense is relevant and appropriate.

9. *The Hypothetical Situation.* Creating a hypothetical situation in which the audience take part through their imagination creates interest and maintains attention by getting them involved in the speech. In a speech advocating stricter law enforcement, for example, you might have the audience imagine themselves being victims of a mugging: "Your car has broken down late one night in a large city. No phone is around, so you have to walk to a gas station you saw about a mile back. As you walk, you notice footsteps behind you . . . ." Your description could go on to describe being confronted by the muggers, being beaten and left on the street, having to stagger to the nearest building, and so on. The more vivid your description, the more involved your audience become. And the more involved they are, the more attentive they are. So with a little imagination—yours and theirs—you can have the audience "in the palm of your hand."

10. *The Principle or Theory.* Although this is one of the most difficult techniques to use effectively, the introductory principle or theory sometimes is an effective attention getter. An unusual and dramatically presented theory compels attention and sustains interest. For example, one student, a black male, began his speech by describing the theory of racial superiority that holds that Caucasians are inherently more intelligent than blacks. Because of the suspense this theory created, and because of the appropriateness of the theory to the topic (racism) and the contrast between the theory and the speaker, who was extremely bright and articulate, audience attention was riveted on him and his message. But all too often, despite the importance which the speaker may place on the theory, introductory theories are dull, pointless, or unnecessary. So be very careful in using this technique—it can also be an effective method of putting your audience to sleep.

11. *Proximity.* Often you can get attention by making a direct reference to things in close proximity to the audience: an actual member of the audience, perhaps referred to by name, some object near at hand, something that occurred at a place near where you are speaking, and so on. To single out members of your audience by name is particularly effective, because it serves to individuate them—to make them specific personalities and to draw them closer to you and to each other. If you have ever been singled out by a speaker in this way, you will also realize that the shock value alone keeps you attentive to the speaker and that the threat of other people being singled out will keep the rest of the audience attentive as well.

12. *Order.* A useful way of maintaining audience attention throughout the speech is to use devices that indicate the order of the things you are discussing. Numbering your points as they come up is particularly helpful; if attention wanders, hearing "second," "third," and so on alerts the listener to the fact that a new idea is about to be considered. Organization by time sequence, physical location, and other structural systems that we will consider in later chapters also help maintain attention by keeping the flow of the speech clear to the audience.

13. *Style.* The words you choose, the patterns of phrasing you use, the ways in which you express yourself—in fact, virtually all elements of your use of language—comprise your style. If you use "good" style, you will be able to maintain attention much more effectively during your speech. Briefly, good style has several characteristics. It is active, depicting things as living, moving objects. It is vivid, causing realistic images to arise in audience members' minds through specific, concrete descriptions. It is dramatic, using words that have an emotional impact upon the audience. Dramatism is particularly a product of effective verb choice. Whenever possible, your verbs should be as specific and unusual as is practical. You should, for example, use *invaded* instead of *entered, assaulted* instead of *hit, raced* instead of *ran,* and so on. Good style, finally, is specific, depicting detailed aspects of the things being described. Through careful attention to your language style, then, you can keep your audience attentive throughout your speech.

14. Silence. This is a guaranteed attention getter. If, during your speech, audience attention seems to be wandering, just stop. And look at them. And keep looking. Pretty soon, everyone in the audience will look back. They'll be wondering why you stopped. Did you forget your place? Are you done? What's going on? The next thing you say after this long pause will be heard by everyone. I guarantee it. But if silence is so effective, why don't all speakers use it all of the time? Because psychologically, it is difficult for the speaker to use silence. When you are speaking, one of your greatest sources of security is the sound of your own voice. As long as you hear noise, everything must be all right. It is a lot like the proverbial first date. On that date, what's the worst possible thing that can happen? All right, the second worst. It's silence. You are both riding along in the front seat of the car, and neither of you can think of anything to say. The silence is nerve racking. You begin to tremble, your stomach tightens, you sweat profusely, and you frantically search your brain for something to say. Anything to end the silence. So it is with public speaking. It is tough to stand, saying nothing, and look at your audience. But if you have the guts to do it, you will get their attention without fail.

15. Variety. The most attention-arousing speeches use a variety of the techniques listed above. They use quotations, tell stories, ask rhetorical questions, refer to recent events, inject humor, depict conflict, create suspense, make startling statements, construct hypothetical situations, build on principles or theories, employ proximity, clarify order, maintain an effective style, and occasionally use silence. Although I never have heard a speech use all of these devices, our goal should be to use as many as possible in the speeches we deliver.

USING ATTENTION-GETTING DEVICES

As we looked at the various devices we can use to stir audience interest, we also saw some criteria for their use. Because adherence to those criteria is the key to successful attention getting, this section will summarize them briefly.

First, attention factors should be used throughout the speech. Granted, it is crucial that you secure audience attention at the very beginning, and most of the techniques described above are designed to do just that. But because people have very limited attention spans, you must continually strive to renew their interest. Your material should be selected, points organized, and delivery designed to sustain audience attention from beginning to end.

Second, the factors you use should be appropriate to the speech. If they do not relate to your topic, they will serve only as distractors or will be seen by your audience as cheap tricks designed solely to get their attention. Moreover, if they are too outlandish, the audience are likely to go away remembering the device but forgetting your main point. The attention devices you use, therefore, should direct audience attention toward the things you want them to remember or do, not toward the devices themselves.

Third, your devices should fit the setting. Jokes fit after-dinner speeches, but usually not funerals; drinking stories fit fraternity meetings, but not sermons. Keep in mind the nature of the situation in which you are delivering the speech, and select and develop devices which are appropriate to it.

Fourth, attention getters should fit the audience. Their interests, attitudes, values, and so on all dictate the extent to which certain devices will be effective. Certainly, you will want to avoid any device (obscenity is a primary example) that might offend them.

Fifth, the devices you choose should fit you. If you are not good at telling jokes, don't try. If silence makes you break out in hives, don't use it. As a general rule, use those devices in which you have confidence rather than force yourself to use things that do not fit your personality or abilities. Forced attention getters get attention, all right, but not the kind we want.

Finally, try as much as possible to foresee and prevent distractions that might divert listeners' attention from you. The wise speaker eliminates unsteady visual aids, distractions behind him or her (such as writing on a blackboard), and if possible, outside noise. He or she avoids bizarre clothing, jangling jewelry, strange hair styles, distracting mannerisms, and other personal characteristics that might draw attention to themselves and away from the speech. And if, despite all precautions, some powerful source of distraction does arise (such as a train thundering by outside), the wise speaker waits for the distraction to end before continuing.

SUMMARY

In this chapter, we have seen a rather lengthy list of attention-getting devices, all geared toward the secondary objectives of drawing attention to the speaker, to the audience, to the situation, or to the message. We also have seen some ideas concerning the use of these strategies so that you can implement them with maximum effectiveness. But one more suggestion must be offered before we move on to other considerations. While the techniques we considered are effective, and while their use will do much to gain and maintain audience attention, we must not become preoccupied with them. Our main objective is to give the audience information, and the bulk of our speech should be devoted to that material. The strategies seen here are important, but we never should lose sight of the principle that their use is intended purely to support the information which we are giving.

EXHIBIT 1

Chester, Pa.: Shawn Armstead shoots himself after apparently finding a .45 caliber revolver in a dresser. His life ends at age 4.

Palm Desert, Calif.: Plinking at tin cans among sand dunes near their home, Juan Diaz, 19, accidentally killed his brother when a companion jostled his arm.

Los Angeles, Calif.: A candidate for president, Robert Kennedy, is fatally shot while celebrating a victory in the primary elections.

The cities, ages, and names may vary, but one pattern is clear: all of these people fell victim to the number one murderer in America, the handgun. Every 48 minutes an American is killed by a handgun. Every 2 minutes a handgun is used to commit a crime. In fact, during the ten years in which the United States was at war in Vietnam, more than twice as many civilians as soldiers were killed, and those civilians were killed here, at home, by guns.

Analyze the attention-getting devices used in this introduction to a speech about gun control. What devices do you see?

EXHIBIT 2

In Boston on October 2, 1973, six youths set upon a young woman carrying a can of gasoline to her car, forcing her to douse herself with the gasoline and then setting her afire. She burned to death. Police noted that the incident followed by two nights the nationwide showing of the movie *Fuzz*, a crime drama set in Boston that contained a scene portraying teenagers burning a derelict to death, just for kicks.

More recently, in Florida a 14-year-old boy robbed and murdered his next-door neighbor, a 78-year-old woman who lived alone. When arrested, he claimed he had developed the plan by watching an episode of "Kojak," in which the same crime had been committed.

Are these isolated examples? A recent survey conducted by Arthur Nielsen estimates that the average child has witnessed 18,000 television murders by the time he (or she) graduates from high school. Could it be that this child receives as much education from the television as he does from school? And what does television teach him to do?

Analyze the attention-getting devices used in this introduction to a speech about television violence. What devices do you see?

PROJECT

THE ANNOUNCEMENT

This sort of speech presents information in a concise, organized, relevant, and clear manner. It tells about something that has occurred in the past (who won some contest, for example), something just about to occur ("There will be an executive meeting immediately after this one"), or something that will occur in the near future ("The Christmas party will be a week from Tuesday"). The purpose of an announcement is to inform; anything else (entertaining, persuading) is secondary. When making an announcement, you must convey your information in an understandable manner during a very brief time; thus, it is important that you prepare the announcement carefully through these steps:

1. Select your topic. While the situation generally will dictate the topic to you (that is, there is something which you must announce to this group), for purposes of this assignment select a topic from the following list:

An upcoming election	A business interviewer on campus
A committee meeting	Results of a questionnaire or survey
An upcoming sports event	Yesterday's sports scores
A future lecture	The formation of an interest group
A new course syllabus	Winners of some contest

2. Develop your material. An announcement must provide complete information; thus, it must answer the questions: Who? What? When? Where? Why? How? Moreover, it should indicate both costs and benefits to the listeners when appropriate. However, it should not contain unnecessary detail; remember, you only have a short time to make the announcement.

3. Organize your material. First, state your main idea—the meeting, results, game, and so on—you are announcing. Then provide the necessary details about who, what, when, where, and so on.

4. Develop an introduction that gets the attention of the listeners. Startling or suspense-building statements are good.

5. Develop a conclusion that summarizes and repeats the essential parts of the announcement.

6. Deliver your speech pleasantly and in a conversational, direct style. There is no need to be dramatic.

Name _____

Date _____

Speech Type _____

Speech Outline, Project Number _____

Speech Topic: _____

Speech Objective: _____

_____

Speech Title: _____

Introduction
    Attention:

    Motivation:

    Credibility:

      Preview

      Body

      Conclusion

Instructor's Comments:

CHAPTER 6
PROMOTING UNDERSTANDING

PRIMARY (PREPARATIONAL) OBJECTIVE:
To promote audience understanding of presented information

Secondary Objectives	Corresponding Strategies
To acquire adequate information	Use self as source
	Use interviews as source
	Use impersonal exchanges as source
	Use written sources as source
	Use surveys/experiments as source
To organize information clearly	Chronological order
	Spatial order
	Causal order
	Topical order
	Process order
	Known-unknown order
	Ascending-descending order
	Experiential order
	Question-answer order
	Constructing an outline
To present information coherently	Introductions
	Transitions
	Conclusions

CHAPTER OBJECTIVES

After studying this chapter, you should be able to:

- Acquire from a variety of sources the information you need
- Organize information using each of the nine patterns presented in this chapter
- Construct a scratch outline, a full-sentence outline, and a topical outline
- Write the introduction to a speech
- Develop transitions between speech sections
- Write the conclusion to a speech

INTRODUCTION

No doubt you have heard the theory that, if you give enough typewriters to enough monkeys, eventually one of them will write the complete works of Shakespeare. Typically, this theory is used to illustrate the workings of probability: by chance alone, a monkey would become the bard of the jungle. But this theory is based on another principle—one which few people (possibly for good reason) have considered. The monkey situation works (or at least has the potential to work) because each monkey has available to him or her the same letters which were available to Shakespeare; all he or she must do is hit them in the right order. In fact, you have an even better chance of writing with Shakespearean quality: you know whole words, and all you have to do is arrange them properly. Indeed, it should be relatively easy for you to write the greatest novel in the history of civilization. You know all the words (practically) that every English-speaking writer has or will know—all you have to do is put them in the proper patterns. Greatness rests, then, in the knowledge you possess, and in the order in which you present that knowledge to others.

Aside from the fact that the great literary works of the world are a function largely of organization (and that this book could easily have been written by a hamster with a Scrabble set), there is another reason why organization should interest us: by creating relationships between ideas, organization promotes and influences audience understanding of our speeches. As we saw in our consideration of listeners' characteristics at the beginning of this section, people learn by making connections and inferring relationships. Thus, the meaning they form based on our words depends largely on the order in which we say those words. Our success in giving information to others, then, depends on the information we give and the order in which we give it.

In order to devise strategies for ordering our information, we first must understand the ways in which our listeners process that information when they receive it. Thus, we will consider briefly some of the factors governing audience understanding and retention.

1. People Learn by Making Connections

When we present information to someone, we want to cause him or her to learn (that is, understand and retain) that information. Research suggests that learning usually occurs through various sorts of connections. First, we make connections according to

We Learn by . . .

Making Connections

similarity. That is, we tend to associate things that are similar in any way: physical appearance, sound, emotional connotations, intellectual meanings, and so on. Second, we also learn through *proximity*. We tend to group together things that are close to each other in space or time, and to remember the sequence through which we typically encounter things. Thus, you are able to remember both the sequence of events comprising the history of the United States (at least in general terms) and to recall the route you follow on your way home.

Third, we learn the *cause-effect relations* between things. By observing events (for example, rain) and their consequences (wet ground), we ultimately discover that certain things cause certain other things. But note one item: we also can learn invalid relationships. Most superstitions fall into this invalid category. Probably, sometime in the dim and distant past, some guy walking down the road had a black cat across his path just before a runaway mastodon trampled him to dust. Seeing this temporal (time) relationship, someone may have concluded that "having a black cat cross your path causes bad luck." A relationship that occurred once through chance alone was attributed to a cause-effect relationship. So the point is this: cause-effect relationships are based upon proximity in time, but don't assume that because something followed a certain event it was caused by that event.

Finally, we learn by *associating the known with the unknown*. When we encounter something new, we naturally ask ourselves, "Now, what is this thing similar to?" Imagine, about one hundred years ago, someone trying to explain what a car was to someone else who had never seen one. Probably, the explanation went something like this: "Well, it's like a horse, only there are wheels instead of legs, an engine instead of muscles, headlights instead of eyes, seats instead of a back, and a trunk instead of a tail." By relating new things to similar things we already understand, we seek to discover and learn the nature of those new items.

As we learn about our environment, we look for relationships—for connections between the people, things, or ideas we encounter. When such relationships are obvious (this house is next to that one), we learn them; when no relationships are obvious (as between black cats and stampeding mastodons), we may invent them. As speakers, then, we must take care to clarify relationships for our listeners so that they learn the connections we want them to learn, not connections they have invented on their own.

2. People Understand and Retain Information Best When That Information Is Organized

As we have seen, people look for relationships and then use those relationships to interpret and remember new things. Organized information, by definition, specifies relationships within the new facts so that the audience do not have to hunt for connections, and it facilitates memory by providing all of the connection keys audience need. Disorganized information, by forcing the audience to hunt for relationships, increases the likelihood that the audience will either infer incorrect relationships or that they will be unable to find any relationships and, out of frustration, simply stop listening.

3. People Understand and Retain Information Best When That Information Is Repeated

The more frequently we encounter cause-effect, similarity, proximity, or known-unknown relationships, the more imprinted upon our minds those relationships become. Thus, novice actors forget their lines, rookie quarterbacks forget their plays, and you get lost on your way home to your new house, all because they and you have not repeated the associations between information often enough. To promote understanding and memory of particularly important points, then, we as speakers must take care to repeat those points fairly often (just as television commercials repeat their points frequently) so that the audience remember them.

4. People Understand and Retain Information Best When That Information Has Some Emotional Impact

As you think back over your life, what events do you remember best? The day you left home for the first time? Your first date? The day someone close to you died? Probably you recall most vividly events that had a powerful emotional impact upon you—things that made you extremely happy, sad, frightened, and so on. Although it is unlikely that we as speakers can produce the same degree of emotional impact upon our listeners' emotions, we still can apply this principle when speaking. Through the use of vivid descriptions, emotional comparisons, dramatic narratives, and other devices we will see later, we can involve audience emotions in our speech and use that emotionalism to get them to remember the information we provide.

5. People Understand and Retain Information Best When That Information Is New and Relevant

As we saw earlier, if the information is new, people will be curious about it, provided they believe that the information somehow is relevant to their own situations. Or even better, they will be motivated to learn that information if they believe it to be relevant to their own need satisfaction, perhaps allowing them to achieve something, escape something, or avoid something. We therefore need to relate our information to our audience, providing them with new information and demonstrating how it might be relevant to their needs and lives.

6. People Understand and Retain Information Best When That Information Can Be Implemented Through Imitation

Briefly, let's focus on a specific kind of information, behavior. Sometimes we may want to teach people how to do something: play a piano, hit a golf ball, build an automobile, and so on. When specific behaviors comprise the information we are trying to impart, modelling becomes important.

Research has shown that several factors are related to the effectiveness of modelling as a teaching device. First, if you want someone to follow your example, it helps if that person likes you. Just as small boys imitate the behaviors of sports heroes whom they idolize, so too do listeners imitate the behaviors of speakers they like and admire. Thus, establishing your credibility is important if you want your audience to do as you do.

Second, imitation is facilitated if you and the audience are similar in relevant respects. Suppose, for example, that you are teaching someone how to play the piano. Suppose, too, that you have six fingers on either hand—a terrific asset when doing an arpeggio. Your pupil probably would be discouraged from imitating you, exclaiming: "I can't do that; I only have three fingers!" You need, therefore, to identify with your audience, saying, in effect, "If I can do this, so can you."

Third, imitation is easier when the task to be imitated is clear and simple. The golf pro who throws a ball on the ground, promptly drives it 450 yards, and then hands the club to his or her student saying, "Here, you do it," probably will not be

A Complete
and Detailed
Compendium
of My
Knowledge

(with Footnotes)

You Are Your Best Information Source

terribly successful. The task must be broken down to its simplest parts so that the behaviors can be imitated one at a time.

Finally, imitation works best when the imitator is motivated. If, for example, he (or she) sees that the model person has been rewarded for performing this behavior (perhaps by winning bets during golf rounds), he will be motivated to obtain the same rewards. Or if the model offers some reward, such as "Learn to weld doors onto cars like this, and you can keep your new job," the imitator will be motivated to learn the behavior. In essence, imitation works best if the listener first is motivated to learn, and then is presented with the specific information or behaviors to be imitated.

At this point, then, we know that people understand and retain information when they see connections, when the information is organized, repeated, emotion rousing, new, and relevant, and when they have the opportunity to implement that information via imitation. With this knowledge, then, we are ready to undertake the achievement of our speaking objectives relating to promoting audience understanding. In this chapter, we will determine three things: ways of acquiring the information we need to achieve our main objective, ways of organizing that information so that it is understandable to our audience, and ways of presenting that information coherently so that audience comprehension is maximized.

ACQUIRING INFORMATION

When you are going to provide information to someone, it helps to *have* some information to provide. Although you probably are aware of most of the sources of information available to you, and although such sources really are limitless in number, we will review a few of them here to ensure that you are using the best information sources available.

The most obvious, most important, most available, and most overlooked source of
information is you—your own experiences, observations, and ideas. Usually, you will
use this source automatically; if you have any sense at all, you will choose a topic
about which you know a little (and preferably a lot) already. Other information
sources then act as supplements to your own knowledge. But there are two problems
commonly encountered when we use ourselves as information sources, and those
problems must be overcome if we are to implement our knowledge successfully.

First, we often tend to undervalue our knowledge, observations, or past experiences. Perhaps you are an example. Maybe you feel that you have never gone
anywhere, done anything, met anybody, or had any fun. You believe your life has
been pedantic, pedestrian, uneventful, and, at times, even boring. Is that your problem? Well, here's news. You *have* done things, gone places, and met people that
listeners are interested in. Honest. Have you ever interviewed for a job? Whether you
were successful or unsuccessful, that's a situation nearly everyone can relate to and
find interest in. Have you ever seen a movie? Probably other people in the audience
have seen it, too, and could relate to a discussion about it. The same goes for
television shows, books, magazines, and the like. In fact, almost anything you care to
talk about concerning your own experience probably will be interesting to your
audience. Just pick something.

Second, when we do choose some aspect of our own experiences to discuss, we
too often are unsystematic in analyzing those things. That is, we rarely get all we can
out of the things we have done, read, heard, and so on. To help overcome this
problem by assisting our thought processes, Wilson and Arnold (1978) developed a
"Topical System for Generating Thoughts," which consists of a list of characteristics of
things we ought to consider as we analyze our knowledge. Although this list looks a
bit intimidating, it really is rather simple and serves as a useful tool in helping us
generate information. This topical system consists of the following:

1. *Existence* or nonexistence of something
2. *Amount* or degree or quantity of something
3. *Location* of something, including adjacency, distribution, and so on
4. *Time* elements of something
5. *Movement* or activity of something
6. *Form,* either physical or abstract, of something
7. *Composition* or substance, either physical or abstract, of something
8. *Changeability* of something
9. *Strength* or power or potency of something, including its capacity to help or
   hinder something else
10. *Desirability* of something in terms of rewards or punishments
11. *Practicality* or feasibility of something
12. *Causality* in relation to something, such as what caused it, or what it causes
13. *Relationships* to something, or things with which it coexists or correlates
14. *Genus-species relationships* of something, or the categories, families,
    groups, and so on to which it belongs
15. *Possibility* or impossibility of something

Suppose, for example, one of your burning interests is space travel, and you have established as your objective informing your audience about some aspect of travel in outer space. Still, you have to narrow your topic and determine precisely what information your speech will contain. Thus, you might go through this list as a means of arriving at specific content. You might talk about recent space ventures (existence), advantages or promises of space travel (desirability), the development of space travel techniques (causality or genus-species relationships), or the possibility of long-range travel in the distant future. Similarly, for any topic area you can choose one or more items from the list to direct your efforts. In so doing, you will both narrow your topic to something more manageable and generate ideas about the topic that otherwise might not have occurred to you.

Interviews

An excellent source of information, interviews involve actually talking to the person or persons who possess information that might be useful to you. Perhaps the primary advantage of interviewing is that it provides you maximum flexibility: you can ask things as they occur to you and probe for additional information when a particular point the respondent brings out strikes your fancy. If you interview several people, interviewing also allows you to compare answers given by those people to the same questions, or it even allows you to ask each person's reaction to the answers given by an earlier respondent. Indeed, if you know what you are doing, "getting it from the horse's mouth" through interviews can be the best source of information after personal observation and experience.

Unfortunately, too many interviewers do not know what they are doing. They decide to interview someone (just whom they are going to interview doesn't make much difference) to collect information (on a topic to be named later), and they run around asking randomly chosen questions of randomly chosen people. This sort of "interviewing" produces little or no useful information. You can avoid this wasted time and effort if you will follow a few simple rules:

1. Choose your respondents carefully. Decide who has the information you want, who would be willing and able to provide that information, and who has the time or inclination to see you. Then contact the people who are left from this process of elimination to see if you guessed right—if they really are willing, able, and so on.
2. Prepare carefully. Plan the questions you want to ask and the order in which you want to ask them. Nothing is more frustrating or annoying to a respondent than to have you sit and fumble for questions to ask him or her. So you probably will want to write out a brief list of questions for the interview.
3. Avoid asking leading, unclear, or argumentative questions. Your purpose is to gather information, not to argue with or embarrass the respondent. Thus, you should try to phrase your questions neutrally and avoid asking questions like "Do you still kick small dogs?" or "Do you still cheat on your income tax?"
4. During the interview: explain the purpose and importance of the interview at the very beginning; keep the interview as brief as possible; express thanks to the respondent at the close.

5. For recording answers: tape recorders obviously are best—they capture the entire response so that you can go over and analyze it at some later time. But first ask the respondent's permission to use a recorder; some people object to being recorded, and this person should be given the opportunity to express whatever reservations he or she might have. If you are taking notes rather than recording, try to keep your note writing as unobtrusive as possible.

6. After the interview, offer the respondent an opportunity to review your notes or listen to the tape. Probably he or she will decline, but you should at least give the respondent a chance to review his or her responses so that he or she can correct any answers which might be unsatisfactory.

By following these few rules, then, you probably will be able to use this valuable information source to its maximum advantage.

Impersonal Exchanges

Interviews involve personal, direct face-to-face exchanges between you and the interviewee. However, there may be times when impersonal, less direct exchanges may be used. For example, programs broadcast over the mass media (radio or television) involve one-way communication between the performer and you; nevertheless, the information you obtain from the broadcast may be useful. Similarly, public speeches often provide useful information, even though you do not have the opportunity to speak directly to the person delivering the message. Finally, letters may also be a good source of information. They are less reliable than interviews because they do not allow you to adapt your questions to the respondent's answers, because they can more easily be ignored and left unanswered, and because they may produce answers that were not what you were looking for, but they still allow you to make contact with a person who may have information you need. Two rules to keep in mind if you use letters: never ask for too much information (people do not like to write long letters in response) and always include a self-addressed stamped envelope for the respondent's use.

Written Sources

Perhaps the most commonly used source of information is the library. The *Reader's Guide to Periodical Literature* is well known as an index to information appearing in magazines, and the card catalog is a useful index to information in books. But some other indexes also are worth noting. Research published in scholarly journals is abstracted in *Psychological Abstracts, Sociological Abstracts, Biological Abstracts,* and the *Business Periodical Index;* newspaper information can be located in *The New York Times Index;* government documents are listed in the *Catalogue of the Public Documents of Congress and of All Departments of the Government of the United States* and in the *Monthly Catalog of United States Government Publications;* books are listed in *Books in Print* and the *Book Review Digest;* and doctoral dissertations are described in *Dissertation Abstracts.* And if none of these tell you what you need, the *Basic Reference Sources* and the *Guide to Reference Books* present lists of reference works that may take you to the sources you need, or the *Bibliographic Index: A Cumulative Bibliography of Bibliographies* may lead you to sources relevant to your topic.

Just as there are some basic rules you ought to follow while interviewing, so too are there some techniques that will make your reading more productive. Some of these include:

1. Have a purpose in mind as you read. Know in advance what you are looking for and use that objective to guide your reading choices.
2. When possible, use the table of contents or the index of the thing you are reading to locate specific topics of interest to you.
3. Read more than one source on a particular topic. This allows you to check the consistency and accuracy of your sources. Moreover, if the topic is a controversial one, try to read at least one source representing each of the various viewpoints. Even if your speech is to present just one point of view on the topic, you should know what the other viewpoints are.
4. Take notes as you read. Generally, 3 × 5 notecards are the most manageable note-taking materials. But no matter what you decide to write on, you should always remember to record complete bibliographic information (author, title, work, publisher, date, volume, page numbers, and so on); to record quotations, sources, and statistics with perfect accuracy; to summarize long ideas in a manner which accurately reflects the meaning of the original words; and to be discriminating in what you write (don't copy down everything you see). When using cards, you might also remember to record only one idea, quotation, or item on each card, and to write at the top of the card the specific topic to which the information relates.

Surveys and Experiments

Researchers gain much of their information through measurement of a descriptive or experimental nature. Descriptive measures are used to assess characteristics of people as they exist at the moment. Such things as questionnaires, surveys, opinion polls, and the like fall into this category. The measures of audience characteristics we saw in Chapter 2 can be used to construct descriptive measures of this sort. Experiments go one step further and try to assess the effects of one thing upon something else. For example, if we wanted to see if our speech produces attitude change, we could measure audience attitudes before the speech, then deliver our message, and then measure their attitudes again to determine whether any changes had occurred. Although it typically is impractical for us to conduct a carefully controlled experiment prior to delivery of our speech, surveys and experiments occasionally may provide us with information previously undiscovered by anyone else.

Tests of Information

You should not immediately accept as fact anything you see, hear, or read. Rather, there are some questions you should ask to assess the quality of your information. These include:

1. Is it accurate? As best you can tell, does it truly represent reality?
2. Is it recent? That is, how close in time to the thing being considered was the

information generated? Do the statistics apply now? Is the authority you read up to date? Were there eyewitness accounts of the incident?

3. Is it complete? Do you have the whole story, or was something likely to have been left out? Viewpoints on controversial issues are particularly susceptible here.
4. Is it reliable? Has the source provided good information in the past?
5. Is it objective? Is it likely to present the facts in an unbiased manner?
6. Is it consistent, both with other sources and with itself?

By applying these tests, you can be more sure that the information you are using is good information.

ORGANIZING INFORMATION

As we have seen, people have a need for order or structure in their lives. They look for relationships and then, based on the relationships they observe or invent concerning their surroundings, they draw conclusions about the things they encounter. It is this need for structure that makes it particularly necessary for us as speakers to carefully organize the information we present. But the advantages of good speech organization go far beyond this adaptation to listeners' needs. Research into the effects of organization has determined several consequences of a speech's organizational quality.

There is evidence, first, that clear organization facilitates understanding and retention. Studies conducted by Thompson (1960), Darnell (1963), Thistlethwaite, deHaan, and Kamenetsky (1955), and Baird (1974) demonstrated that disorganized speeches are not understood or remembered well by the people who hear them, while well-organized speeches usually are comprehended and retained. These studies found, too, that inclusion of previews (which quickly summarize the main points of the speech at the very beginning of the talk) and reviews (which summarize the main points at the conclusion of the speech) also facilitate comprehension and memory.

Second, organization seems related to attitude change. Smith (1951), for example, found in an early study that minor changes in speech organization produced no effects upon audience attitude change, but that large-scale disruption of a speech's organizational pattern caused the audience to turn against the speaker and his or her viewpoint. It would seem, therefore, that small errors in organization are overlooked by an audience, but that large problems in organization have a negative impact upon the effectiveness of the speech.

Organization may also have a third effect: it may influence audience perceptions of the speaker's credibility. Thompson (1967) observed that while disorganization had a negative effect upon audience comprehension of the speech and upon their perceptions of the speech's quality, it did not influence their perceptions of the speaker's competence. But Sharp and McClung (1966), using the same speeches Thompson had, observed a substantial decrease in credibility ratings produced by disorganization of the speech. Since Sharp and McClung used more sophisticated measuring devices than had Thompson, it seems likely that good speech organization enhances credibility, while poor organization damages it.

Finally, as most of the studies reported above demonstrated, perceptions of speech quality are influenced by organization: people hearing a well-organized speech think it is a good one, while people hearing a poorly organized speech think it a bad one. And they are right. However, even minor elements of organization influence these quality judgements. In his brilliant study, Baird (1972) observed that previews and reviews serve to create an impression of organization so that speeches having them are rated as good, while speeches not having them are rated somewhat lower. This effect is seen most clearly when the speech is disorganized: including a preview and a review in a randomly organized speech caused the audience to think they were hearing a well-organized message, while leaving the preview and review out allowed the audience to see the speech as the mess it truly was. So if you begin with a preview ("In this speech, I will cover three points, which are . . .") and end with a review ("So I have covered three points, which were . . ."), you convince your audience that they have just heard a clearly organized speech, even if what occurred between the preview and review actually was disorganized garbage.

Clearly, it is important that we organize our speech well. Our effectiveness in informing, persuading, and establishing credibility rests upon our organizational clarity to a large degree. Thus, we move now to some patterns that we might use as we seek to organize the information we have collected.

Patterns of Organization

The standard patterns for organizing speeches may be divided into two categories. *Logical* patterns are structures used because they make sense—because they present information in a straightforward, understandable way. *Psychological* patterns are structures used in order to adapt to the psychology of the audience, particularly to their attitudes and values. For example, some psychological patterns are used when the audience are initially favorable, others are used when the audience are initially unfavorable. But this is beyond our immediate concern; our purpose here is to discover ways in which information can be communicated more clearly to our listeners; thus, we will consider only logical patterns below.

Chronological Order

This pattern is based upon time, as it reviews occurrences in the sequence in which they happened or gives directions according to the time sequence in which things should occur. Most historical accounts follow a chronological pattern: "In the French Revolution, the peasants seized power by force and quickly changed all the locks on the palace doors so that the nobles could not get back in. Then they had a big party in which they gorged themselves and became sick. When the nobles recaptured the palace the next day, they were forced to clean up and found many stains and cigarette burns." Or a recipe for baking a cake can follow a similar pattern: "Preheat the oven to 450°. In a large bowl, beat three eggs, 6 oz. of horseradish sauce, 1 slice of Limburger cheese, and a red pepper. When the mixture stands in stiff peaks (probably after about 45 minutes), pour it into a paper bag and place it in the oven. Wait 30 minutes. Remove the bag, and throw the whole mess away."

The chronological sequence is an excellent pattern for speeches introducing another speaker, historical lectures, speeches of nomination, and the like. However, it does have a weakness in that such important considerations as cause, effect, desirability, form, spatial relationships cannot be discussed without interrupting the flow of time the speech creates.

Spatial Order

As the name implies, this pattern is based upon the relationships of things as they exist in space. When giving directions, for example, you use this pattern: "Go straight ahead two blocks, and then turn left at the Standard station. Go until you hit the first stoplight, and turn right. Go four more blocks (you'll see a little grocery store on your left at the corner), and then turn right again. It's the first house on your left." The problem with spatial patterns, though, is that you have to indicate the type of spatial order you are using. When giving directions, it's the from-here-to-there order. But with other situations, it can be a top-to-bottom order, a right-to-left order, a front-to-back order, and so on.

Causal Order

We have seen that people learn according to causal relationships. To capitalize on this tendency, we can organize our materials in cause-effect terms. Such causal patterns can move in either of two directions: from a description of present causes to a prediction of future effects, or from an analysis of present conditions to a consideration of the causes which produced them. Thus, a speech on pollution control might examine present water and air pollution problems and then project the future consequences of pollution, while a speech on the current crime rate might present recent incidences of crime and then examine the social forces that made the participants into criminals.

When using this pattern of organization, certain things must be accomplished. First, you must prove to the audience that causal relationships exist. Through the facts and supporting materials you present, you must demonstrate beyond doubt that the effects you describe truly are produced by the cause and are produced *only* by that cause (that is, no other causal factors exist). Moreover, you must show that if the cause is removed (if in fact that is what you are suggesting), the effects will disappear and no undesirable side effects will arise. Finally, you may also have to prove that the effects are truly undesirable (if you are suggesting that the cause be eliminated) or that the effects will truly be advantageous (if you are suggesting that some causal element be implemented). While some of these considerations move into the area of persuasive speaking, they nevertheless are related to the informative use of causal organization as well.

Topical Order

To some degree, this sort of pattern represents a catchall category: if your materials lend themselves to no other pattern of organization, arrange them by topic. A speech on the governmental system of the United States; for example, might be divided into three subtopics: the legislative branch, the judicial branch, and the executive branch. Or a speech on how to develop and give a public speech might be divided into two topics: preparing to speak and delivering the speech. And a speech on the social effects of legalizing abortion might be divided into the topics of "advantages" and "disadvantages." Thus, the topical pattern really is an arbitrary grouping of themes relevant to your speech topic and purpose, and the one demand to be met is that the groupings be understandable and reasonable to you and your audience.

Process Order

This pattern of organization is similar to the chronological order in that it considers things in the sequence in which they occur. When we describe the steps of some operation in their natural order, we are using the process pattern even though the steps also may occur in chronological sequence. If, for example, we are describing the workings of an internal combustion engine, we could consider in order everything that occurs: the injection of fuel into the cylinder, the spark from the spark plugs, the explosion and movement of the piston, and so on. But we might want to become even more complex than that and describe processes that occur simultaneously, such as the electrical system, the fuel system, and the piston-cylinder system. Then we would use a topical order to divide the engine into its three subparts, and within each subpart/subtopic describe in order the things that occur in the process. Similarly, a golf pro when giving a lesson will tell you what to do simultaneously with your hands, head, arms, hips, knees; he divides his little speech into subtopics (areas of the body), and then describes in sequence the process through which each part goes.

Known-Unknown Order

Earlier we saw that people learn new things by associating them with things they already know and understand. Occasionally, you can use this principle throughout your entire speech, basing your organizational pattern upon the analogy principle we discussed above. That is, you do three things. First select something the audience already understand to use as a point of comparison (such as the horse to compare with the car). Second, select one of the preceding patterns of organization with which to structure your speech (for example, a spatial arrangement moving from front to back or a topical arrangement looking at the topics of locomotion, care, and passenger accomodations). Then, third, move through your organizational pattern comparing the old to the new. Through this extended use of analogy, then, you use a known-unknown organizational pattern to clarify the information for your audience.

Ascending-Descending Orders

With this pattern, you first select some criterion for ordering your material and then arrange the material according to the amount of that criterion each point possesses. Suppose, for example, you use importance as the criterion. You then could present your points in order of increasing importance (ascending order) by starting with your least important point and moving to increasingly more important ones, or you could present them in descending order, starting with the most important and moving to the least. Or when describing a series of objects according to size, you might move from smallest to largest (ascending), or largest to smallest (descending). Similarly, topics might be arranged according to their familiarity to the audience, their complexity, their interest to the audience, and so on.

Experiential Order

Sometimes, it is effective to organize our speech according to our own experience with the topic, describing how we came to acquire our knowledge or to arrive at the conclusions we are presenting to the audience. In recounting how we became a world-famous tennis star, for example, we could describe our early failures and later triumphs. Or in telling how to fix a car, we could describe some of the commonly made mistakes we committed when we first undertook repairing our old Edsel. Or if we are describing the religious commitment we now feel, we could describe the periods of life and noncommitment through which we passed before reaching our current state of mind. In so doing, then, we accomplish two objectives: we demonstrate to our audience our familiarity with and commitment to the topic, thus enhancing our credibility, and we clarify the information for the audience by organizing it.

Question-Answer Order

Suppose we can anticipate in advance the audience's questions concerning our topic. One way to organize our speech would be to list those questions at the beginning and then provide answers to them one at a time. The order in which we take those questions also must be considered, however; we might want to organize them by topic, by ascending-descending order of importance, by cause or effect, by chronology, or by one of the other patterns we have seen. By doing this sort of double organization, we can both clarify the issues for the audience by grouping questions together, and we can maintain their interest by stating and answering questions on their minds. But note one important thing: for this pattern to be effective, you must be quite sure that the audience are asking the questions you present. Nothing is more boring than to have someone answer questions you do not care about in the first place.

Obviously, a great many of organizational patterns are available to you. Your choice should depend upon a variety of considerations: the sort of information you are presenting, the psychology of the audience, the nature of the situation, and your own perceptions of what is reasonable. And that choice should be made carefully, for the effectiveness with which you organize your speech will have a significant impact upon the effectiveness with which you speak to your audience.

Constructing an Outline

When the main ideas of your speech have been selected and made clear, and when your information has been gathered and you have selected an organizational pattern, it is time to outline the whole. A good outline serves several useful functions. It allows you to review the entire structure of your speech to see if you have covered all the important points, if you have given each point the emphasis it deserves, and if you have fitted the parts of the speech together in a logical fashion. Moreover, it allows you to judge whether you have developed and clarified adequately each of the points and subpoints you will cover. And it helps you remember the entire speech by fixing in your mind the main points you will cover and the sequence in which you will present them. So outline building is far more than just a speech-preparing exercise required by instructors of public speaking; it is a crucial step toward achieving the objective you have established for yourself.

An outline, as you should know, consists of an organized, symbolized, indented list of main points, subpoints, and supporting materials. As a rule, an outline will take this form:

I. First main point
  A. First major subpoint
    1. Supporting statement number 1
      a. First piece of specific information
      b. Second piece of specific information
    2. Supporting statement number 2
  B. Second major subpoint
    1. Supporting statement
    2. Supporting statement
      a. Specific information
      b. Specific information
        (1) More specific information
        (2) More specific information
          (a) Even more specific information
          (b) Another bit of even more specific information
  C. Third major subpoint
II. Second main point
  A. Major subpoint
  B. Major subpoint
III. Third main point

Within this sort of format, there are several requirements that must be met. First, each point should contain only one piece of information or one idea. For example:

I. Prostitution should be legalized in order to decrease crime and increase state tax revenues.

Or

I. Prostitution should be legalized.
  A. Legalization would decrease crime.
  B. Legalization would increase state revenues.

The second example is correct. The main idea is presented with the Roman numeral; the two subpoints are given with the capital letters. Similarly, all parts of the outline should contain one and only one separate thought.

Second, the outline should accurately reflect relationships between ideas. That is, the most general ideas should be listed with Roman numerals, the next most general with capital letters, the next with Arabic numbers, and so on. For example:

I. Unregulated prostitution encourages other forms of crime.
  A. Prostitution should be legalized and regulated.

    B. Customers often are robbed.
    C. Drug abuse and prostitution go hand in hand.
       1. Prostitution is a victimless crime.
       2. No one is harmed by it.

Or

I. Prostitution should be legalized and regulated.
    A. Unregulated prostitution encourages other forms of crime.
       1. Customers often are robbed.
       2. Drug abuse and prostitution go hand in hand.
    B. Prostitution is a victimless crime.
       1. No one is harmed by it.
       2. People should not be punished for harmless activities.

Again, the second example is correct. Points A and B are reasons supporting I. Points 1 and 2 are facts supporting A and B. Probably, you would want to support the 1 and 2 statements with specific examples, quotations, statistics, and so forth. But in any case, the outline must establish the logical relationship among the points you cover. Thus, done correctly, outlining guarantees a well-organized speech.

Third, you must use a consistent system of symbolization and indentation. All main points should be listed with Roman numerals; all major subpoints should have capital letters; all supporting statements immediately below major subpoints should have Arabic numbers, and so on. In other words, stick to the system illustrated above. In addition, when an entry runs longer than one line, indent the second line the same amount as the first line. For example:

I. If this main point runs longer than one line, the second line should be
   indented so that it matches the first line.
    A. If the subpoint runs longer than one line, it should be indented to match
      the first line of this entry
       1. If this specific statement runs beyond one line, you know what to do.

By using this sort of consistent indentation, you establish visually the logical relationships among the points, with main points farthest left (including the second line if there is one), major subpoints four typewritten spaces to the right, supporting statements four more spaces to the right, and so on.

Fourth, you should avoid having single subpoints. Generally, subpoints indicate subdivisions of the main points they fall under. Similarly, supporting statements indicate divisions of subpoints, specific pieces of information indicate subdivisions of supporting statements, and so on. So for every A you should have a B; for every 1 there should be a 2; for every a there should be a b. Occasionally, though, there are exceptions: sometimes a main point is defined by a single subpoint, or sometimes a single example is used to prove the statement it follows. But for the most part, there should be two points every time you subdivide a point on the outline.

Finally, there should be only one symbol for any one heading. For example:

I. A. Prostitution causes other forms of crime.
   B. Prostitution can provide additional governmental income.

Or

I. Prostitution should be legalized and regulated.
   A. Prostitution causes other forms of crime.
   B. Prostitution can provide additional governmental income.

The second example is correct; no point should have more than one symbol.

Although these five requirements for outlining seem rather simple and straightforward, they are at times rather difficult to implement. You must analyze your points, subpoints, and supporting materials carefully in order to discover their relationships and then apply the rules of outlining form in order to structure them properly. But through careful adherence to these requirements, you will arrive at an outline that will achieve all of the advantages we discussed at the beginning of this section.

Types of Outlines

Outlines can take several forms, although only two usually are recommended. We will look at four types of outlines but examine in detail only two of them.

1. The Scratch Outline. This is the sort of outline you put together on a moment's notice—perhaps because you've been called upon to speak without expecting it or because you neglected to do your assignment the night before. Usually, scratch outlines consist only of two or three main points, perhaps with major subpoints listed beneath each. For example, suppose you are sitting in public speaking class early one Monday morning, and you suddenly discover (when the instructor reads the names of students scheduled to speak) that you must deliver an informative speech. On the piece of kleenex you find in your pocket, you might scratch out the following outline:

HOW TO CURE HICCUPS
  I. Introduction: The problem of hiccups
 II. Cures
    A. The breath-holding method
    B. The paper bag method
    C. The fright method
III. Conclusion
    A. The best method
    B. Action step

Obviously, such an outline does little more than remind you of your major points while you speak. But when you have time to prepare, you ought to produce something considerably more substantial than a scratch outline.

2. The Brief. A "Brief" is anything but. It consists of *all* the information you can lay your hands on, *all* points and subpoints you can think of, *all* arguments

relevant to your topic (both for and against your viewpoint)—in fact, everything
relevant to your topic except the kitchen sink (and that, too, if your speech is on
methods of remodeling houses). The brief is used most commonly in legal settings,
where lawyers must be prepared to counter every argument their opponents offer plus
construct a few of their own. Although you might want to construct this sort of
thorough outline just to be sure that you have covered everything in your speech, the
brief outline usually is reserved for overachievers and masochists.

3. The Full-sentence Outline. As the name implies, this sort of outline uses
complete sentences for each point listed in the outline. Suppose, for example, we
were constructing an outline of the speech, "How to Use Public Speaking by Objectives." Our full-sentence outline might look like this:

   I. The first step is to prepare the introduction.
      A. The first thing the introduction must do is get attention.
         1. Startling statements often attract the attention of the audience.
            a. (example)
            b. (example)
         2. Rhetorical questions involve the audience.
         3. Personal stories interest the audience.
      B. The second thing the introduction must do is motivate interest.
      C. The third thing the introduction must do is establish credibility.
  II. The second step is to prepare the body of the speech.

And so the outline would go, developing step by step the process through which one
proceeds in developing a speech.

While the complete-sentence outline has the advantage of putting the entire
thought down in writing so that it cannot be lost during the speech, there also is the
danger that, if we deliver the speech from this outline, we will end up reading it to the
audience. In fact, such an outline practically becomes a speech manuscript, except
that it is in outline form rather than in a paragraph structure. Since read speeches are
usually dull speeches, this temptation must be avoided. Thus, while this sort of
outline might be useful in preparing the speech, it ought not be used as notes from
which to talk.

4. The Topical (or Key Word) Outline. Rather than complete sentences, this
type of outline uses key words or topics to indicate the points to be covered. For
example:

   I. Introduction
      A. Attention
         1. Startling statement
            a. (example)
            b. (example)
         2. Rhetorical questions
         3. Personal stories

B. Motivation

C. Credibility

II. Body

The ideas covered in this outline are the same as those seen in the full-sentence example above, but now just one or two words are used to indicate the topic or subtopic to be discussed. Thus, this sort of outline serves to jog your memory while you speak, but it does not present the temptation to read the outline to the audience. For these reasons, then, this is the best sort of outline to use while speaking.

To assist you in developing your own (preferably topical) outline, here is a form with which you can fill in each part of an informative speech:

I. Introduction

    A. Attention-getting statement(s)

        1. _____

        2. _____

    B. Interest-motivating statement(s)

        1. _____

        2. _____

    C. Credibility-building statement(s)

        1. _____

        2. _____

    D. Preview of main points in body

        1. _____

        2. _____

        3. _____

II. Body

    A. First main point: _____

        1. First subpoint: _____

Construct an Outline That Does Not Require Study During the Actual Presentation

a. Specific information: _____

b. Specific information: _____

2. Second subpoint: _____

a. Specific information: _____

b. Specific information: _____

B. Second main point: _____

1. First subpoint: _____

a. Specific information: _____

b. Specific information: _____

2. Second subpoint: _____

a. Specific information: _____

b. Specific information: _____

C. Third main point: _____

   1. First subpoint: _____

     a. Specific information: _____

     b. Specific information: _____

   2. Second subpoint: _____

     a. Specific information: _____

     b. Specific information: _____

III. Conclusion

   A. Review of main points in body

     1. _____

     2. _____

     3. _____

   B. Concluding statement: _____

Of course, you may want to modify this outline statement, using more or fewer main points, subpoints, or pieces of specific information or becoming even more specific in some of the things you say so that parts of the outline are broken down still further. Nevertheless, this outline form does serve to indicate the way in which your final speech outline should appear when it is complete.

DEVELOPING COHERENCE

Information is coherent when it forms a unified, smoothly flowing, complete body of knowledge. To some degree, we already have set about developing coherence, as we have sought to place our information into a logical, unified sequence. But there are some other things we must accomplish in order to achieve a truly coherent speech: we must develop an introduction to the speech, transitions that connect the parts of the speech, and a conclusion that effectively ends the speech. When these elements are added to the material we already have developed, then and only then will we have a truly coherent speech.

The Introduction

In previous chapters, we developed some understanding of what a good introduction should do. We will review those things here only briefly. First, an introduction must get attention. Using some of the devices we discussed in Chapter 5, you must cause the audience to pay attention to you rather than to something or someone else in the setting. Second, the introduction should motivate. In a later chapter, we will examine some motivational techniques; at this point, simply note that you must give the audience some reason to listen, by promising them some reward for doing so or by threatening them with some adverse consequence if they do not do so. Third, the introduction should establish your credibility. If your audience are to believe you, they must be convinced that you are a credible source. Again, a later chapter will outline some strategies for gaining credibility. At this juncture, we will note simply that, to be credible, you must prove your competence with the topic, your trustworthiness, your good intensions, your likeability, your dynamism, and your admirability. And finally, the introduction should introduce the topic, telling the audience what you are going to be talking about and listing briefly the main points to be covered.

Transitions

When you have developed and outlined the points that will comprise your speech, you still must have some means of moving smoothly from one point in the speech to the point that immediately follows. Generally, that is accomplished through transitions.

The primary function of transitions is to alert your listeners that a new idea is being developed and to show them the relationship between this idea and the one which preceded it. Thus, transitions are words, phrases, and sentences which summarize, clarify, and forecast main points and subpoints in speeches.

Transitions come in two forms: primary and incidental. Primary transitions serve to move you from one major point of the speech to the next. Often they are used in conjunction with internal summaries; for example:

"So we have seen three characteristics of my first point . . . ." (Reviews characteristics.) "Now, let's go on the second point, which is . . . ."

Or

"Now that we have analyzed the _____, the _____, and the _____, let's move to the next topic I'd like to cover today."

By quickly restating specific subpoints of a main point, the internal summary serves to review and emphasize those points and to tie them up so that discussion of the next section can be undertaken. The transition that immediately follows the internal summary ("Let's move to the next topic . . .") tells the audience that the new subtopic has arrived.

Incidental transitions show relationships between ideas within subpoints. Consisting of single words or phrases, they take these forms:

Adding Material	Summarizing Material	Contrasting Material
Furthermore	Therefore	However
Moreover	Finally	On the other hand
Also	On the whole	Still
In addition	So	Although
Similarly	In sum	While

Elaborating Material	Reason Giving Material	Process-time Movement Material
More specifically	Because	Then
That is to say	Since	Next
For example	For	First . . . second . . . third
In other words	As a result	As
For instance	Consequently	When

Of course, this by no means constitutes a complete list of incidental transitions you might use. But it does illustrate the sorts of things you need to include in order to smooth the flow of your ideas as you present them to your audience.

One final point concerning transitions. Occasionally, you might want to use them to call attention to particularly important points in your speech. For example:

"We come now to the most important idea I want to consider."
"Give this point particular attention."
"This idea is so important that I'll repeat it."
"Even if you forget everything else, remember this."

These kinds of transitional sentences do two things. They signal the audience that a new idea is coming, and they emphasize that idea so that the audience are more likely to catch it. If there are two or three things you particularly want the audience to remember, use these emphasis-giving transitions.

The Conclusion

The last part of an informative speech (you doubtless will be surprised to learn) is the conclusion. Too often an inexperienced speaker will run out of things to say (having covered all the points in the body of the speech) but find himself (or herself) still standing up in front of the audience. After a long, embarrassing silence, he'll blush, mutter "Thank you," and beat a hasty retreat to his seat. Hardly an impressive finish, and certainly not the sort of thing that leaves a positive impression in the minds of the listeners. To be truly effective, you must prepare the last part of your speech every bit as carefully as you planned the first parts.

A good conclusion does three things. First, it summarizes the main points of the speech, providing the "review" we discussed earlier in this chapter. In so doing, it demonstrates that the speech in fact was clearly organized (or at least causes the audience to *think* it was organized), and it provides one final view of the major ideas the speech covered. It is crucial, then, that the conclusion begin with a review.

Second, the conclusion should leave the audience in a particular frame of mind. If you want them to be thoughtful and to reflect on what you have said, your conclusion should promote that; if you want them to be running around the room in a frenzy, the conclusion should cause that, too. Hence, you must decide what sort of response you want—serious thought, happy feelings, frenzied activity, warm sympathy, and so on—and then design your conclusion so that the response is elicited. Some devices you might use to achieve such responses include:

1. Issuing a challenge or appeal to the audience, perhaps demanding that they do something.

2. Providing an appropriate quotation.
3. Providing a narrative story illustrating what you want them to feel, think, or do.
4. Offering them additional reasons to do what you want.
5. Telling them what you personally intend to do, thus offering yourself as a model.
6. By asking questions, causing them through their answers to commit themselves to your proposal.

Typically, informative speeches do not conclude with strong emotional appeals; thus, quotations and stories are the most appropriate devices here. In a later chapter, we'll look at some of the emotion-arousing devices you can use at the conclusion of persuasive speeches.

Finally, the conclusion should end the speech, and do it decisively and completely. Few things are as annoying to an audience as a speaker who behaves like a car with a bad idle setting—you turn off the key, and it still keeps sputtering and coughing and going on, and on, and on. . . . When you have summarized and created the proper mood, give a final, concluding sentence, and stop.

SUMMARY

While the objectives and strategies we considered in this chapter may not enable you to write *War and Peace,* they will allow you to prepare speeches understandable to your audience. Our primary objective being to promote audience understanding of information we present, we examined the three secondary objectives that must be achieved. First, we saw that, in order to acquire adequate information, we should rely on several sources of information, including ourselves, interviews, impersonal exchanges, written sources, and surveys of experiments. Second, when we have collected that information we must organize it clearly, use the chronological, spatial, causal, topical, process, known-unknown, ascending-descending, experiential, or question-answer pattern, and develop an outline that puts those patterns into action. Then, third, when our materials are arranged, we must present them in a coherent, unified whole, using an effective introduction, clear transitions, and a well-developed conclusion. All of these strategies, when implemented, will greatly aid achievement of our informational speaking objective.

THE SPEECH
(Informative)

PART I: INTRODUCTION

Get attention
Motivate interest
Enhance credibility
(Preview)

10 percent of speech

PART II: BODY

A. First main point
  1. First subpoint
    a. Specific information
    b. Specific information
  2. Second subpoint
    a. Specific information
    b. Specific information
  (Primary transition)
B. Second main point
  1. First subpoint
    a. Specific information
    b. Specific information
  2. Second subpoint
  (Primary transition)
C. Third main point
  1. First subpoint
  2. Second subpoint

85 percent of speech

PART III: CONCLUSION

Summarize
Create mood
Conclude

5 percent of speech

REFERENCES

Baird, J. E., Jr. "The Effects of 'Previews' and 'Reviews' Upon Audience Comprehension of Expository Speeches of Varying Quality and Complexity," *Central States Speech Journal* 25(1974):119–127.

Darnell, D. K. "The Relation Between Sentence-Order and Comprehension," *Speech Monographs* 30 (1963):97–100.

Sharp, H. and T. McClung. "Effects of Organization on the Speaker's Ethos," *Speech Monographs* 33(1966):182.

Smith, R. G. "Effects of Speech Organization Upon Attitudes of College Students," *Speech Monographs* 18 (1951):292–301.

Thistlethwaite, D., H. deHaan, and J. Kamenetsky. "The Effect of 'Directive' and 'Non-directive' Communication Procedures on Attitudes," *Journal of Abnormal and Social Psychology* 51(1955):107–118.

Thompson, E. "An Experimental Investigation of the Relative Effectiveness of Organizational Structure in Oral Communication," *Southern Speech Journal* 26(1960):59–69.

————. "Some Effects of Message Structure on Listeners' Comprehension," *Speech Monographs* 34(1967):51–57.

Wilson, J. and C. Arnold. *Public Speaking as a Liberal Art,* 4th ed. Boston: Allyn and Bacon, 1978.

EXHIBIT 1

I. A strong correlation exists between crime and handgun possession.
   A. Most crimes involve guns, particularly handguns.
      1. Over 50 percent of all murders last year involved handguns.
      2. Robberies require threats, and handguns threaten in most instances.
   B. Evidence disproves the adage that "guns don't kill people; people kill people."
      1. Most murders are spontaneous; 70 percent were unplanned and might not have occurred had no gun been available.
      2. Twenty percent of all gun attacks are fatal; only 5 percent of knife attacks end in death.
      3. Psychologically, guns are easier to use than any other weapon; they require less physical effort or initiative.
II. Guns are not desirable methods of self-protection.
   A. Self-defense laws restrict use of force.
      1. Only "reasonable force" is permitted.
      2. Use of a gun is unjustified if the danger can be avoided.
   B. Guns are neither safe nor effective as protection for the home.
      1. Safety
         a. A gun is six times more likely to kill a family member as it is to kill an intruder.
         b. Mistaken identity may cause an innocent person to be shot.
      2. Effectiveness
         a. The intruder has the element of surprise on his side.
         b. The threat of a gun may precipitate extreme action by the intruder; the situation is made more dangerous.

Above is a partial outline for the speech on gun control. What pattern of organization is used: How might the information be presented more effectively?

EXHIBIT 2

I. Television violence teaches real-life violence.
   A. Short-term learning occurs through imitation.
      1. Imitation theory
         a. Evidence exists that children learn by copying behavior.
         b. Increasing frequency of observation increases learning.
      2. Much behavior on television is violent, and children imitate that behavior.
         a. Zamora case modeled after "Kojak" episode.
         b. Rape case modeled after "Born Innocent."
   B. Long-term effects also occur.
      1. Eron and Huesmann study: aggressiveness at age 19 directly related to amount of television violence seen.
      2. Gerbner and Gross study: distrust of others related to frequent television viewing.
II. Entire value systems taught by television violence.
   A. Aggressive behavior taught as effective method for solving problems.
      1. Television shows that violence works.
      2. H. J. Skornia study: television teaches children to solve problems violently.
   B. Gerbner and Gross study: people exposed to television violence ultimately develop fear of the real world.

Above is a partial outline for the speech on television violence. What pattern of organization is used? How might the information be presented more effectively?

PROJECT

THE PROGRESS REPORT

As its name indicates, this sort of speech reports the progress of something presently taking place. Such reports are typified by business meetings in which engineers describe the ongoing development of some new product or by professional conferences in which scholars report on their continuing research efforts. Their primary objective is to promote understanding by the audience of the thing under development. Typically, they describe the purposes (if any) underlying the thing, the stages completed, the stages to be completed, and the outcomes to be expected. You should prepare this report by proceeding through the following stages:

1. Select a topic. Choose something going on right now. You might be involved in it personally (such as in some community project or in some recreational activity), or it might be something you know about (such as the current professional football/basketball/baseball season or some construction in the vicinity). In any case, it should be something under way but not yet completed.
2. Gather your information. Learn what you need to know about the history, present stage, and future of the thing.
3. Organize your material. Use one of the organizational patterns described in the preceding chapter to describe the development, past and future, of this thing.
4. Develop an introduction that gets attention, motivates interest, shows your acquaintance with the topic, and previews the main points you will cover.
5. Develop a conclusion that summarizes your main points and refers back to the things you said in the introduction.
6. Use some sort of visual aid that will demonstrate the progress of the thing you are discussing.

Name _____

Date _____

Speech Type _____

Speech Outline, Project Number _____

Speech Topic: _____

Speech Objective: _____

_____

Speech Title: _____

Introduction

    Attention:

    Motivation:

    Credibility:

      Preview

      Body

      Conclusion

Instructor's Comments:

CHAPTER 7
PROMOTING RETENTION

PRIMARY (PREPARATIONAL) OBJECTIVE:
To promote audience retention of presented information

Secondary Objectives	Corresponding Strategies
To make information intense	Details
	Examples
	Definitions
	Analogies
	Contrasts
	Quantification
	Visualization
To make information associable	Same first letter
	Rhyme
	Same number of letters
	Combining relationship

CHAPTER OBJECTIVES
After studying this chapter, you should be able to:

- Develop details supporting your general speech materials
- Develop examples supporting your general speech materials
- Develop definitions clarifying your speech materials
- Develop analogies illustrating your speech materials
- Develop contrasts illustrating your speech materials
- Develop quantifications illustrating your speech materials
- Develop visualizations clarifying your speech materials
- Develop devices that create associations between your major speech points

INTRODUCTION

A few years ago, I was asked to judge a speech contest sponsored by the local chapter of an international organization devoted to the improvement of its members' speaking skills. After delivering what I considered to be an insightful, poignant lecture on the craft of public speaking and then listening to five speakers who clearly had not heard a word I said, I was treated to lunch. While I and the members sat busily munching our rubber chicken, we were favored with an address delivered by the featured speaker, a man who, if the master of ceremonies was to be believed, was one of the world's foremost practitioners of the speaking arts. Toward the end of his speech, this gentleman offered the following summary: "This organization is like a garden. First, you have a row of peas: *Pleasantness, Persuasiveness,* and *Power.* Second, you have a row of lettuce: let us speak, let us listen, let us think. And third, you have a row of turnips: turn up at meetings, turn up the corners of your mouth." I turned up my lunch. But I remembered the speech. Even now, years later, I wake up screaming in the middle of the night, hearing voices murmuring about peas, lettuce, and turnips.

Believe it or not, this true example of public speaking illustrates the third primary objective we must achieve when giving information: making that information as easily retainable as possible for our audience. It is crucial that our listeners not only attend to and understand us, but that they also remember the things we have said. Thus, in this chapter we will examine some techniques for promoting audience retention.

INTENSIFYING INFORMATION

While we can simply present our audience with the pure, bare facts we gathered and outlined in the previous chapter, such information probably will not be very memorable for them. Bare facts often lack impact, vividness, emotionality, or any of the other characteristics that, as we saw at the beginning of this entire section, make information memorable. Thus, we need to "flesh out" our bare facts with material that adds impact (and hence memorability) to our skeletal information. These materials also clarify our information so that audience understanding is also improved. Let's consider, then, some of the more commonly used types of intensifying strategies.

Details

Providing specific characteristics, parts, and features of the things we discuss helps the audience understand and retain the points we cover. Speaking about auto safety and Ralph Nader's book *Unsafe at Any Speed* (in which the old Chevrolet Corvair, among others, is proclaimed hazardous to our health), for example, we could simply say, "I had a '65 Corvair, and it fell apart." Not terribly illuminating or memorable. Or we could provide some details: "The first time I drove it, the car's steering wheel came off in my hands. That allowed me to test the brakes, which promptly failed. This in turn gave me the opportunity to test the bumper protection as it held up against a large building. After my release from the hospital . . ." Such details clarify our point, make it more concrete, and make it memorable. Whenever possible, then, we should use details to intensify the general point we want to make.

Examples are specific instances of the thing in question—the action, object, situation, or experience we are talking about. We can divide examples into several categories. First, they can be either real or hypothetical. *Real examples* are things that actually exist or have existed. If we are trying to illustrate the Communist plot to take over the world, we might cite the instances of Poland, Vietnam, Cambodia, Cuba, and other countries where Communist influence has become predominant. On the other hand, *hypothetical examples* are fictitious; we make them up to clarify and illustrate the thing we are discussing. Most of the examples in this book are hypothetical, beginning with such phrases as "Suppose we are . . ." or "If we are. . . ." Hypothetical examples do not prove anything (real examples often do), but they can clarify the point we are trying to make.

Second, examples can be singular or serial. A *singular example* is, as the name implies, a single instance of the thing under consideration. Our discussion of communism might focus exclusively on Vietnam, for example, or our speech about the dangers of Chevy Corvairs might cite only the instance of our own car. Indeed, you could even take a singular example and use it as the foundation for most or all of your speech, making it an "extended" example. For instance, as I was preparing this book, parts of it were sent out to experts in communication for review and criticism (which reminds me: if there are parts of it that you don't like, blame them, not me). One critic suggested that I create a hypothetical situation at the beginning of the book and then lead you through that situation throughout the book in order to illustrate how speaking by objectives works. Obviously, I decided against that suggestion. But it would have been an instance of an extended singular example, as you were put into that situation and then shown how to deal with it in each phase of preparation and presentation. Come to think of it, it still sounds like a good idea.

Serial examples consist of a series of brief instances of the thing under discussion. Suppose you are talking about the nutritional value (or lack of it) in breakfast foods. You might cite the instances of Wheaties, Cheerios, Post Toasties, Raisin Bran, and Frosted Flakes to illustrate your point. In that case, you would, of course, have (you guessed it) serial cereal examples.

Definitions

Sometimes we must use terms or concepts unfamiliar to our listeners. Rather than hope that they will guess the meaning from the context in which the word is used, we should supply some sort of definition. There are several ways in which we can define such words:

1. *Synonym:* we can supply another word which means about the same thing and which the audience understands. For example, we might tell the audience that the word *gauche* means "tactless or lacking in social grace."
2. *Classification:* we can define the thing by telling what class of things it falls into. A *framus,* for example, "is a rare type of sea creature with the body of a crab and the head of a C.P.A."
3. *Function:* things also may be defined by their use. A *muffler,* for example, is "a long strip of cloth you wrap around your neck to keep warm."

4. *Differentiation:* we can define things by telling what they are not. "By *muffler*, I do not mean that metal tube that goes on the tailpipe of your car to deaden noise." Or "When I say *public speaking*, I am not talking about conversations in public places, meetings held in front of passers-by, or messages broadcast over radio or television."

5. *Etymology:* occasionally, we can define a word by describing its development. The word *spiffy*, for example, comes from Sir Irving Spiffy, a well-known figure in Victorian England who spent millions on his wardrobe and was the first person to wear tiny sandals on his ears. No kidding.

6. *Example:* we can give an instance of the thing in order to define it. One *crustacean* is a crab, another is a lobster, and still another is the framus we saw earlier.

Obviously, your choice of definitional device will be determined by the sort of word you must define and the sorts of things your audience already understand. But again, the point is this: if you think there is even the slightest possibility that they will not understand a particular term or phrase, define it rather than risk confusing or frustrating them.

Analogies

We can intensify something by demonstrating to our listeners the ways in which that thing is similar to something the audience already understand. Like examples, analogies can be divided into several types. *Literal analogies* compare two or more real things, such as a Ford to a Chevrolet, American to British educational systems, or Canadian to Australian agriculture. *Figurative analogies,* on the other hand, compare things not physically similar but which share some common property that illustrates the point being made. Telling your audience that "Communism is like a cancer spreading across the face of the globe" draws an analogy between two dissimilar things that share one commonality: uncontrolled spread. Franklin D. Roosevelt used this device when he talked about the Lend-Lease Bill, telling Americans that it was like lending your neighbor a garden hose when his house is on fire. As a rule, literal analogies are used to illustrate the actual new thing by comparing it with something the audience already understands, while figurative analogies are used to give emotional impact to the thing under consideration. Finally, analogies also may be *isolated,* or a brief comparison of the things ("Communism is like cancer"), or they may be *extended,* offering a drawn out comparison of the concepts (an entire speech on education using comparisons between unknown and known educational systems, such as the British and American).

Contrasts

Analogies and contrasts operate according to the same principle, intensifying by comparing, but they do opposite things. Analogies show similarities, contrasts show differences. Our earlier example comparing an automobile to a horse is an instance of contrasts. Specifically, we might say: "Both horses and cars touch the ground in four places, but horses do it with legs while cars do it with tires. Both have steering mechanisms, but horses use bridles while cars have steering wheels. Both require fuel (oats versus gasoline), both carry riders (saddles versus seats), and both break down occasionally (but you can't shoot your car). And both pollute, but while cars give off carbon monoxide, horses give off . . . ." Well, you get the idea.

Quantification

If you can provide numbers, these often clarify and dramatize the point. Consider, for example, these three statements about highway casualties: "Last year, an awful lot of people were killed on the highways." "Last year, about 45,000 people were killed on the highways." "Last year, 45,000 people were killed on the highways—enough people to populate the entire city of Ypsilanti, Michigan." The first gives only very general information; the second gives specific information; the third makes the information specific *and* dramatic. Any time you can present quantities—in totals, fractions, percentages, proportions, or ratios—it makes the information more concrete, more interesting, and more memorable for the audience.

Visualization

In an earlier chapter, we attended to the construction and use of visual aids. Here simply note: any sort of pictorial version of your information you can present to your audience will help them better understand and remember the information. Charts, diagrams, graphs, pictures, cartoons, models, maps, and so on can all be used to illustrate and dramatize your points, and the more of them you use (assuming you use them properly), the more interesting and memorable your message will be.

Tests for Intensifying Materials

While details, examples, definitions, analogies, contrasts, quantification, and visualization all typically serve to make your information more understandable, interesting, and memorable, their impact is by no means guaranteed. Indeed, unnecessary details, dull examples, unneeded definitions, senseless analogies, and so on can produce the opposite effect: make the speech a long, drawn-out bore. We need to use some criteria in determining whether our supporting material will be helpful.

1. Is the material needed? That is, does it actually clarify a potentially muddy point or add interest in a dull part of the speech or make memorable information that otherwise might be forgotten? If the initial point you want to make already is clear, interesting, and memorable, don't use the additional materials; they will only lengthen the speech unnecessarily. If, however, you truly believe that clarification and so forth are needed, then and only then should you incorporate the materials we discussed above.

2. Is the material relevant? An example, an analogy, a contrast, a visual aid—all must relate to the point of the speech they are intended to clarify. If you give an example just because it is humorous or show a cartoon just to "give the audience a break," you probably will only confuse them because they are looking for direct relationships among the things you say. Be sure, then, that the materials you include are directly relevant to the main points of the speech.

3. Is the material correct? Obviously, it is important that the examples you cite, details you present, statistics you list, and so on be correct. You have an ethical responsibility to be accurate in your information, but you also have a stake in that

To Intensify Information, Give Details, Quantify, and Add Visual Appeal to the Material

accuracy: the audience judges your credibility according to the accuracy of your information. Moreover, since the main objective of this sort of speaking is to teach the audience information, to present them with incorrect facts is to completely misuse this sort of communication. For all these reasons, it is crucial that your supporting materials be accurate.

4. Is the material specific? It had better be. The real function of intensifying materials is to make things more clear and less abstract. Numbers make things more real; examples add specificity to the points they illustrate; details provide additional substance to the things they describe. But if your supporting materials are vague or general, they do not play this clarifying, deabstracting function. Thus, unless they are specific, they are wasted.

5. Is the material clear? Suppose you are giving a speech describing the process of nuclear fission. You might be extremely specific and detailed, giving multiple examples of each principle you describe and using analogies that are remarkably inventive, but there still could be one problem: no one knows what the heck you are talking about. Details do not help if the audience do not know what the words mean, and statistics are useless if the audience do not understand what the numbers represent. So just as you must assess the clarity of your main points, so too must you evaluate your supporting material to see if it also is understandable to your audience.

6. Is the material interesting? Examples, analogies, statistics, and the rest are not inherently interesting; you can construct a dull analogy just as easily as you can create an interesting one. As we saw in an earlier chapter, material that is new, relevant, somewhat humorous, vivid, and full of devices like rhetorical questions or startling statements typically is also interesting to the audience. Thus, to make your

clarifying and interest-building materials truly interesting, you should ensure that they
contain attention-getting devices.

7. Is the material appropriate in amount? For instance, how many examples do
you really need to clarify the point you are making? Will one do it? Will two do it
better? Three even better? Where do you reach the point of diminishing returns—the
point at which additional examples start to detract rather than add? The same questions apply to all of the other clarifying devices: how much detail, how many
analogies, how much quantification, and so on are really needed and useful? You
certainly don't want too little of this material because the points then will not be
clear. But you also don't want too much because the points then become belabored.
Seek the midpoint by evaluating carefully the number of statistics, examples, and so
on you need.

ASSOCIATING INFORMATION

Making information intense can help your audience recall that information at a later
time, but there also are some other strategies to promote audience retention. These
strategies all are based on a principle we have seen before: that people learn and
remember relationships between things. Thus, if we can create some association or
commonality between the ideas in our speech, people will be more likely to remember those ideas. A number of books have been written proclaiming that they can
help us remember things—people's names, birthdays, anniversaries, and so on. All of
those books, and all of the systems for memory which they offer, rest on this same
principle. To remember someone's name, they tell us, we have only to isolate some
physical characteristic of that person and then to associate his or her name with that
characteristic. Thus, next time we meet that person we can very quickly recall the
name. For example, we might meet someone named Walter at a party and notice that
he has a large wart on his nose. "Aha," we think "Walter and wart start with the same
letter." Then, when we see him the following week at another party, we stride
confidently across the room, extend our hand, and bellow, "Hi, Wart."

There are any number of techniques we can use to create an association between the points we want our audience to remember.

1. Have each point you want them to remember start with the same first letter.
If you can phrase those points in one word (for each point), and if you can have those
words start with the same letter (and tell your audience that they do), they will find it
easier to remember all of those points later on. At the beginning of this book, for
example, we saw that the three major stages of speaking by objectives are preparation, presentation, and preservation. I could just as easily have called those stages
"getting ready," "delivering," and "handling questions," but I wanted them all to
begin with the same letter so that they would be easier for you to remember. After all,
speaking by objectives is like a garden: first, you have a row of peas. . . .

2. Have the points rhyme. Again this creates a commonality so that, if the
audience remember one of the points, that point stimulates recollection of the others.
An instructor of sales techniques once told me that sales presentations consisted of
the pitch, the close, and walking away before the customer could change his or her
mind; as he put it, these steps were: "talk, sock, and walk." His rhyme works—I still
remember those cornball steps.

3. Have the words to be remembered consist of the same number of letters. When summarizing your main points, for example, you might say something like: "I only want you to remember three little four-letter words: talk, sock, and walk." Again, you provide the audience with a key for remembering those points.

4. Provide some combining relationship. That is, give them some framework they can use to relate the points. Our "this organization is like a garden" example is a terrific illustration of this technique.

The point, then, is this: do anything you can to relate the points you want your audience to remember. Creating some association between them helps each point to become a trigger for the other points so that, by remembering only one of them, the audience are better able to recall the remainder. And don't worry about being corny; the main idea here is to have the audience walk away remembering the key ideas you presented, and the sacrifice of a little dignity to achieve that seems justified.

PACKAGING INFORMATION: TYPES OF
INFORMATIVE SPEECHES

Throughout this and the preceding chapters, we have considered the primary objectives, secondary objectives, and corresponding strategies relevant to the achievement of information main objectives. We have seen ways to get and maintain audience attention; we have observed techniques for acquiring, organizing, and developing coherence in our information; we have considered methods for intensifying and associating information. We now are ready to put all of these things into a single package: an informative speech.

Although informative speeches can be categorized in a variety of ways, we will consider here five types of informative speeches. Each involves slightly different approaches to and applications of the concepts we have discussed in the preceding sections. We will analyze the topics, patterns, and special considerations relevant to each speech type so that, as you construct your objectives and strategies prior to delivering each sort of informative speech, you can be more certain that you have considered all the options available to you.

Instructional Speeches

This sort of speech tells the audience how to do something or how to make something. As the name implies, it is designed to instruct the listener in specific behavioral techniques.

Topics. Any sort of "how to" subject: how to play golf, how to repair an automobile, how to improve your tennis backhand. Generally, topics geared toward teaching the audience specific behaviors fall into this category.

Patterns. The most commonly used patterns facilitate explanation of the behavior to be performed: chronological, spatial, causal, and process.

Special Considerations. Be sure that your audience follow the flow of behaviors. Summarize often so that they know what you have covered and where in the process you are. If special equipment is needed to do this thing (such as repairing a car, or

playing golf, or baking a cake), be sure the listeners know what that equipment is and
how it should be used. Finally, whenever possible promote audience participation.
Just as the golf pro has you actually swing while he or she explains the mechanics of
hitting a golfball, so should you make the audience an active part of the speech. If it is
impractical to have them actually perform the behavior, use a lot of visual aids so that
they mentally become involved in the activity. And, as we have seen, take advantage
of imitation as a teaching device.

Descriptive Speeches

As you might guess, these speeches are designed to describe people, places, events or
things. Their primary objective is to make the thing described as clear and vivid in the
audience's minds as possible.

Topics.   Almost any sort of topic can fall into this category. Such things as "My most
unforgettable character," or "My three days in Paris," or "The Boston Tea Party," or
"A pencil sharpener" all require description.

Patterns.   Chronological, spatial, causal, topical, known-unknown, ascending-
descending, experiential, and question-answer patterns all work well.

Special Considerations.   Since the ultimate test of a descriptive speech is whether it
allows the audience to visualize the object being described, a great deal of detail
probably is desirable. Indeed, most of the speech will be spent providing that sort of
clarifying and intensifying material. Care must be taken, too, that the descriptive
materials provide a complete view of the object (remember the old story of three
blind men who, upon encountering an elephant, concluded that it was a snake, a
tree, or a wall, depending on which part of the elephant each touched) and that the
materials be carefully organized so that the audience know exactly what aspect of the
object is being described. The language used in the speech, finally, must be planned
carefully so that it paints a vivid, clear picture for the audience.

Explanatory Speeches

Speeches that explain things, such as ideas, processes, theories, or other complex
things that need clarification and analysis fall into this category. The goal of explanatory speeches is to achieve audience understanding—to have them comprehend
something previously foreign to them.

Topics.   Any sort of complex thing, process, event, theory, and so on can serve as a
topic for an explanatory speech. For example, "The Federal Government," "The
Internal Combustion Engine," "The Nature of Communism," and "Nuclear Fission"
all would be topics for explanatory speeches.

Patterns.   Chronological, causal, topical, process, known-unknown, ascending-
descending, experiential, and question-answer patterns can be used.

Special Considerations. Since the things being explained are usually complex (hence the need to explain them in the first place), great care must be taken to make the explanation as clear and understandable as possible. Therefore, the more clarifying material you can incorporate into your speech, the better off you will be. In addition, internal summaries should be used frequently to keep your audience oriented toward the progress of your speech, and you should "read" audience feedback carefully to see that they understand each point before you move on to the next one. Interest-arousing materials must also be included; explanations of extremely technical things can be deadly unless you maintain audience attention and interest.

Critical Speeches

If your purpose is to evaluate something—a book, movie, television program, work of art, and so on—you are delivering a critical speech. Specifically, critical speeches establish criteria for judging the thing under consideration and then apply them to that thing in order to render an overall judgment of quality.

Topics. Any person, place, thing, or event which can be evaluated lends itself to a critical speech. "My Favorite Book," "A Critical Analysis of 'Star Wars'," or "An Evaluation of the Nixon Administration" are representative of this speech category.

Patterns. Topical, ascending-descending, experiential, question-answer, known-unknown patterns can be used.

Special Considerations. A major problem with a speech of this sort is resisting the temptation to move away from objective evaluation toward persuasive appeals. Remember, your purpose is to present information as objectively as possible, not to convince the audience that they should feel a certain way or act in a particular manner toward the subject of the speech. In addition, the audience must understand thoroughly the criteria which you apply to the thing. For example, if you criticize a movie because it has "jump cuts," you should explain to the audience what jump cuts are and why they detract from the quality of the picture. Lastly, you must also be sure that your audience are familiar with the thing you are criticizing. If they haven't read the book, seen the movie, or heard of the person, then you must both give some justification for talking about that thing and tell them all about the thing at the outset.

Report Speeches

Unlike the other speech forms, this final type of speech is based exclusively upon your own personal experience. The purpose of reports is to provide the audience with information concerning something in which they are interested and in which you were actively involved.

Topics. Any activity in which you were or are actively engaged can serve as a report topic. Ongoing or completed research projects, committee meetings, financial operations, travel, direct observations, and so on are the sorts of things about which reports typically are given.

Patterns. Experiential is the most common pattern, although you might use

chronological, spatial, causal, topical, ascending-descending, or question-answer patterns.

Special Considerations. As a rule, reports should begin with some statement of problem: the purpose of the research study, the reason for the committee meeting, the objective of the financial manipulations, the purpose of the trip, and so on. Next, a brief explanation of procedure usually is provided. For research reports, the equipment, subjects studied, experimental treatments, and statistical analyses are described. For meetings, the length, location, times, dates, and attendees are listed and the topics discussed are mentioned. Similarly, travel experiences would describe methods of transportation, the itinerary, and so forth. In essence, you report who, what, when, where, how, why, and how many. Third, if information gathering was an important part of the process (for example, if members gathered information prior to conducting the meetings about which you are reporting), you might review the sources of that information or the procedures followed to gather the materials. These first three steps are accomplished rather quickly, as they serve primarily to introduce your speech. The remainder of the report (that is, the body of the speech) is devoted to the results of the study, the decisions of the committee, the product of the financial transactions, the discoveries of the trip, or whatever the results of the activity were. Note, however, that *progress reports,* which relate activities which still are going on, are often unable to offer a complete set of results. Rather, such a report may have to present tentative findings, or it may even have to conclude after the description of procedure, saying, in effect, "This is what we are doing now; we will give you results when we have them." The conclusion of the report, lastly, may offer implications of the study, recommendations for further courses of action, suggested financial strategies, and so on. Again, though, it is important to remember that this should be an informative speech, not one designed to persuade the audience.

TABLE 7-1   TYPES OF INFORMATIVE SPEECHES

	INSTRUCTIONAL	DESCRIPTIVE	EXPLANATORY	CRITICAL	REPORT
TOPICS	"How to" subjects: golf, auto repair, tennis, brain surgery, and so on	Almost anything: people, places, things, events, and so forth	Complex or abstract things: ideas, theories, processes, events, and so on	Things which can be evaluated: books, movies, television programs, art and so on	Any activity in which you have engaged: research projects, meetings, travel, and so on
PATTERNS	Chronological Spatial Causal Process	Chronological Spatial Causal Topical Known-unknown Ascending-descending Experiential Question-answer	Chronological Causal Topical Process Known-unknown Ascending-descending Experiential Question-answer	Topical Ascending-descending Experiential Question-answer Known-unknown	Experiential Chronological Spatial Causal Topical Ascending-descending Question-answer
SPECIAL CONSIDERATIONS	Keep behavior sequence clear Summarize often Explain necessary equipment Promote audience participation	Provide much detail Clarify as much as possible Provide complete view Organize carefully Use vivid, clear language	Include maximum amount of clarifying material Summarize often Adapt to feedback Arouse interest	Avoid becoming persuasive Clarify criteria Clarify thing being evaluated	Begin with problem statement Describe procedure Describe information gathering Present results (if available)

SUMMARY

Consider Raquel Welch or Robert Redford. While the skeletons of each undeniably are important, it is the way in which those skeletons are developed—"fleshed out," if you will—that makes them so memorable. And the same is true with our speeches: the bare information is vital, but the material we use to intensify and amplify that information is what gives it its real impact. Thus, in this chapter we examined some techniques for making information memorable. First, we looked at strategies for intensifying information and considered the use of details, examples, definitions, analogies, contrasts, quantification, and visualization. Then, second, we briefly discussed some techniques by which we can associate our points to assist the audience in remembering them at a later time. By promoting audience retention of our speech materials, then, we have achieved the third primary objective leading to the achievement of our main speech objective, giving information to our audience. Lastly, we studied five specific types of informative speeches, noting the considerations and strategies unique to each. By combining this information with the material presented in the two chapters before this one, then, you should be able to construct informative speeches that your audiences will listen to, understand, and remember.

TABLE 7-2   TO PROVIDE INFORMATION

FIND IT	→ CLARIFY IT	→ ORGANIZE IT	→OUTLINE IT	→ SMOOTH IT	→ MAKE IT MEMORABLE	→ CONCLUDE IT

Sources =
Yourself
Interviews
Impersonal
  exchanges
Written
  materials
Surveys and
  experiments
	Materials =
	Details
	Examples
	Analogies
	Contrasts
	Visualization
		Patterns =
		Chronological
		Spatial
		Causal
		Topical
		Process
		Ascending-
		  descending
		Experiential
		Question-answer
			Types =
			Scratch
			Brief
			Full
			  sentences
			Topical
				Transitions =
				Primary
				Incidental
					Devices =
					Same first
					  letter
					Rhyme
					Same number
					  of letters
					Provide
					  relationship
						Methods =
						Summarize
						Create mood
						Kill it

PROJECT

THE SPEECH TO ENTERTAIN

As the title implies, this speech seeks to entertain an audience. Too often, however, we confuse "entertain" with "amuse." The speech to entertain may be amusing, but it may also have a serious purpose. Typically, such speeches have a light touch and a tone of humor and optimism, but the message they ultimately convey may be quite serious. Or the purpose may be solely to amuse, with no ultimate message intended. The nature of the occasion and the situation usually determines what the ultimate purpose is. In any case, these speeches are difficult to deliver effectively, and they must be carefully prepared. You should proceed through these stages:

1. Select a topic. Generally, the best speeches to entertain have a novel topic or an unusual view of things. For example:

   Your friend, the vampire bat   Gadgets: The threat to mankind
   The worst job in the world   Television rots minds
   The saddest words ever spoken   Cockroaches: The best pets
   The joys of motherhood   Sports for masochists
   If I ruled the world   The literature of advertising

2. State your objective. What do you want to do? Amuse your audience? Give them a sugar-coated but serious message? Show them the folly of their ways? Decide specifically what your purpose is.

3. Develop your material. Stories, hypothetical or real examples, and similar specific, concrete things typically have more appeal than do abstract ideas or arguments. Like your topic, your material should also be novel or approached in an unusual fashion. It also should be in good taste and not offensive to anyone present.

4. Organize your material. Like any speech, the speech to entertain should have main ideas and supporting subpoints and should be arranged in some logical sequence.

5. Develop an introduction that arouses interest. Establishing your credibility is probably less important with this sort of speech, but a personal example or two may simultaneously entertain your audience and show your familiarity with the topic.

6. Develop a strong conclusion that refers back to the introduction. Nothing ruins the effect of a speech to entertain so much as a conclusion that ends with a whimper.

7. As you deliver the speech, use lively, graphic language, an active and varied set of gestures and movements, and almost continuous eye contact. Vocal variety is particularly important: changes in rate, inflection, and volume, and the use of "pregnant pauses" do much to heighten the dramatic effect of the speech. Humorous visual aids may also be effective in enhancing your listeners' enjoyment.

Name _____

Date _____

Speech Type _____

Speech Outline, Project Number _____

Speech Topic: _____

Speech Objective: _____

_____

Speech Title: _____

Introduction

    Attention:

    Motivation:

    Credibility:

      Preview

      Body

      Conclusion

Instructor's Comments:

PROJECT

SPEECHES TO INFORM

In the preceding chapters, we analyzed several types of informative speeches, including:

1. *Instructional speeches,* which show an audience how to do things.
2. *Descriptive speeches,* which make people, places, or things vivid in the listeners' minds.
3. *Explanatory speeches,* which clarify and analyze things for the audience.
4. *Critical speeches,* which evaluate things.
5. *Report speeches,* which summarize activities in which you are or have been involved.

All of these speech types provide information to the audience, even though they may also persuade, entertain, and so on. If the information presented in such speeches is to be comprehended and retained by the audience, you must prepare carefully by proceeding through these stages:

1. Select the topic. Possible topics for each speech type are listed in the preceding chapter.
2. Gather your material. Draw upon your own knowledge, interviews, library research, or your own surveys or experiments. Be sure, too, that you have clarifying materials to support or illustrate any points that might be unclear to your audience.
3. Organize your material. Use one of the organizational patterns presented in Chapter 6; appropriate patterns are suggested in the consideration of each informative speech type (in this chapter).
4. Develop an introduction that gains attention, motivates interest, and establishes your credibility.
5. Develop a conclusion that summarizes your main points, makes those points memorable for your audience, and refers back to the attention-getting statement you presented in the introduction.
6. In delivering your speech, use any visual aids you think will make the information more clear and memorable. Be enthusiastic, use a lot of gestures, and move freely about the front of the room. Maintain maximum eye contact with your audience. Speak loudly and clearly and try to vary your rate of speaking, the pitch of your voice (that is, how high or low it is), and the volume of your voice.

Name _____

Date _____

Speech Type _____

Speech Outline, Project Number _____

Speech Topic: _____

Speech Objective: _____

_____

Speech Title: _____

Introduction

    Attention:

    Motivation:

    Credibility:

      Preview

        Body

      Conclusion

Instructor's Comments:

Name _____

Date _____

Speech Type _____

Speech Outline, Project Number _____

Speech Topic: _____

Speech Objective: _____

_____

Speech Title: _____

Introduction

    Attention:

    Motivation:

    Credibility:

      Preview

      Body

      Conclusion

Instructor's Comments:

PART IV
PREPARATION FOR PERSUADING

In preceding chapters, we have examined some important principles of public speaking: organization, clarity, memorability, and so on. But there are times when being clear, organized, and memorable is not enough. For example, after interviewing you for a position in her company, a personnel officer might decide that, based upon the clear, organized, memorable information you presented about yourself, she would not hire you even if your father was the chairman of the board. Or, after hearing your clear, organized, memorable speech favoring legalization of marijuana, the members of the audience, all of whom belong to the local chapter of the Society to Keep America Pure at Any Cost, might decide to organize a tar-and-feathering party with you as the guest of honor. No, in situations like these, you need to be more than organized, clear, memorable, and so on—you must also be persuasive.

Simply put, persuasion consists of influencing people's beliefs, values, attitudes, and behaviors. You persuade someone when you somehow convince him (or her) to think what you want him to think, feel what you want him to feel, or do what you want him to do. But the key thing is, he thinks, feels, or does as you want because that is what *he* wants to do. Put in the most basic (and, some would argue, most crass) terms, then, persuasion occurs when you make someone want to think, feel, and act the way you want him to.

Excluded from the realm of persuasion is the related concept *coercion,* in which someone is forced to do something against his will. Some of the most influential speeches have been delivered by muggers in dark alleys, as they tell their "audiences" things like: "Gimme your bread or I'll blow off your head." Those little speeches get results, but they are not persuasive; they coerce people into doing things they really do not want to do. Thus, the problem we face in this chapter goes beyond mere influence to encompass the question, How can we get people to want to think, feel, or do what we want them to do?

When considered in the abstract terms used above, persuasion seems like a very esoteric, unachievable objective of communication. In truth, though, we persuade people every day, often without even realizing it. On our way downtown, for example, we might arrive at a four-way stop intersection at the same moment as does a car on our right. We might persuade that driver to let us go first by aggressively nudging our car (which also happens to be an extremely battered '65 Cadillac) into the intersection. Or later, at a restaurant, we might persuade a waiter to bring us caviar and Dom Perignon 1959 simply by asking for it. The waiter naturally wants to bring us these goodies because, first, he expects us to pay for them and, second, he expects a large tip. And later in the day we might try to persuade the boss to give us a raise, to persuade a friend to pay for lunch just this once, to persuade our insurance agent to pay us $1,000 for that classic Cadillac that was totalled at the intersection, or to persuade a close friend to bail us out of jail. In fact, any time we cause someone to change (voluntarily) a belief, value, attitude, or behavior, we have achieved persuasion.

But don't be misled. People aren't always as easily persuaded as the above examples might suggest. Indeed, there are times when people are downright resistant to your persuasive attempts. A great deal of research effort has been devoted to the nature of resistance to persuasion, and the findings have indicated that there are certain types of persons who are likely to be resistant. First, people who are highly ego-involved in the issue under consideration are difficult to persuade for they have a great deal of themselves invested in their beliefs, attitudes, or behaviors. The American businessperson's attitudes toward capitalism, for example, are so closely tied to all he or she is or does that changing them would be virtually impossible. Second, those who have already adopted a polar or extreme position on the issue will be difficult to persuade for they tend to become "locked in" to their attitude set. Moreover, if the individual's attitudes are well organized and consistent, those interrelationships will make it difficult to change any one belief or attitude; people's need for consistency would make it necessary to change several beliefs or attitudes at the same time. Characteristics of the individual, as we saw in Chapter 2, also are important. People who are older, male, intelligent, anxious to avoid conflict or anxiety, and who possess the personality characteristics of dogmatism, low self-esteem, or authoritarianism all tend to be more resistant to others' attempts to persuade them. And finally, if the individual has stated his (or her) position publicly so that others know how he feels, or if he has been rewarded for his opinions or actions, or if he has too little correct information concerning the topic, his mind will be difficult to change. All of these things can serve to make persuasion very difficult to achieve.

The question remains, then: How do we overcome these sources of resistance in order to achieve persuasion? The next three chapters will provide some answers to that question, but at this moment we need to consider some principles upon which those answers will be based. These principles include:

1. People want to do the "right" thing.

The importance of this first principle cannot be overemphasized. When people choose to believe something, or to feel a certain way, or to engage in some behavior, they do so because they think the belief, attitude, or behavior is correct or proper. Even when people do things they know to be "wrong" (such as committing a crime or "fudging" on income taxes), they do them because, in their minds and given their circumstances, it is "right" (for example, they see crime as the best way to obtain funds quickly, or they think income taxes to be disgustingly high so that cheating is justified). While the things people think and do may make little sense to us, then, we must remember that they make sense to the people who think and do them.

2. Three factors enforce persuasion: credibility, reasoning, and emotion.

Aristotle called these factors *ethos, logos,* and *pathos.* According to his observations (and the observations of nearly everyone else for the past 2,000 years), people are persuaded through their perceptions of the source of the persuasive message, through the logic and reasoning the message employs, and through the emotions in the audience the message arouses. Any one of these factors can be enough to produce persuasion; however, the most effective appeals for persuasion take advantage of all three.

3. The less the audience are asked to, the more easily persuaded they will be.

If you ask your listeners to do something extremely easy or to believe something rather insignificant or to change a relatively unimportant attitude, you probably will have little difficulty in succeeding. After all, very little is required of your audience to do, think, or feel these things. But if you ask something major of them ("Give all you own to the poor and follow me") or ask them to believe something having tremendous implications ("I personally have encountered life forms from other planets") or try to change an attitude that is extremely important to them ("Human life is worthless and murder is valuable to the world's economy"), you will find it much more difficult to achieve persuasion. To achieve major changes, then, you probably would be most successful if you asked for a series of minor, progressive changes over an extended period of time.

4. The more the audience trust, like, and respect the speaker, the more likely it is that they will be persuaded by him or her.

This is the credibility or ethos factor we saw in **2** above. When someone we admire asks us to do something, we probably will do it, often without even asking for reasons. However, if someone we loathe asks us to do the same thing, we probably will simply refuse, or we may ask for a substantial set of reasons (and even challenge those reasons when they are given). Indeed, many theorists feel that this factor of source credibility is the single most important element of persuasion.

5. To achieve persuasion, we have to give people good reasons.

Overcoming resistance to persuasion is, to a large degree, a function of giving the audience reasons—reasons to change their beliefs, attitudes, values, behaviors, and so on. Such reasons can take many forms, some of which we will see in the chapters that follow. There are, for example, credibility-based reasons (as when a mother says to her son, "Do it because I told you to"), need-based reasons ("Do it and people will like you, so that your need for affection will be satisfied"), consistency-based reasons ("Do it because doing so is consistent with what you already believe and do"), and a variety of other reasons, any of which can produce successful persuasion. But all of these reasons rest on the principle we saw at the beginning of this list: people do what they think is right. Reasons demonstrate "rightness" to our listeners.

6. Persuasion is most effectively achieved when audience emotions can be aroused.

Convincing an audience that a particular behavior is "right" is achieved through reasoning; obtaining commitment or a determination to perform that behavior is best achieved through emotion. Or, to put it in terms of the "direction" and "intensity" characteristics of attitudes, the direction (positive or negative) of an attitude is best changed through logic, but the intensity (strength) of an attitude is best influenced through emotion. Thus, we not only need to give people reasons for doing or thinking things, we also need to stir their emotions so that those actions or thoughts are strong, long-lasting ones.

In the three chapters that follow, we will study some primary objectives taken directly from the principles above. Those objectives are:

1. Enhancing credibility so that the audience are inclined to do or think as you ask simply because *you* ask it.
2. Proving arguments so that the "rightness" of what you advocate becomes evident to your listeners.
3. Constructing appeals so that the feelings of the audience are involved in order to increase the strength of their attitudes and commitment.

For each of these objectives, there are secondary objectives and speech strategies that lead to their achievement. We will explore those objectives and strategies in the following chapters.

CHAPTER 8
ENHANCING CREDIBILITY

PRIMARY (PREPARATIONAL) OBJECTIVE:
To cause the audience to attribute high credibility to you as a speaker

Secondary Objectives	Corresponding Strategies
To establish perceived competence	Demonstrate acquaintance with topic Affiliate with credible sources Show familiarity with vocabulary Organize speech Provide much information
To establish perceived character	Use accurate facts Tell things known to be true Demonstrate consistent behavior Be as explicit as possible Use consistent verbal-nonverbal cues
To establish perceived good intent	Be candid Demonstrate benefits to audience Show acceptance and benefits by others Establish identification
To establish perceived dynamism	Be active in delivery Use forceful language Indicate own behavioral commitments
To establish perceived likeability	Show liking for audience Show respect for audience Show similarity to audience Show disassociation from disliked things

To establish perceived admirability   Demonstrate valued traits
Avoid vicious criticism
Present similarities and differences
Show composure and dignity

CHAPTER OBJECTIVES
After studying this chapter, you should be able to:

- Define the concept *credibility*
- Describe how credibility changes from one receiver to the next
- Describe how credibility changes across time
- Describe how credibility changes across topics
- Describe how credibility changes across settings
- List and explain the dimensions of credibility
- Develop a statement that establishes your competence in the minds of your audience members
- Develop a statement that establishes your character in the minds of your audience members
- Develop a statement that establishes your intent in the minds of your audience members
- Develop and implement a strategy that establishes your dynamism in the minds of your audience members
- Develop a statement that improves your likeability in the minds of your audience members
- Develop a strategy that establishes your admirability in the minds of your audience members

INTRODUCTION

Quick, now; what do Joe Namath, Danny Thomas, Catherine Deneuve, Dick Van Dyke, and Telly Savalas have in common? They're all celebrities, certainly, but what else? Well, for one thing all of them have at one time or another advertised on television products about which they are hardly experts. Savalas has advertised liquor, Van Dyke fire prevention techniques, Thomas coffee makers, and Deneuve automobiles. And Namath has advertised panty hose! But why? Why would advertisers spend hundreds of thousands of dollars to have these people say things to the American public that some unknown (like your author) would say for $99.95? The reason: these people are considered credible, at least by the advertisers who pay them to tout their products.

For our purposes, credibility will be defined as "the amount of believability a receiver attributes to a source." In this definition we find a couple of important points. First, the concept of believability. Source credibility consists of the willingness of a particular audience to believe what a particular source says. Thus, high credibility is a key to successful speaking: if our audience are willing to believe what we tell them, influencing them is fairly easy. If, however, our audience are unwilling to believe us,

Credibility Is Given by Audiences to Speakers

then we might as well give up—there is nothing we can say or do to achieve our objective. The development of at least some credibility therefore is absolutely necessary in order for us to achieve our objective.

The second important point embodied in the definition above is the idea that credibility is something an audience "attributes to a source." That is, in spite of its name, "source credibility" is not a characteristic of sources at all, but of receivers. They decide whether or not they will believe what the source tells them. Naturally, what a source does has an impact upon this decision, but it still is important to remember that ultimately, source credibility is a receiver phenomenon, not a speaker characteristic.

In this chapter we will examine the nature of credibility in an effort to discover some methods by which we can convince audiences to believe the things we tell them. Specifically, we will examine three topics. First, we will look at the dynamics of credibility, noting the changes through which audience judgments of credibility pass. Second, we will analyze the dimensions of credibility, or the particular judgments audiences make about sources while trying to decide whether to believe them. And finally, we will develop some credibility devices, or some strategies by which we might be able to persuade our audiences to believe us so that we might be better able to influence them.

DYNAMICS OF CREDIBILITY

Audience judgments of source credibility are not stable—they change literally from one moment to the next. Since we naturally want to influence those changes so that they occur for us rather than against us, it is useful to understand the sorts of changes which typically occur. Specifically, source credibility changes across receivers, across times, across topics, and across settings. Let's look at those changes individually.

Changes Across Receivers

This one is obvious. Just as beauty is in the eye of the beholder, so too is credibility in the eye of the receiver. And like beauty, credibility is perceived slightly differently by everyone. Consider, for example, the case of Charles Manson. To most people, Manson is virtually a monster—a person who masterminded the bloody murder of Sharon Tate, the La Bianca family, and others. But to his group of followers, Manson was and is even now the most credible source to walk the earth. The same principle applies to Adolf Hitler and the Nazis, Reverend Jim Jones and the People's Temple, and almost every other public figure you can name. Some people find these individuals credible and believe everything they say, even to the point of giving up their lives for them. Other people find these same individuals despicable. And that's why elections almost never are unanimous: sources are perceived credible by some receivers but not by others.

As public speakers, it is important that we remember this changing nature of credibility. All audiences perceive us differently so that we always must be conscious of establishing our credibility with them. But even within audiences, each individual sees us a little bit differently so that the more reasons we can provide the audience for believing us, the greater the likelihood that we will convince the individuals comprising that audience of our credibility (remember, different reasons appeal to different people). In the last section of this chapter we will examine a variety of credibility-building devices. The more of them you can use, the better off you probably will be.

Changes Across Times

Source credibility changes across times just as it changes across receivers. Such temporal changes can be divided into two categories: internal changes, which occur during the time speaker and audience confront one another, and external changes, which occur between the times a particular source and a particular receiver meet. Let's consider these categories one at a time.

Internal Changes

The changes in perceived credibility that occur while speaker and audience meet can be subdivided into three categories: preinteractive, which occur before the speaker begins to talk; interactive, which happen while he or she talks; and postinteractive, which happen right after the speaker quits. Again, let's look at these separately.

Preinteractive Credibility. When the audience first enter the speaking situation, they form an immediate impression of the source, and from that impression they draw conclusions about his or her credibility. Generally, the impression they form is derived from several sources. First, the reputation of the source—a reputation typically based upon earlier speeches and comments made about those speeches by other people—influences audience opinions. If the source is reputed to have misrepresented the facts in the past, he or she is likely to be viewed with some suspicion now. If he or she has been an outspoken opponent of drinking in the past, the present audience of W.C.T.U. Local 313 probably will be favorably disposed. Reputation thus consists of the audience members' previous experiences, direct or indirect, with the source—things about the source's beliefs, attitudes, character, and abilities which they hold to be true because of their own observations or observations reported to them by other credible sources.

A second determinant of preinteractive credibility is the status the audience perceive the source to have. Research by Harms (1960) demonstrated that, regardless of their own social position, receivers generally assign high credibility to speakers perceived to be of high status and low credibility to those of low status. Such judgments of status seem to come from two primary sources: the source's appearance, as we shall see shortly, and the source's occupation. In our society, one's occupation is a major status determinant. Research summarized by Davis (1972), for example, shows that people in our culture tend to rank/order various occupations according to status in a very consistent fashion. Typically, chief justice of the Supreme Court is ranked highest, followed by president, senator, college professor, physician, and so on. The rank/order of these specific occupations is not important; the fact that so many people rank them in the same way is. But surprisingly, even within occupational groups status differences are found. Often, these differences are unexplainable. Research by Whyte (1948) discovered status differences among restaurant cooks, as cooks who handled primarily chicken had higher status than those who usually handled other types of meat. But even among the chicken workers there were status differences: cooks primarily handling light meat had higher status than those primarily handling dark meat.

The source's appearance is a third influencer of credibility judgments. Studies of general attractiveness suggest that people perceived to be attractive tend to be more credible and hence more influential than people judged unattractive. In one such study, Singer (1964) found that attractive female students generally are able to obtain higher grades from male instructors than are females rated unattractive. Mills and Aronson (1965) conducted an even more dramatic study. They took a female speaker and had her deliver the same speech to two different audiences of males. For the first audience, she was made up to look as attractive as possible; for the second, she was made as unattractive as possible. Even though she delivered the exact same speech to both audiences, the results she obtained were dramatically different. When she was attractive, she was extremely credible in the eyes of her drooling audience and thus able to persuade them to her viewpoint. But when she was unattractive, her credibility was low and she had no impact at all. Since other studies have found the same effect with male speakers and female audiences and with same-sex situations, we can conclude that perceived attractiveness and perceived credibility go hand in hand.

Clothing also influences credibility, largely because we judge a source's status to some degree on the basis of how he or she is dressed. The famous "streetwalker" study (Lefkowitz, Blake, and Mouton, 1955) illustrates the point. In this study, an experimental confederate wandered about a large city violating the "Don't walk" sign at street corners. He would walk up to a corner, wait for the light to change so that it said, "Don't walk," wait for other pedestrians to gather around him, and then take off across the street. He performed this bizarre behavior on two consecutive days. On the first day, he was dressed in a high-status outfit—three-piece suit, tie, and so forth. On the second day he was dressed in a low-status outfit—overalls, a mop over his shoulder, and so on. The experimenters were curious to see whether the streetwalker would be able to influence other pedestrians to follow his example and jaywalk, and whether his influential abilities would at all be affected by his pattern of dress. The results again were dramatic. When he was dressed in his high-status outfit, a substantial number of people followed him across the street. When he was dressed in low-status clothing, however, virtually no one followed him. The status indicated by a speaker's clothing therefore seems another element of appearance that influences credibility judgments.

A fourth determinant of initial credibility is the introduction the source is given just before he or she starts to speak. If the audience do not know much about the speaker prior to their arrival, the introduction they are provided probably will be the most important factor influencing their initial evaluations. For instance, Haiman (1949) presented the same tape-recorded speech to three different groups. However, for each group the tape was attributed to a different speaker. The first group was told that the speaker was the surgeon general of the United States; the second was told that the speaker was secretary of the Communist Party in America; the third was told that the speaker was a college sophomore. After hearing the speech, each group was asked to evaluate the speaker and his topic. Haiman found that the speaker introduced as the surgeon general was rated significantly more competent than the other two, and that his speech was significantly more persuasive.

Surprisingly, however, even when the speaker is known to the audience, the introduction he or she is given influences perceptions of his or her credibility. Kersten (1958) compared the effects of two introductions: one designed to focus attention on the speaker and his subject and to build his prestige and one that did not try to accomplish those things. The individuals hearing the favorable introduction exhibited significantly more shift of opinion than did those hearing the poor introduction or no introduction at all.

While the content of the introduction given to the audience makes a difference, so, too, does the source of the introduction. That is, how do the audience feel about the person who presents you to them? If he (or she) is credible, then the nice things he says about you probably will help. But if he is not credible, the compliments he gives you will probably not help, and they might even hurt. After all, the audience are likely to reason, If this jerk thinks this speaker is great, chances are they both are jerks. Turkeys of a feather flock together. So the moral is, choose carefully those who will introduce you.

Preinteractive credibility, then, seems the product of several things, including your reputation, status, appearance, and introduction. At this point the audience already have formed an opinion of you, and you haven't even opened your mouth. So let's open it.

Interactive Credibility.   Changes in credibility judgments continue while the source speaks. Generally, two categories of message elements seem to influence audience evaluations of a speaker: elements that reveal information about the source and elements directly related to the content of the speech.

Elements revealing information about the source are many, but we will devote attention to only a few here. First, factual accuracy gives the audience insight about the source: To illustrate, suppose you are listening to a speech, and the speaker gives you a piece of information you know to be wrong. What can you assume about the source based upon this mistake? Three things: that he (or she) is ignorant, that he is careless, or that he is dishonest. Obviously, he loses no matter which of these you choose. The lesson is clear: be sure when you are speaking that you have your facts right.

Another revealing element of the speech is grammar. Even though the audience may themselves consistently use ungrammatical language, you can't get away with it when you are speaking. Grammatical errors will cause them to perceive you as uncultured, uneducated, ignorant, or all of the above, and you lose again. Take care to avoid grammatical mistakes because they can be costly to your credibility.

Third, characteristics of your delivery affect perceptions of you and your credibility. The study by Harms (1960), for example, determined that listeners make quick and relatively accurate judgments of a speaker's status (and hence his or her credibility) on the basis of his or her vocal characteristics alone. Moreover, a speaker's overall delivery style has an effect; a very listless, inactive speaker often is perceived to be uninterested in the topic or the audience, and his or her credibility suffers as a result. Thus, delivery acts along with informational accuracy and grammatical correctness to influence credibility by revealing information about the source to the audience.

Message elements more directly related to content also seem to influence judgments made about speakers. First, studies investigating the effects of including evidence in persuasive speeches suggest that credibility judgments and attitude change both are facilitated through authority-based information. Gilkinson, Paulson, and Sikkink (1954), who included or excluded authority citations (that is, quotations from accepted authorities) in two versions of the same speech, found that the speech containing evidence produced more attitude change than did the speech containing no quotations. Since other studies have found the same effect, including evidence seems an effective device for improving perceptions of one's credibility.

The effects of evidence upon credibility are not as simple as the preceding paragraph might suggest, however. Research cited by McCroskey (1969) indicates that the effects of evidence are to some degree determined by the source's initial credibility level. If the speaker has initially high credibility, she (or he) does not need to use evidence to be effective. Since the audience already believe her, citing authoritative evidence probably will contribute little to her appeals. However, if the source has low preinteractional credibility, she often can improve her image by presenting the audience with evidence of which they previously were unaware. That is, if the audience are already aware of the facts you cite, your credibility probably will not rise beyond its initial level. On the other hand, if you are able to present them with information they have not considered before, they are likely to increase their respect for you and your topic.

A second message element affecting audience evaluations of speaker credibility is the use of one-sided or two-sided arguments. Research by Hovland, Lumsdaine, and Sheffield (1949) determined that this aspect of speech content interacts with certain characteristics of the audience. If the members are well educated, the two-sided strategy enhances credibility and promotes attitude change. If, however, the audience are poorly educated, the one-sided approach is more effective. Thus it is important that we analyze our audience carefully in order to select the most effective strategy.

Fear appeals are a third message element influencing credibility judgments. As their name might indicate, fear appeals essentially are persuasive attempts based upon the assumption that the best way to get someone to do something is to scare him or her into it. While controversy over the effectiveness of fear appeals continues, there is some evidence that the use of this technique does impact the user's credibility. Hewgill and Miller (1965) presented two speech forms—one containing strong fear appeals and the other containing mild appeals—to four different audiences. Two audiences heard the strong message, with one audience having it attributed to a highly credible source and the other having it credited to a noncredible source. The same procedure was used for the two groups hearing the mild message. The results showed that strong appeals were more persuasive than mild ones when used by a credible source, but that no differences between the strong and mild appeals appeared for the low-credibility sources. However, the noncredible source received lower credibility ratings when he used strong appeals than he did when using mild ones. Therefore, it would appear that fear appeals serve to exaggerate the credibility you already have: if it is high, fear appeals improve it; if it is low, fear appeals reduce it.

In summary, changes during the speech result largely from two categories of message elements. Elements that reveal information about the source to the audience (such as factual accuracy, grammatical correctness, and aspects of delivery) impact audience judgments of the source, as do such content-related factors as using evidence, structuring one-sided or two-sided arguments, and including or omitting fear appeals. Obviously, knowing the impact of each of these factors can help us develop strategies to improve our credibility in the eyes of the audiences we confront.

Postinteractive Credibility. Really, this last credibility stage, which occurs when the speaker stops talking, simply represents the combination of preinteractive and interactive credibility factors. If, for example, the audience initially were favorable in their judgment of the source (based upon his or her reputation, appearance, introduction, and so forth), and then they heard a speech full of factual errors, grammatical mistakes, and the like, their final assessment of the speaker would represent a combination of the favorable first impression and the miserable second impression. Similarly, if the speaker's preinteractive credibility was neutral or low but he or she delivered an impressive message, the postinteractive credibility would substantially improve the initial credibility level. This final level of credibility remains with the receivers when they leave, but, as we shall see, it is not necessarily the level they will carry with them the next time they show up to hear this same speaker.

External Changes

In the preceding section, we considered the changes internal to the speaking situation that occur in audience members' credibility perceptions. But changes do not cease to occur when the audience leave. Rather, credibility changes between speaking occasions just as it occurs during them. These external changes also can be categorized into three types. First, *reality* can change. New facts may emerge or events occur that change audience perceptions of a particular source. The plight of Richard Nixon is an excellent example. Between each of his televised addresses to the nation during the

Watergate scandal, reality changed. New facts were uncovered, new testimonies heard, and new allegations made, all affecting the masses' attitudes toward him. Thus, every time he spoke, Nixon faced an audience with perceptions of his credibility that were radically different from the perceptions they had held even a week earlier. That made audience analysis just a little bit difficult.

Second, audience members themselves may change. In fact, since people are changing continuously, we can guarantee that the audience will change. The question is, How do those changes impact their perceptions of a source's credibility? Perhaps they have no impact at all. But perhaps, by adopting new beliefs or attitudes, internalizing new values, adopting new behaviors while discarding old ones, and so on, the members of the audience have changed to a degree that they no longer are compatible with the source. Certainly, their perceptions of his or her credibility would change in a situation like that.

Finally, the *source* himself or herself may change. Consider, for example, the metamorphosis of Timothy Leary some years ago. Late in the 1950s, he was an eminent psychologist, respected in academic circles. Then he "dropped out," becoming a leader of the drug-oriented counterculture. In so doing, he gained credibility with the youth he associated with, but lost credibility with the academic types who previously had admired him. Neither the academics nor the members of the counterculture changed any of their fundamental ideas or values, but their perceptions of Leary's credibility changed because his values and beliefs ceased to fit those of one group and became like those of the other. Similarly, any change in the source between speaking events will produce changes in audience perceptions of his or her credibility.

Changes Across Topics

The credibility of a source usually changes according to the topic on which he or she is speaking. No one is extremely knowledgeable about everything. The chief justice of the Supreme Court is a smart person and an expert in legal matters, and when he talks about the law, we should believe him. But when he ventures into other topic areas, such as finance or foreign relations, we ought to be a bit more critical of his views. Similarly, most speakers have areas of expertise and areas about which they know comparatively little. Thus, when a speaker discusses a topic in which he (or she) is an expert, his credibility is high; when he discusses a topic with which he is less familiar, his credibility is lower.

There is, however, an exception to the rule that credibility changes across topics. Some individuals, because of their high credibility in certain areas, are considered credible when they talk about other topics as well. This tendency for audiences to generalize their perceptions of credibility across topics is called the *halo effect*, for some sources apparently come to be seen as having halos around their heads so that, no matter what they talk about, audiences believe them. Advertisers capitalize upon the halo effect when they have celebrities (such as the ones named at the beginning of this chapter) speak about their products to an apparently believing public. And the public seems to be influenced by those endorsements, buying the advertised products in spite of the fact that the celebrities know little if anything about the products they recommend. Certainly, these are instances of source credibility gone wrong. We should believe people only when they know what they are talking about, and we should guard against falling prey to the halo effect.

Changes Across Settings

The surroundings in which a speech is delivered are a fourth factor influencing audience credibility judgments. A professor accorded high credibility in her classroom might receive somewhat lower evaluations were she to deliver the same lectures while standing on the counter at a local bar. Moreover, the number of people present may affect credibility. Some speakers who are ineffective when speaking before large crowds might be extremely persuasive and believable on a one-to-one, face-to-face basis. Thus, both the physical setting and the social surroundings influence attitudes toward the source.

Clearly, then, credibility is a dynamic process rather than a static object. It changes constantly, fluctuating from one receiver to another, one moment to the next, one topic to another, and one setting to another. To be successful in enhancing our own credibility, we must keep all of these change factors in mind and try to adapt ourselves and our message to them.

DIMENSIONS OF CREDIBILITY

In the preceding section, as we talked about changes in credibility, you might have been mislead just slightly. It may have sounded to you as though credibility is a single, unified judgment audiences make about speakers, so that audience members simply decide whether a source is extremely credible, extremely incredible, or somewhere in between. In fact, this is not the case. A great deal of research has been conducted into the nature of credibility, and virtually every study done has determined that audiences make several specific judgments about a speaker when they assess his or her overall credibility. These judgments comprise the dimensions of credibility, and their importance cannot be overemphasized. When the audience are trying to decide whether or not to believe us, it is these dimensions that they consider. Therefore, to enhance our credibility we must be able to influence those audience judgments about the credibility dimensions. And to do that, it helps to know what those dimensions are in the first place.

But first, a disclaimer. While everyone agrees that credibility is multidimensional, not too many people agree exactly on what those dimensions are. As Cronkhite (1969) points out, credibility experiments have isolated such dimensions as "trustworthiness," "dynamism," "competence," "sociability," "evaluation," "agreeableness," "extroversion," "emotional stability," "conscientiousness," "culture," "objectivity," or "identification," depending on who did the experiment, what kinds of experimental subjects were used, what kinds of speakers were used, what kinds of speech topics were used, what kinds of measurement items were used, and what kind of statistical analysis were used. So no one knows for sure exactly what or how many dimensions comprise credibility. What follows, therefore, is a review of some of the more prominent views of credibility dimensions and a summary list of those dimensions. The summary list presents the dimensions which pass the ultimate test: they make sense. At least to me.

these was Aristotle's. He claimed that credibility consists of character, sagacity (or

wisdom), and good will. Character refers to the general moral fiber of the speaker—his or her trustworthiness, integrity, honesty, and so on. Sagacity considers general intelligence and competence in dealing with the particular topic about which he or she is speaking. Finally, good will takes into account the speaker's attitude toward the receivers; that is, whether he or she is working in their best interests or is out for some personal gain without concern for the listeners' well-being. Interestingly, even though this list came from Aristotle's own ruminations about speakers and audiences, more recent "scientific" studies of credibility using computers, numbers, laboratories, and all of those other things we value so highly have produced very similar lists. And the really nice thing is that this list makes sense: we hardly would believe the things a speaker tells us if we perceive him or her to be dishonest, ignorant (or stupid), or out to cheat us for his or her own personal benefit. That, of course, is why so many used-car salespersons go hungry.

One of the earliest "scientific" examinations of credibility was conducted by Hovland, Janis, and Kelley (1953), who used the semantic differential measurement (the one we saw in Chapter 2 that uses opposite adjectives at either end of a seven-point scale) to evaluate a variety of speakers. When they combined all of their scales into categories by using a statistical factor analysis, they discovered that, no matter how many scales their subjects filled out, there really were only three judgments actually being made: judgments about the source's expertness, trustworthiness, and intent. Sound familiar? It should: expertness is much like sagacity (although it implies topic-specific rather than general competence) trustworthiness is virtually synonymous with character, and intent parallels good will. This research, then, lent additional credence to Aristotle's three-dimensional view of source credibility.

More recent studies, however, have suggested some modifications in the three-dimensional system. Andersen, for example, found only two dimensions in his research: evaluation, which takes into account all three of the dimensions which Aristotle identified, and "dynamism," or the extent to which the source is perceived to be aggressive, forceful, and emphatic (Andersen, 1971). Similarly, Berlo, Lemert, and Mertz (1969) discovered three dimensions: qualification, which corresponds to expertness/sagacity, safety, which includes elements of both trustworthiness/character and intent/good will, and dynamism, was added to our list.

Still more recent studies have added still more dimensions. McCroskey, Larson, and Knapp (1971) suggested five: competence, character (similar to trustworthiness), intention, dynamism, and personality (which considers the speaker's apparent friendliness and pleasantness). Burgoon (1978) suggests the dimensions of competence, character, composure (the source's apparent ability to remain cool under stress), sociability (similar to personality), and extroversion (the willingness of the speaker to interact with others). And Hart, Friedrich, and Brooks (1975) list seven: power (the speaker's ability to control rewards and punishments for the audience), competence, trustworthiness, good will, idealism (the extent to which the speaker is perceived to possess qualities which the audience admires), similarity (the extent to which he or she is judged to resemble the audience in significant ways), and dynamism.

Having seen the views of several students of source credibility, then, let's arrive

TABLE 8-1   DIMENSIONS OF SOURCE CREDIBILITY

ARISTOTLE	Sagacity	Character	Good will				
HOVLAND, JANIS, AND KELLEY	Expertness	Trustworthiness	Intent				
ANDERSEN		Evaluation		Dynamism			
BERLO, LEMERT, AND MERTZ	Qualification	Safety		Dynamism			
McCROSKEY, LARSON, AND KNAPP	Competence	Character	Intention	Dynamism	Personality		
BURGOON	Competence	Character			Sociability	Composure	Extroversion
HART, FRIEDRICH, AND BROOKS	Competence	Trustworthiness	Good will	Dynamism	Similarity	Idealism	
SUMMARY	Competence	Character	Intent	Dynamism	Likeability	Admirability	Power

at some sort of summary list of credibility dimensions. Such a list probably should   **215**
consist of the following:

Enhancing Credibility

   1. Competence.   Does the speaker know what she (or he) is talking about? Has she had first-hand experience with the topic? Has she researched it thoroughly? Is she smart enough to understand it? Many of the message elements we saw earlier have an influence upon these judgments: factual accuracy, grammatical correctness (which indicates education and hence the likelihood of competence), delivery (in that speakers who deliver their speeches fluently often are perceived as competent in other respects as well), and so on. Of course, your reputation, the introduction you are given, and to some degree your status influence this judgment as well.

   2. Character.   Is the speaker trustworthy? Is she (or he) reliable? Is she consistent in her views, or does she change with the wind? Such judgments of character are much more subjective than are judgments of competence, which can be based upon such tangible things as education or experience. Here audiences must rely upon the speaker's reputation and upon their own observations of her truthfulness and consistency and willingness to follow through on the promises she makes.

   3. Intent.   Is the speaker trying to promote the welfare of the audience? What's in it for her (or him)? Even when the answer is at least partially obvious, as when political candidates give speeches because they want to be elected, the listeners still want to know what the speaker has in mind for them. Thus, they must be convinced that the speaker cares about them and has their interests, as well as her own, at heart.

   4. Dynamism.   Is the speaker dynamic in her (or his) delivery? Is she involved, physically as well as mentally, in her speech? Although this does not seem like it should be an important consideration, it is, for this reason: audiences infer attitudes of the source based upon observable behaviors. If her delivery is too casual, or too lackadaisical, or too inactive, the audience and likely to assume that she doesn't really care, or that she is insincere. But if she is dynamic, forceful, active, and so on she certainly must be sincere about and interested in the things she is saying, right? Well, not necessarily. But audiences assume that, and dynamism therefore is an important dimension of credibility.

   5. Likeability.   Is the speaker's personality pleasant? Is she (or he) friendly? Is she similar to the audience in beliefs, attitudes, values, and so on (remember, we tend to like people who are similar to us)? Does she treat the audience with respect? Virtually everything the audience learn about a speaker influences this dimension. And to complicate things, this dimension is related to all the others: we tend to like people who are competent, trustworthy, well meaning, and dynamic. Consequently, this probably is the most difficult dimension for us as speakers to control. But if we can convince an audience to like us, our credibility and hence our influence will be increased immensely.

To Improve Your Credibility, Demonstrate a Thorough Knowledge of Your Speech Topic

6. *Admirability.* Is the speaker someone whom the audience can look up to and admire? Does she (or he) possess traits or qualities which all of us would like to have? Has she done things which have earned our respect? Like likeability, this judgment is a subjective one encompassing other dimensions of credibility and much more. And like likeability, this judgment is based upon everything the audience learn about the source so that it is difficult for a speaker to control. Nevertheless, if an audience truly admire us, our ability to influence them will be extremely strong.

In this second section, then, we saw the sorts of judgments people make as they assess our credibility or decide whether or not to believe us. With this knowledge, we now are ready to devise some strategies that might be useful in enhancing our credibility in the eyes of the audiences we encounter.

CREDIBILITY STRATEGIES

In looking at some of the things you can do to enhance your credibility, we will consider each dimension in turn, isolating the behaviors you might use to improve audience judgments of that dimension.

Competence
1. Demonstrate your personal acquaintance with the topic. Tell your audience about the experiences you have had that are relevant to your speech topic or about the research you have done in it. Let them know why you have chosen this particular topic to speak about and why you care about and are personally involved in it.
2. Affiliate yourself with other credible sources. If you are going to be intro-

duced to your audience, try to make sure that the person doing the introducing is perceived as credible by that audience. In addition, if you have the opportunity to do so, supply that person with information about yourself that he or she can use in the introduction and that will demonstrate your competence to the audience.

3. Show familiarity with the special vocabulary of the topic. By using the correct terminology and defining for the audience topic-related words with which they might be unfamiliar, you demonstrate your acquaintance with the subject matter.

4. Show familiarity with recognized experts in the topic field. Citing authorities as evidence during your speech lends you credibility by showing that you have researched the topic and that leading, credible experts agree with your point of view. To be sure that your citations have the desired effect, you should do two things: analyze your audience carefully so that you know which sources they are likely to think credible and give the qualifications of your sources when you cite them so that all doubt of their expertise (and your acquaintance with it) might be removed.

5. Organize your speech carefully. Audiences are funny: if they can't follow the progress of your speech, they blame it on your speaking, not their stupidity. Thus, while a clearly organized speech may not help your credibility, a poorly organized one probably will damage it by causing the audience to question your speaking competence.

6. Provide a lot of information. The more knowledge you demonstrate to your audience (within reason, of course), the more competent they will perceive you to be. In essence, demonstrate that you have learned something from your experience and research.

Character

1. Be sure your facts are accurate. We've seen this one before.

2. Tell the audience things they know to be true. Accurate facts do not demonstrate honesty if the audience have no way of determining their accuracy. Thus, it is sometimes helpful to tell them things they know to be true as well as to tell them new information they may not be able to verify immediately.

3. Demonstrate consistent behavior. It might be useful to remind your audience of your past behaviors so that they can see that your current actions are consistent.

4. Be as explicit as possible. Don't create the impression of wishy-washiness or evasiveness by speaking in vague generalities. If the audience determine that pinning you down is akin to nailing jello to a wall, they probably will be hesitant to trust you.

5. Be sure that your verbal and nonverbal behaviors are consistent. As we shall see in a later chapter, people get suspicious when your words do not match the actions that accompany them. For example, if you swear to your audience that you are committed to them and your topic while, at the same time, you are casually propping yourself up on the podium, they are likely to wonder how truly involved and committed you are. Thus, you must take care to match your words with your actions.

Intent

1. Be candid with your audience. They know you want something, so why not let them know what it is? Your objective in speaking doesn't have to be a big secret.

In fact, since the best objectives benefit both the speaker and the receiver, it might be to your advantage to tell them what you are after.

2. Demonstrate how your proposal will benefit them. In effect, use one or more of the motivational devices we saw in the previous chapter.

3. Show that other audiences have accepted your point of view and benefited from it. Obviously, you won't be able to do this every time, but if possible, it is useful to use other similar audiences as silent witnesses to your good will.

4. Establish "identification" with the audience. Show how you share a common fate with them—how what happens to them also happens to you. Obviously, if you are "in the same boat" they are, you are not going to sink it.

Dynamism

1. Be active in your speech delivery. Use a large number and wide variety of movements and gestures and make maximum use of your voice by varying the rate, pitch, and volume with which you speak. When we considered delivery in an earlier chapter, we saw in greater detail some of the techniques you can use to develop a dynamic delivery.

2. Use forceful language. Again, we don't want to offend our audience with the language we use. But within the limits of good taste, the more dramatic and intense the language we use, the more dynamic and credible we will be perceived to be.

3. Indicate precisely the behavioral commitments you have made to the topic. By showing how you yourself have been actively involved in this thing, you demonstrate to your audience your sincerity and commitment. The credibility of Martin Luther King and Jesse Jackson grew from their active involvement in and personal sacrifices for the ideas they advocated.

Likeability

1. Show your audience that you like them. Compliment them (sincerely). Show how you want the best for them. Talk about the relationship you have had with some or all of them (provided, of course, that it has been a good one). In effect, show them that you are friendly toward them and care about them.

2. Show respect for them. Even though you are the star of the show and the resident expert on the topic, do not, under any circumstances, "talk down" to your audience. Treat them as equals, as people worthy of respect, and they will treat you the same way.

3. Show similarity to them. Even if you disagree with them in most respects, emphasize the beliefs, attitudes, values, and so on that you have in common with them. Or show how your background or experiences are similar to theirs. Or demonstrate how you share their interests and concerns. As any good politician will tell you, it pays to find some point of commonality or similarity with your audience, even if you have completely different backgrounds, purposes, and ideas.

4. Disassociate yourself from ideas or things that the audience dislike. If your audience intensely dislike "pinko commie perverts" and suspect you might be one, you obviously will need to convince them that you are not. Or if you are talking to a group of workers who perceive you to be a member of management, you may have to identify with them and disassociate yourself from the management group. So the basic principle is that if the audience are likely to believe that you hold ideas or associate with people they do not like, you may have to disassociate yourself from those ideas or people, provided that in fact you do not believe or associate with them. But don't turn into a gutless wonder who betrays everything and everyone when the pressure is on. If you really do believe those things or associate with those people, don't lie about it; stand up for it. The audience will respect you for your courage.

Admirability

1. Demonstrate how you possess traits the audience values. If, for example, they value courage, then tell them of an incident in which you exhibited that trait. Or if compassion is important to them, show that you have exhibited that trait in the past. But the key to doing this well is to do it modestly and subtly. In our culture, remember, modesty is a valued trait, too. Thus, most audiences would not be impressed if you stood up and said, "Hi, there. I'm brave, strong, kind, cheerful, courteous, and dignified; I help little old ladies and small dogs across the street; and I'm working on my seventeenth merit badge." Instead, you have to subtly reveal these qualities through your behaviors, past and present.

2. Avoid vicious criticism of opposing viewpoints or spokespersons. You can disagree with your opposition, of course. But if you become insulting, vicious, nasty, and so on, you will sink in the eyes of your audience. People usually do not respect those who are nasty or petty.

3. Present yourself as both similar to but different from your audience. This is difficult to do. We know that people admire those who share their beliefs, attitudes, values, interests, or concerns. But on the other hand, an audience would have little reason to look up to someone who was just like them. Thus, through your message, appearance, reputation, or introduction, you must also show them that in some ways you are different—that you embody some of the things they would like to be but are not now. And again, you must do so modestly and subtly.

4. Show composure and dignity. People who become upset or rattled under pressure are not admired in our society; those who remain cool, calm, and stoical are. Thus, even though you might be frightened out of your wits by giving a speech, try not to show it.

SUMMARY

At the end of the last chapter, you knew how to attract your audience's attention and motivate them to sustain their interest. Thus, in this chapter we moved to the next step: convincing them to believe the things they hear you say. Their willingness to believe is primarily a function of the credibility they attribute to you, so we spent some time dissecting credibility. First, we looked at the dynamics of credibility, or the changes through which audience assessments of credibility go. We saw that it changes from receiver to receiver, from time to time (both internal and external to the speaking situation), from topic to topic (except when the halo effect causes this principle to be violated), and from setting to setting. Then, secondly, we tried to specify the dimensions of credibility and decided, after a review of prominent theorists, that when an audience judge a particular speaker's credibility, they assess her or his competence, character, intent, dynamism, likeability, and admirability. Finally, armed with this knowledge, we developed some strategies through which we might enhance our listeners' evaluations of each of these six dimensions.

REFERENCES

Andersen, K. *Persuasion: Theory and Practice.* Boston: Allyn and Bacon, 1971.

Berlo, D., J. Lemert, and R. Mertz. "Dimensions for Evaluating the Acceptability of Message Sources," *Public Opinion Quarterly* 33 (1969):563–576.

Burgoon, M. *Human Communication.* New York: Holt, Rinehart and Winston, 1978.

Cronkhite, G. *Persuasion: Speech and Behavioral Change.* New York: Bobbs-Merrill, 1969.

Davis, K. *Human Behavior at Work.* New York: McGraw-Hill, 1972.

Gilkinson, H., S. Paulson, and D. Sikkink. "Effects of Order and Authority in an Argumentative Speech," *Quarterly Journal of Speech* 40(1954):183–192.

Haiman, F. "An Experimental Study of the Effects of Ethos in Public Speaking." Ph.D. dissertation, Northwestern University, 1948; reported in *Speech Monographs* 16(1949):190–202.

Harms, L. S. "Social Judgments of Status Cues in Language." Ph.D. dissertation, Ohio State University, 1959; abstracted in *Speech Monographs* 27(1960):87.

Hart, R., G. Friedrich, and W. Brooks. *Public Communication.* New York: Harper & Row, 1975.

Hewgill, M., and G. Miller. "Source Credibility and Response to Fear-Arousing Communications," *Speech Monographs* 32(1965):95–101.

Hovland, C., I. Janis, and H. Kelley. *Communication and Persuasion.* New Haven: Yale University Press, 1953.

———, **A. Lumsdaine, and F. Sheffield.** *Experiments in Mass Communication: Vol. III of Studies in Social Psychology in World War II.* Princeton: Princeton University Press, 1949.

Kersten, B. "An Experimental Study to Determine the Effect of a Speech of Introduction upon the Persuasive Speech That Followed." M.A. thesis, South Dakota State College, 1958.

Lefkowitz, M., R. Blake, and J. Mouton. "Status Factors in Pedestrial Violation of Traffic Signals," *Journal of Abnormal and Social Psychology* 51(1955):704–706.

McCroskey, J. "A Summary of Experimental Research on the Effects of Evidence in Persuasive Communication," *Quarterly Journal of Speech* 55(1969):169–176.

———, **C. Larson, and M. Knapp.** *An Introduction to Interpersonal Communication.* Englewood Cliffs, N.J.: Prentice-Hall, 1971.

Mills, J. and E. Aronson. "Opinion Change as a Function of the Communicator's Attractiveness and Desire to Influence," *Journal of Personality and Social Psychology* 1(1965):73–77.

Singer, J. "The Use of Manipulative Strategies: Machiavellianism and Attractiveness," *Sociometry* 27(1964):128–151.

Whyte, W. *Human Relations in the Restaurant Industry.* New York: McGraw-Hill, 1948.

EXHIBIT 1

There is a reason why I have chosen this particular topic to present to you today. I carry with me scars inflicted by a handgun. The scars are not the kind you can see; I have never been shot. Rather, the scars are deep inside me, and they were put there when a burglar shot my brother to death late one December night two years ago. I hope none of you have similar scars, and my aim in this speech is to help all of us from being scarred in the future.

Analyze the credibility-building statement used in this introduction to the speech about gun control. What dimensions are considered? How might additional dimensions have been built?

EXHIBIT 2

During the past two years, I have worked as a part-time reporter for the *Ann Arbor News*. During that time, I have reported a number of crimes committed locally. I have also been an avid television watcher, and several months ago I began to notice what seemed to me to be a strange relationship between television programming and the sorts of crimes which I was reporting. I began to investigate this correlation, and I arrived at the conclusion based on my own observations and my reading that, in fact, television violence and real-life violence are related. I want to describe that relationship for you today.

Analyze the credibility-building statement used in this introduction to the speech about television violence. What dimensions are considered? How might additional dimensions have been built?

PROJECT

THE SPEECH OF INTRODUCTION

This type of speech introduces another speaker to the audience. Your purpose in such a speech is to tell your audience about the speaker and to motivate them to listen to the speaker's message. Since your introduction significantly influences the speaker's chances for success, it is important that you prepare carefully through the following stages:

1. Select the topic. In most situations, your topic will be the speaker and his or her speech; for this assignment, however, you may need to select one of the following situations:

A minister to college students	A movie star to your class
A scientist to your class	A businessperson to a civic group (Rotary, Lions, and so forth)
A sports star to a church group	A fire marshal to grade school students
An author to a literary club	A nominating speaker to a political convention
A politician to a commencement group	A military hero to a group of antiwar demonstrators

2. Gather your material. Learn all you can about the speaker and the speaker's topic by interviewing the speaker, conducting library research, interviewing people who know the speaker, and drawing upon your own knowledge. Seek material relevant to the dimensions of credibility.
3. Organize your material. Divide your material into three or four main points, such as stages of the speaker's life, the speaker's leading accomplishments, events particularly illustrative of the speaker's character and expertise, and so on. Use the specific information you have gathered as support and amplification for those main points.
4. Develop an introduction that arouses interest (perhaps by creating suspense or referring to audience characteristics) in both the speaker and the speech and demonstrates your own competence to speak about the speaker.
5. Develop a conclusion that summarizes the main points you have stated about the speaker, introduces the topic or title of the speech, and then presents the speaker to the audience.
6. When delivering the speech, remember that the audience came to hear the speaker, not you. Thus, keep your remarks brief and to the point and use a conversational and not overly dramatic delivery style.

Name _____

Date _____

Speech Type _____

Speech Outline, Project Number _____

Speech Topic: _____

Speech Objective: _____

_____

Speech Title: _____

Introduction

    Attention:

    Motivation:

    Credibility:

      Preview

      Body

      Conclusion

Instructor's Comments:

PROJECT

THE GOOD-WILL SPEECH

Speeches of this type, as their name implies, are designed to elicit good will from the audience—to cause them to think better of the speaker and the topic. Superficially, the purpose of such speeches seems to be informative, for their content consists solely of information about the topic; the speaker does not offer obvious persuasive appeals. Nevertheless, the ultimate purpose of such speeches is persuasive: the speaker wants to change listeners' attitudes so that they feel more favorably toward the topic. It is important to note, too, that the term *good will* refers not only to the desired result, but to the speaker's method as well. To secure good will from the audience, the speaker must first show good will toward them. The "intent" dimension of credibility thus lies at the heart of this type of speech. Preparation of good-will speeches involves several stages, including:

1. Select a topic. Decide what you want your audience to feel more favorably toward. Possible good-will speech topics include:

    An automobile safety association   A consumer's advocacy group
    A chemical manufacturing company   A private college
    A conservationist organization   A fraternity or sorority
    A religious organization   A newspaper publisher
    A social service organization   A political party

2. Gather your material. Through your own experience, interviews, library research, and so on, obtain information about the topic that will demonstrate to your audience good will toward them. In effect, show your audience what your organization has done or will do for them.
3. Organize your material, probably by dividing your material into three or four major benefits your topic provides your audience.
4. Develop an introduction that arouses the curiosity of your audience and demonstrates your expertise and your good will toward the audience.
5. Develop a conclusion that *does not* make a persuasive appeal but makes the topic memorable to the audience.
6. Deliver the speech in a friendly, conversational manner. Present your information in a modest manner (bragging does not promote good will), and if you find it necessary to discuss competitors of or opponents to your topic group, do so kindly and graciously.

Name _____

Date _____

Speech Type _____

Speech Outline, Project Number _____

Speech Topic: _____

Speech Objective: _____

_____

Speech Title: _____

Introduction

    Attention:

    Motivation:

    Credibility:

      Preview

      Body

      Conclusion

_____

Instructor's Comments:

CHAPTER 9
PROVING ARGUMENTS

PRIMARY (PREPARATIONAL) OBJECTIVE:
To prove your arguments so that your audience believe them

Secondary Objective	Corresponding Strategies
To prove the correctness of your arguments	State claim Use evidence
To reason clearly	Use deductive reasoning Use inductive reasoning Use Toulmin reasoning model Avoid improper reasoning

CHAPTER OBJECTIVES
After studying this chapter, you should be able to:

- Phrase a claim of fact, value, and policy
- Prove claims through the use of examples, statistics, presumptions, and opinions
- Construct a valid deductive argument using either a syllogism or an enthymeme
- Construct a valid inductive argument using reasoning by example, analogy, sign, or cause
- Construct a valid argument using the Toulmin model
- Identify and avoid fallacies of language and argument

INTRODUCTION

Imagine that a close friend of yours smokes. Imagine that you do not smoke, and that you want to influence your friend so that he or she also does not smoke. Your attempt to persuade your friend might go something like this:

> You: "Chris, you really should stop smoking."
> Chris: "Why?"

Now you face a choice. You have given Chris your topic (smoking) and revealed your main objective (to get Chris to stop smoking as soon as possible). But now you have to give something else. Thus, you might say one of the following:

> "Because smoking causes cancer."
> "Because if you do, I'll give you a penny."
> "Because your smoke may cause birth defects in my unborn children."
> "Because if you do, I'll give you $1 million."
> "Because if you continue to smoke, Santa won't leave you any toys."
> "Because smoking is expensive, smelly, and unpleasant to people around you."

All of these "because" statements are reasons that support the statement you made at the very beginning of the conversation. As we saw at the beginning of this part, reasons comprise the basis of persuasion; people want to do what is "right," and rightness is demonstrated by the reasons you provide. However, these "because" statements also demonstrate some important characteristics of reasons. In order for reasons to be persuasive, they must be two things: *believable* to the listener and *important* to the listener. To demonstrate, consider again the six reasons listed above.

"Because smoking causes cancer." Probably, cancer is important to the listener; chances are, Chris wants to avoid contracting cancer if possible. However, Chris may not believe that smoking truly does cause cancer (or Chris may believe that cause-effect connection, but still thinks, "It can't happen to me"). Your task is to prove to Chris the accuracy of your reason.

"Because if you do, I'll give you a penny." Chris probably believes this (unless you are perceived to be an incredible tightwad), but it is unlikely that this reason carries much importance in Chris' mind. It is unlikely, then, that this reason alone would be persuasive (unless you could add importance to the reason by saying something like, "The penny is a 1789 Turkey head, the only penny of its kind in existence. It could be worth millions").

"Because your smoke may cause birth defects. . . ." The persuasiveness of this argument rests on two things: Chris' concern about you and your yet-to-be-born children (importance), and Chris' evaluation of the truth of your statement (believability). To achieve your objective, then, you would have to establish concern about you and the accuracy of your facts.

"Because if you do, I'll give you $1 million." Probably this would be important to Chris, but no way is it believable (unless you happen to have the cash in hand).

"Because Santa won't leave you toys." Get serious.

"Because it is expensive, smelly, and unpleasant." You may, in this instance, have to prove that the statement is true and that it should be important to Chris.

These statements indicate, then, that in order to be effective, our reasons must be important and believable to our listeners. But where do these things come from?

To Prove Correctness, Establish Your Claim

What makes a reason important and believable to our listeners? Importance seems to spring from several things: the value system of the audience (and the extent to which the reason is tied to audience values), the perceived consequences presented in the reason (getting a penny is considerably less important than getting $1 million), the credibility of the source (reasons given by credible sources generally carry more weight than do reasons given by noncredible sources), the importance of the reason to the source, and so on. If we analyze our audience carefully, we should be able to determine what reasons would be considered important by that particular group of people.

Believability also is a function of several factors. Credibility is one, of course: we are more likely to believe what credible sources tell us. Consistency is another—we believe things consistent with what we already know to be true. But there are two other determinants of believability that we as speakers can control must use to make our reasons effective. First, people believe things when those things are *proven* to be true. That is, if the facts indicate that something is correct, people will believe it. Our first task thus is to prove the correctness of the reasons we give. Second, people believe things that make sense. If our ideas all fit into a coherent, sensible pattern, people will be more likely to accept those ideas. We therefore must also reason properly. In this chapter, then, we will examine those two things—proof and reasoning—as we seek to develop arguments which our audiences will accept.

PROVING CORRECTNESS

Persuasion, as we know, involves change. Our listeners must be convinced to change their beliefs, attitudes, and so on. And, as we also know, people must be shown reasons for making changes, and they must be made to believe that those reasons are good ones. But how do we do that—how can we prove to people that our reasons are good? Generally, we prove correctness through two steps. First, we offer a "claim," and then we show that this claim is correct by supporting it with facts. Let's examine each of these steps in turn.

Claims

A *claim* is something you want your audience to accept. It might also be called an *assertion,* an *argument,* a *reason,* or a *conclusion,* but by all these names it is the same thing: the idea that you want your audience to buy. Generally, claims are divided into three categories: fact, value, and policy. Claims of *fact* are aimed directly at audience members' beliefs, for they deal with past, present, or future states of affairs. Such claims as: "Television causes insanity," "Cancer cures smoking," "Adolf Hitler was a female impersonator," or "Contact will soon be made with beings from other planets" all fall into this category.

A claim of *value* is aimed toward audience values and attitudes. Specifically, it holds that something or someone is good or bad, valuable or worthless, desirable or undesirable, justified or unjustified. For example: "Jogging is a waste of time," "Capitalism is the best economic system yet developed," or "The Chicago Bulls are the worst basketball team in the history of humankind."

Claims of *policy,* finally, recommend specific behaviors in which audience members should engage. Typified by the word *should,* claims of this sort might suggest that: "The President should tighten wage and price controls," "Victimless crimes should be legalized," or "The national highway speed limit should be set at 90 miles per hour."

When you make a claim, the audience are likely to ask (at least themselves) certain questions. Claims of fact and value often elicit the questions, "How can I be sure that this statement is accurate?" or "How well does the situation or thing described fit the criteria which we must apply to them?" Claims of policy might elicit these questions and others: "Why should I do this?" "How should I do this?" "When and where should I do this?" "What other, better things might I do instead?" "What reasons are there for my not doing this?" All of these questions or concerns must be satisfied if persuasion is to occur. And one of the best ways to satisfy them is through the use of our next topic, evidence.

Evidence

In Chapter 7, we saw some devices that can be used for clarification: details, examples, definitions, analogies, contrasts, quantification, and so on. Evidence consists of many of the same devices, but in persuasion they are used to prove as well as to clarify. Thus, evidence is information which serves to convince an audience of the correctness of the claims the evidence supports. For our purposes, evidence can be divided into two categories: fact and opinion. Factual evidence in turn can be divided into three subtypes: examples, statistics, and presumptions. We will consider each in turn.

Examples. As we saw in Chapter 7, examples are specific instances of the issue in question, they can be real or hypothetical, and they can be singular or serial. In

Use Statistics and Examples to Support the Claims You Make

informative speeches, examples serve to clarify; in persuasion, they serve to prove (but note that only real, and not hypothetical, examples have proof value). Suppose your claim is that the Big 10 is the best basketball conference in the country—a claim of value. To support it, you might cite one example ("A couple of years ago Indiana and Michigan finished first and second in the NCAA tournament") or a series of them ("Against nonconference opponents, Michigan was 5–0, Michigan State was 5–0, Ohio State was 6–1, Indiana was 6–2," and so on). Or to prove your claim that there is a need for strict gun control laws, you might cite instances in which guns have been misused: political assassinations, accidental shootings, and the like.

When using examples, there are certain criteria you ought to keep in mind. By asking yourself the following questions you can increase the likelihood that the examples you employ add impact to the claims you advance:

1. Is the example representative, truly typifying the class of things which it is supposed to represent, or is it just a chance occurrence?

2. Is the example truly relevant to the claim it is supposed to support?

3. Are enough examples used, or have just one or two isolated events been offered?

4. Are the examples timely; that is, did they occur during a time period, past or present, relevant to the time with which the claim is concerned? Examples of cannons backfiring on Spanish galleons 400 years ago would hardly add weight to your claim that gun control laws are needed now.

5. Are there negative examples (that is, instances that disprove what you are claiming)? If so, are they important? Can they be answered? If there are such examples and they are important, you had better have some sort of answer prepared.

Statistics. As we saw in Chapter 7, quantifying your claim through the use of statistics can both clarify and prove. To claim that a certain drug causes birth defects is, without support, not very persuasive. To add the information that 8 out of every 10 mothers taking that drug during pregnancy gave birth to a deformed child gives the claim considerable force. Indeed, statistics are probably the most persuasive sort of evidence you can use; perhaps that is why so many commercials tells us things like, "Nine out of ten doctors recommend. . . ."

Like examples, statistics should be used with some care. You might ask yourself these questions as you prepare to use this type of evidence:

1. Are the statistics from a reliable, unbiased source? Organizations that specialize in gathering statistical data (such as the Gallup or Harris polls) usually are more trustworthy than are casual or biased data collectors. Beware of statistics that might have been carelessly gathered or that might have been released for self-serving purposes (as when the tobacco industry releases studies that prove statistically that smoking isn't so bad for you after all).

2. Is the sample upon which the statistics are based truly representative? Briefly, a sample is a group of things chosen from a whole population of things as being representative of that population. A voter's poll, for example, telephones a few thousand New Yorkers and then, based upon the responses of that sample, predicts how the entire city's population is likely to vote. When evaluating sample-based statistics, you must pay close attention to the nature of that sample. If it is too small (only five New Yorkers are called) or in some way biased (only registered Republicans are called), then the generalizations made about the entire population based upon the responses of the sample must be held in question (such as the conclusion that, based on our sample, New York City will unanimously vote Republican).

3. Do the statistics relate to the period of time in question? A voter's poll taken 30 years ago probably would not tell us much about how voters are likely to behave during the upcoming election.

4. Are the things compared statistically really comparable? Or are they the proverbial apples and oranges that cannot be compared in terms of the statistics at hand. For example, a few years ago some "experts" argued that some racial groups are innately more intelligent than other groups and offered as proof the average I.Q. scores obtained by members of the racial groups in question. Other people argued, however, that those scores were not comparable—that cultural differences made I.Q. tests an inadequate measure of true intelligence. Similarly, if the testers had measured only 10-year-olds of one group and 30-year-olds of another, or if they had tested one group at noon and the other at 3 a.m., one could have argued that incomparable groups were being compared. For comparative statistics to be valid, the groups measured by those statistics must truly be comparable.

5. Do the statistics hide significant variations within the groups? For example, consider a situation in which we compare two averages, one of a group whose scores were 11, 1, 1, 1, and 1 and the other of a group whose scores were 3, 3, 3, 3, and 3. Both averages are 3 so we must conclude that the groups are identical, right? Hardly. But averages can hide other characteristics of the groups from which they were drawn, and we must learn all we can about the other statistics that characterize those

6. Is enough information given about the statistics? An average, for example, can be any one of three things: the *mean* (or arithmetic average of the scores), the *median* (which is the score above and below which 50 percent of the group's scores fall), and the *mode* (the most frequently obtained score). You should know which of these averages is used. Similarly, you should know the size of the sample, the range of scores and so forth.

Really, statistics are just abstractions representing some characteristic of a group of people or things. The more you know about those statistics, the less abstract they become and the more understanding you obtain of the actual group.

Presumptions.   Based upon past occurrences, we sometimes can predict or presume that certain things are likely to happen again in the future. For instance, it seems reasonable to presume that the sun will rise in the East and set in the West tomorrow—that has been a consistent pattern in the past. And to predict that in the next mayoral election in Chicago the Democratic candidate will win has almost as much certainty. But other presumptions are not so readily accepted. During a trial, for example, character witnesses often are called to testify on behalf of the accused. Their function is to establish a pattern—to create in the jury's mind the presumption that a fine, upstanding pillar of the community like the defendant would never commit the sort of crime with which he or she is accused. Such a presumption probably would require additional forms of evidence, such as examples of his or her contributions to the community welfare, to impress the jury. Nevertheless, if presumptions of the sort just described can be established in the minds of audience members, they serve as powerful support for the claims to which they relate.

Evaluating presumptions requires asking two questions:

1. Does a true pattern exist? That is, does the sun rise in the same place every morning, or does it just seem that way? Is this man truly an outstanding citizen, or are we jury members just being shown isolated, atypical behaviors he exhibited in the past?

2. Do past patterns still apply to present situations? Sure, the defendant was an upstanding community leader in the past, but that was before he had his frontal lobotomy. Maybe he is different now.

While examples, statistics, and presumptions comprise factual forms of evidence, there exist yet another type of evidence, *opinion*. Although this is a weaker, less certain type of evidence than is factual, opinion evidence also is the type most commonly used in persuasive speeches. Unlike statements of fact, opinion statements cannot be proven true or false. When a movie star says, "I think candidate *X* is the best person for the job," who is going to say "No you don't"? Others may argue that opposing candidates are more desirable, but one fact is indisputable: the star favors candidate *X*. And as we saw in Chapter 8, opinions expressed by credible sources can be extremely influential. Thus, when you begin with the claim that "Aspirin is the best medicine for relieving the discomfort of athlete's foot" and then add the evidence that "Professors Jones, Smythe, and Heffenpeffler all have endorsed aspirin for the treatment of athlete's foot," your claim takes on added acceptability in the eyes of the audience—provided, of course, that they consider those professors to be credible sources.

Before we accept and use statements of opinion as evidence, there are certain questions which we should ask:

1. Is the source qualified to render an accurate opinion? Is the topic within his or her area of expertise (that is, does this source meet the dimension of "competence")? Has the source proven to be trustworthy? What were the source's intentions in making the statement? In sum, is this a credible source?

2. Is the opinion consistent with known facts? A spokesperson for the United Tobacco Company may state that, in his view, smoking makes people more healthy and promotes their hair growth, but most of the facts presently known indicate otherwise. Obviously, opinion statements which conflict with existing factual evidence should be viewed with some skepticism.

3. What are the implications of this opinion? That is, does the opinion make sense if you take it to its logical conclusion? Suppose someone argues that the president of the United States ought not have the sole power to launch nuclear attacks on other countries—that the Congress must also approve such an attack. While this opinion seems reasonable, does not contradict existing facts, and really has in the past been advanced by credible sources, its implications must be examined if its merits are to be judged. Is it practical, for example, to try and convene a meeting of Congress when another country has launched on attack on the United States and dozens of missiles are screaming toward us? Probably we would all be blown to smithereens before the end of the first filibuster. And do members of Congress have any expertise that would make them better able to decide how our nuclear weapons should be deployed? Would they improve at all upon the decision making of the president? Probably not. Thus, the implications of this opinion, when examined, might cause us to doubt the validity of the argument it makes and its utility as a piece of evidence.

As we examined each type of evidence above, we saw some of the tests you should apply to each type before you use it to support your claims. But before leaving this topic, let's consider briefly six criteria that should be applied to all types of evidence, including fact and opinion.

1. Accuracy. The information should, of course, be accurate. To test the accuracy of a given piece of evidence, we should compare it with other evidence we already have collected and know to be true. If this new evidence contradicts the other information, we might have a problem.

2. Recency. The information should be as close in time as possible to the thing in question. Current events should be discussed using today's information; past events should be discussed using the reports of eyewitnesses rather than of people rehashing those events at some later time.

3. Completeness. The information should tell the whole truth, leaving out nothing important. Opinion statements particularly are troublesome here as authorities tend to give only their own viewpoints and omit those of the opposition.

Check as many sources of information as you can to be sure that you are getting the whole story on the topic you are examining.

4. Reliability. The information should come from a source who has a good "track record"—who has provided accurate information in the past. Sources who repeatedly have been incorrect in the past usually are not more reliable now.

5. Objectivity. The information should come from an unbiased source—someone who has nothing to gain from stating the opinions or facts he or she offers. Even opinion statements can be objective: "I have examined all the available pain relievers, and in my judgment aspirin is best" would be perfectly objective if offered by an independent doctor who has been conducting her own research without influence or support from the drug industry. But the best sources are the so-called reluctant witnesses who offer opinions opposite to the biases we would expect them to have. The tobacco industry executive who admits the harmfulness of smoking or the automotive executive who says that cars are overpriced and pollute too much would be believed because they are testifying against their own interests. Thus, these people are not objective, but the information they offer certainly is.

6. Consistency. The information should be consistent with itself (internal consistency), with other things the source has said, and with the things from other sources that we already know to be true (external consistency). Sources who repeatedly contradict themselves and the known facts obviously must be regarded with some suspicion.

All of these considerations must be kept in mind when you are collecting evidence for your own use or listening to evidence provided by another speaker. Only by carefully evaluating the evidence we hear will we avoid falling into the halo effect trap we saw in Chapter 5.

Using Evidence

Research has been conducted concerning the sorts of situations in which evidence is most useful, and from that research three conclusions have emerged. First, McCroskey (1967; 1969) determined that moderate-to-low-credibility sources are most effective if they use evidence, but that highly credible sources gain nothing by using evidence to support their claims. High-credibility sources already are believable to their audiences and thus do not need to use evidence to prove their points. Low-to-moderate-credibility sources, on the other hand, are not particularly believable to audiences so they must improve their own credibility by drawing upon the credibility of the sources they quote (Warren, 1969). While all of this makes sense, additional research findings concerning evidence and credibility give one pause. Cathcart (1955) and Bostrum and Tucker (1969) found that when a low- or moderate-credibility source cites evidence to improve his own credibility, he need not cite the sources of that evidence. In other words, they did not find support for the common sense assumption that, when using evidence, you should tell who the source of that evidence is. Very strange. In addition, Ostermler (1971) determined that you can use yourself as evidence: by relating your own experiences and knowledge, you both enhance your own credibility (even when your credibility was low at the outset) and increase the persuasive effect of your speech. Despite these findings, however, it still seems reasonable to cite the source of your evidence (if that source is likely to be credible to your audience) and to use sources other than your own knowledge and experiences to prove your claims.

A second situation calling for the use of evidence is one in which the audience already know a great deal about your topic. When delivering a speech, you must prove to your audience that you are a competent source. If you appear to know less about the topic than they do, you hardly will be perceived as competent. But if, through your use of evidence, you demonstrate knowledge that surpasses theirs, they will be more likely to perceive you as credible. Thus, the principle is: the more your audience know, the more evidence you need to use.

Finally, your use of evidence also must take into account the attitudes of the audience. If, at the outset, they are in agreement with you, then evidence may be unnecessary—why prove something to them that they already believe? But if, on the other hand, they initially disagree with you, then you must use evidence to prove that your viewpoint is correct and that they ought to modify theirs.

The bottom line of all of this, then, is that in most situations you should use evidence to prove your claims. Rarely if ever will you find yourself speaking to an audience who think you extremely credible, who know nothing about your topic, and who agree with you completely. In all situations other than this one, using evidence both enhances your credibility and increases your persuasiveness.

REASONING

As we already know, it is not enough simply to prove that what you say is true. You also must demonstrate that it makes sense—that it is reasonable. This you accomplish through the way in which you string your claims and proofs together, a process that might be called *reasoning*. Generally, reasoning is divided into two types: deductive and inductive. We will consider each in turn.

Deductive Reasoning

The deductive reasoning process moves from general principles to specific conclusions. Consider this famous example of deductive logic:

> All men are mortal.
> Socrates is a man.
> Therefore, Socrates is mortal.

Here we begin with a general statement of principle, move to a specific instance, and then, by taking those two statements into account, arrive at some conclusion about that specific instance. A jury member might go through this same process as she listens to the testimony of character witnesses: "Upstanding citizens do not steal; the defendant seems, based upon testimony, to be an upstanding citizen; therefore, he probably did not commit the robbery of which he is accused."

The form of reasoning just described is called a *syllogism*. As the preceding
examples illustrate, syllogisms consist of a three-part sequence of argument:

1. A "major premise," which states some general principle (All politicians are sneaky).
2. A "minor premise," which states a specific case relevant to the generalization (Joe Furschluginer is a politician).
3. A "conclusion," which necessarily follows from the premises (Therefore, Joe Furschluginer is sneaky).

Using this form of reasoning, then, your persuasive speech would seek to prove both of the premises and, in so doing, automatically prove the conclusion you want your audience to accept.

Although the syllogism seems rather simple and straightforward to use, things become considerably more complex when we examine the three types of syllogisms: categorical, disjunctive, and conditional. *Categorical syllogisms* begin with a statement about an entire category of things: *all* men are mortal, *every* politician is crooked, *each* professional football linebacker is nasty, or *any* Republican is conservative. At times, these allness terms may simply be implicit (Republicans are conservative; politicians are crooked), but they describe an entire category of things nonetheless. The minor premise then follows with a statement about some specific case, and the logical conclusion is drawn.

Categorical syllogisms must conform to some very strict rules concerning their structure. First, they must deal with three terms—no more and no less. In our classic Socrates example, the terms were *men, mortal,* and *Socrates.* Second, each of these terms must be used twice in the syllogism, but only one time in a specific premise. In the Socrates example, you will observe that each term is used twice, and that each term appears only once in each particular statement. Third, the term that appears in both premises but not in the conclusion (called the *middle term*) must be used at least once in an unqualified, allness sense. Since *men/man* is our middle term, and since the first premise states that "*All* men are mortal," the syllogism is proper. Fourth, a term in the conclusion can be used in an allness or unqualified manner only if it was used that way in one of the premises. It would, for example, be improper to say that "All men are mortal; all mortals are baseball players; therefore, all baseball players are men" because the unqualified term in the conclusion, *baseball players,* was not used in an unqualified sense in the minor premise. Finally, at least one of the premises must be stated positively, and if one premise is negative (containing words like *no, not,* or *none*) the conclusion also must be negative. For example, the syllogisms "No baseball players are fish; no fish are athletic; therefore, no baseball players are athletic" and "All baseball players are strange people; no strange people are communists; therefore, all baseball players are communists" would be invalid, while the statements "All baseball players are fish; no fish are athletic; therefore, no baseball players are athletic" and "All baseball players are strange people; no strange people are communists; therefore, no baseball players are communists" would be valid although senseless.

Disjunctive syllogisms begin with a major premise that contains mutually exclusive alternatives indicated by the words *either* and *or*. For example: "Either the president will reduce inflation or the nation will rise up against him; the president will not reduce inflation; therefore, the nation will rise up against him." The function of the minor premise, then, is to affirm or deny one of the alternatives, so that in the conclusion the alternative not considered in the minor premise is affirmed or denied.

Three rules govern the use of disjunctive syllogisms. The major premise must include all possible alternatives, the alternatives must be mutually exclusive (that is, it must be impossible for both to happen), and the minor premise must affirm or deny one of the alternatives presented in the major premise. For example, a syllogism beginning with "Either it will rain today or it will snow" would be invalid, for there are other alternatives such as hail or sunshine; a syllogism with the premise "Either the president will reduce inflation or the nation will revolt" would be invalid because both things could happen; and the syllogism "Either it will rain today or it will not rain; the moon is green; therefore, . . ." Would be invalid because the minor premise does not select one of the alternatives presented by the major premise.

Conditional syllogisms, which also are called *hypothetical syllogisms,* begin with a major premise that deals with uncertain or hypothetical events that may or may not happen. Usually, this conditionality is indicated by the use of such words as *if, assuming that,* or *supposing that* in the major premise. The major premise uses these words to express an antecedent, or a statement of the hypothetical situation under consideration, and a consequent, or a statement of what will happen if the antecedent takes place. The minor premise then affirms the antecedent or denies the consequent, leaving the conclusion. For example:

"If we eat a pound of chocolate for every meal, we will become extremely fat."

| "We will eat chocolate for every meal." | *Or* | "We will not become fat." |

Therefore:

| "We will become fat." | *Or* | "We will not eat chocolate for every meal." |

If we do what the antecedent says, the consequent will follow, and if the consequent does not occur, then we must not have done what the antecedent suggested.

Conditional syllogisms must follow two rules: the minor premise, as we have seen, must either affirm the antecedent or deny the consequent, and the causal relationship expressed in the major premise must in fact be true. Thus, to state that "If it rains today our dog will throw up; our dog did not throw up; therefore, it must not have rained" would make little sense because the causal relationship offered in the major premise does not exist (or we have an extremely unusual dog).

The categorical, disjunctive, and conditional syllogisms constitute the most complete forms of deductive reasoning. There is, however, another form of deduction called the *enthymeme,* which operates in the same fashion as does the syllogism but leaves out one or two parts of the syllogistic structure. An enthymeme may, for example, state two premises and leave the conclusion implied: "Either Congress will amend the bill or the president will veto it, and Congress will not amend that bill." Or it may even offer just one premise: "Anyone who thinks that way is a dirty commie pervert" leaves implied the premise "You think that way" and the conclusion "Therefore, you are a dirty commie pervert." Enthymemes are encountered much more often than are complete syllogisms, but they operate according to the same rules of logic. Thus, to evaluate the validity of an enthymeme you first must fill in the unstated parts of the syllogism it represents and then apply the rules that govern the sort of syllogism with which you are dealing.

Before leaving the concept of the enthymeme, there is one other distinction between syllogisms and enthymemes we should note. Syllogisms deal with certainty, reaching definite conclusions drawn from their premises. Enthymemes, however, can deal with probabilities. Words like *may, might, could,* and other expressions of tentativeness have no place in syllogisms, but are appropriate for enthymemes. Since much of life is uncertain, enthymemes therefore seem better suited than syllogisms to the sorts of reasoning you will be doing in your persuasive speeches.

By analyzing the form of your deductive arguments (using the rules we observed for each type of syllogism), you can be sure that those arguments are valid—that the conclusion follows logically from the premises. However, if you analyze only the formal validity of your logic, you will be overlooking another important consideration: whether or not your arguments are true. The problem with analyzing the form of syllogisms or enthymemes is that such analyses do not take into account the truth of the premises those arguments employ. For example, in terms of form it would be perfectly valid to argue: "All frogs are enchanted princesses; Harold Stassen is a frog; therefore, Harold Stassen is an enchanted princess." But it would hardly be true. So you must examine not only the form of your deductive arguments, but the truth of your premises and conclusions as well.

Should you decide to employ deductive argument, then, you will face two tasks. First, you will have to construct major and minor premises that logically lead to the claim or conclusion you want your audience to believe. Then, secondly, you will have to develop evidence that proves the truth of the premises you advance. If you can thus combine accurate information and logical reasoning, you will be assured of considerable success in persuading your listeners.

Inductive Reasoning

Unlike deductive reasoning, which moves from general principles to specific cases, inductive reasoning moves from specific cases to general conclusions. Sherlock Holmes used this sort of reasoning to solve his cases. By observing mud on a suspect's shoes, the suspect's length of stride, and the footprints at the scene of the murder, he inferred that the suspect committed the crime. Dr. Watson was, of course, impressed. Until he saw the mud on his shoes.

There are several forms of inductive reasoning. *Reasoning by example* consists of presenting several specific cases and then inferring a general conclusion. If we are advancing the argument that it helps to be tall if you want to be a successful basketball player, you might cite such examples as: Wilt Chamberlain (7'2"), Kareem Abdul-Jabbar (7'2"), Elvin Hayes (6'11"), and so on, ultimately arriving at the startling conclusion that, yes, the best basketball players are tall. *Reasoning by analogy* draws a comparison between two similar cases, inferring that what is true concerning one case must also be true with the other. As we saw in a previous chapter, there are two types of analogy, literal and figurative, and only literal analogies can serve as proof. People predicting the doom of American civilization, for example, draw a parallel between that civilization and the Roman culture just before the fall of the Roman Empire, concluding that, since both civilizations shared common characteristics, they will share common fates as well. So watch out for Vandals and Visigoths.

Sign reasoning is based upon relationships between things that are not causally related; they simply tend to appear at about the same time. Stock market forecasters look continually for signs indicative of what the stock market is about to do. One forecaster, in fact, developed (with statistical evidence) the theory that when the SuperBowl is won by a team from the old NFL, the market drops during the next year, but if the game is won by a team from the old AFL, the market rises. In this and similar instances, we draw conclusions based upon signs we observe, basing our conclusions on the belief that when one thing appears, another thing will soon appear as well.

Causal reasoning, finally, goes a step beyond sign reasoning to infer that a certain factor or cause serves to produce some effect. But this sort of reasoning can move in two directions: cause to effect, where we predict something based upon the causal factor we now observe ("It is now raining; therefore, the inside of my car will be flooded because the windows are open"), or effect to cause, where we observe something and infer that its typical cause must have taken place earlier ("Water is pouring out of my car as I open the door; therefore, it must have rained while my windows were down"). The difficulty with causal reasoning lies in trying to isolate causes for any one event. In order to reach valid conclusions, you must be able to state with some certainty that only one cause can produce the effect with which you are concerned and that the cause you are discussing really does produce the effect in question. Rain usually does flood cars left outside with open windows, but so do passing street-washing trucks and smart-alecky kids playing with garden hoses. And if the wind is blowing in the right direction or the rain is very light, it may not flood the car in the first place. Thus, to be sure that your causal reasoning is accurate, you should ask yourself these questions: Is the alleged cause truly relevant to the described effect (that is, could the cause really produce this effect)? Are there other causes that could have produced the observed effect? Are there counteracting causes that could prevent this cause from producing the effect? By considering these things, we can be more certain that our causal conclusions are indeed legitimate.

The Toulmin Model

A contemporary British philosopher, Stephen Toulmin (1958), has developed a model of argument with which we can implement the deductive and inductive forms of reasoning we examined above. This model, which Brockriede and Ehninger (1960) claim can be applied to develop any argument, consists of six parts, represented in the drawing seen in Figure 9-1. Those parts can be defined as follows:

Data: the evidence upon which you base your arguments
Warrant: the justification or general belief or assumption underlying your argument
Backing: support or proof for the warrant
Qualifier: any reservations about the claim or situations in which the claim might not hold true

Figure 9-1: The Toulmin Model for Constructing Arguments

Claim: the conclusion you want the audience to accept
Reservation/Rebuttal: conditions to which the claim might not apply

Let's consider each of these parts briefly.

1. *Data,* as we have seen, consist of the evidence you use to prove the truth of your claims or arguments. As McCroskey (1968) points out, data can be of three types. Audience beliefs are the most powerful data. If you can take things your audience already believe to be true and use them to support your arguments, the truth of what you are saying probably will go unquestioned by that audience. Source assertions are less powerful but still can be effective data. These are your own expressions of fact and opinion that you offer to your audience based upon your own expertise with the topic. If they perceive you to be credible, these data will be effective; if they do not think you credible, then you probably should resort to the third data type, evidence—the sort of proof-providing material we discussed earlier in this chapter. But again, audience-based data are best, followed by credibility-based data.

2. *Warrants,* as we saw above, are general beliefs held by an audience that certify the acceptability of the claim you ultimately advance. According to Ehninger and Brockriede (1963), these also can be of three types: motivational, authoritative, and substantive. Motivational warrants are based upon audience needs and emotions, suggesting that acceptance of the claim will lead to need satisfaction or emotional gratification or both. For example, we might offer data indicating that people who complete the Dale Carnegie Speaking Course tend to have greater financial success after the course than they had before. Since, our warrant might state, all of us desire financial success, we ought to adopt the claim that we should all attend the Dale Carnegie Course. Authoritative warrants, on the other hand, are based on the credibility of the source of the data. For example: "The surgeon general of the United States says that smoking causes lung cancer (datum). Since he is an expert in this area (warrant), we should do as he suggests and stop smoking (claim)." The substantive warrant, lastly, is based upon our assumptions concerning the nature of the external world. Such warrants employ causal, sign, analogy, and example reasoning to carry the audience from the data to the claim. Consider these examples:

Causal: The murder rate is extremely high (*datum*).
            Since most murders are committed with guns (*warrant*),
            institution of gun control laws will reduce murders (*claim*).

Sign: The sky at dawn is red (*datum*).
Since red morning skies usually signify storms (*warrant*),
we had better prepare for the storm which is likely to hit (*claim*).

Analogy: The Roman Empire collapsed when morality broke down (*datum*).
Since America and the Roman Empire are similar (*warrant*),
we too will collapse if we do not improve our moral climate (*claim*).

Example: Abdul-Jabbar, Walton, and Gilmore are extremely tall (*datum*).
Since these people are typical NBA centers (*warrant*),
we can conclude that NBA centers are tall (*claim*).

3. *Backing* is additional evidence used to prove the warrant. In the examples above, we might want to cite statistics concerning gun-related murders, authority statements about the significance of red morning skies, statements concerning the immorality of the last days of the Roman Empire and how that immorality led to the empire's fall, or statistics indicating how tall selected NBA centers are. When the warrant is motivational, you may need to establish that the audience truly do desire the thing you indicate they do, and when the warrant is authority based you may need to offer evidence that the source should be considered credible.

4. *Qualifiers* typically are single words, such as *usually, often, probably,* that indicate that your claim is tentative—that you recognize its limitations. Such qualifiers are expanded upon in the *reservations* or *rebuttals* you offer, where you state circumstances under which your claim might not apply and, if appropriate, offer answers to objections members of your audience might raise. As the conclusion of our NBA centers argument, we might state our claim, qualifier, reservation, and rebuttal as: "Therefore, *NBA* centers are, and will probably continue to be, extremely tall (qualified claim), unless the game changes significantly in nature (reservation) or a short person who jumps incredibly well gets into the league, and such a person has not existed in the past (reservation with rebuttal)." Under certain circumstances, you might even have to offer data in support of your rebuttal, proving, perhaps, that even short high-jumpers could not succeed as centers in the NBA.

To use the Toulmin model of argument, then, you should go through these steps:

1. State your claim, incorporating any qualifiers you think necessary to make the claim acceptable to the audience.
2. Develop warrants related to the claim: What assumptions must be accepted if the audience are to accept the claim?
3. Discover data that support your claim and do so in accordance with the warrants.
4. If the warrants need to be proven, discover data that can be used as backing.
5. Anticipate objections the audience may have and develop answers to those objections, either by admitting that your claim does not hold true under certain circumstances or by using additional data and warrants to prove that the objections are not well founded.

The Toulmin model can become extremely complicated when one begins to
string chains of arguments together or to offer proofs of warrants, rebuttals, and so on,
or to combine inductive and deductive reasoning patterns. Nevertheless, even when
used at the most simple level, the model is an extremely useful tool for developing
and organizing persuasive messages.

Improper Reasoning

Having seen what good reasoning looks like, let's examine some instances of improper reasoning. Commonly called *fallacies,* these misuses of logic appear in persuasive speeches all too often, and you should be alert to them so that you can both
avoid using them in your own speeches and spot them in speeches delivered by other
people. We will consider two categories of fallacies: those of language, and those of
argument.

Fallacies of Language

1. Deliberate Ambiguity.   Some speakers, notably politicians, will allow the
audience to fool themselves by deliberately using vague terms that the audience can
interpret in many ways. For example, a candidate might announce: "I stand for the
farmer, and I, promise to do all I can to promote the welfare of the farmers of
America." Someone who just happens to have a nice crop of cannabis and vegeta-
bles growing in his backyard might say to himself, "Hey, I'm a farmer! This guy's for
me. I guess I'll vote for him." When the candidate is elected and passes legislation
cracking down on illegal drug traffic; our "farmer" discovers his mistake. Whenever
you deliberately use vague, general terms designed to allow the audience to mislead
themselves, you are committing this fallacy.

2. Loaded Language   Rather than offer logical proof, some speakers will instead use emotionally loaded words in order to appeal to audience members' emotions and avoid their thinking about the issues at hand. Such loaded language can
be either positive (such as referring to police officers as "defenders of the peace") or
negative (such as calling those same officers "pigs") in its reference to the object in
question. When used to obscure thinking and inflame emotions, these emotional
labels constitute a second type of fallacy.

3. Technical Language.   Sometimes, the use of technical language is unavoid-
able. If you are giving a speech on nuclear physics, for example, you will find it
difficult to avoid using words your audience find complicated or difficult to understand. There are other times, however, when technical language is used by speakers
not because it is necessary, but because it might impress, confuse, or intimidate the
audience. I, once observed a college professor use precisely this strategy. When asked
a question to which he apparently had no answer, he paused a moment and then
angrily shouted, "If you were aware of Festinger's theory of cognitive dissonance, you
wouldn't be asking such an ignorant question." The student, having no idea what a
Festinger was (to say nothing of the theory the professor mentioned), sat down,
thoroughly humiliated. By using technical language which, in this case, had nothing

to do with the issue at hand, the speaker succeeded in intimidating the audience—and in committing our third fallacy.

Fallacies of Argument

4. Hasty Generalization   Related to reasoning by example, this fallacy occurs when we reach a conclusion on the basis of too few examples. If, for instance, we find two NBA centers who are each 5'7" tall and then conclude that all centers are short, we have been hasty in arriving at that generalization. Be sure that you have enough examples and that those examples are truly representative before you draw conclusions about the group from which the examples came.

5. Transfer.   A fallacious application of reasoning by analogy or sign reasoning, this error in logic occurs when we assume that, because two or more things are related in some way, they are related in other ways as well. For example, we might believe (based on our experiences with one or two individuals) that people from the South are racially prejudiced. Thus, upon first meeting someone from Mississippi, we might infer that he or she, too, is prejudiced. Or we might believe that all people having beards are politically liberal so that when we meet a bearded person we assume that he, too, is liberal. We thus draw analogies between people or infer attitudes from physical signs when, in fact, these inferences are not warranted. People are individuals, and to group them according to locality or appearance is to commit the transfer fallacy.

6. Faulty Cause.   Occasionally; we observe two events occurring within a brief time of one another and conclude that the first event produced or caused the second. Most superstitions fall into this "after it, therefore because of it" trap in causal thinking. "Black cats bring bad luck" probably grew from the experience of some individual who, shortly after a black cat crossed his path, suffered some catastrophe and assumed that the cat was the cause (what else would cause a catastrophe?). But there are other, more widely accepted instances of reasoning that commit the same fallacy. The old argument that, since most drug addicts smoked marijuana at one time, marijuana causes drug addiction is an example. One might just as legitimately argue that, since most drug addicts at one time blew their noses, Kleenex causes drug addiction. The argument seems (and is) silly but, like the marijuana argument, it takes two events related only sequentially and infers a causal relationship.

7. Shifting Ground.   Occasionally, a speaker will change his (or her) arguments during the course of his speech or, even more commonly, during the question-and-answer session that follows. He might begin with the assertion that, by passing gun laws, almost all murders could be eliminated. Later, he might say that gun control would eliminate most murders. Still later, he could assert that the murder rate would be substantially reduced if gun control laws were enacted. If the audience were not listening carefully, they might miss this shift in argument. If, however, they were vigilant, they would realize that the speaker was shifting ground, taking up a new position he could more easily defend.

8. *Appeal to Irrelevant Authority.* As we have seen, authority-based appeals are perfectly legitimate, provided the authority is relevant to the issue at hand. There are times, however, when a speaker will cite some emotion-arousing source who, in fact, has nothing to do with the claim the speaker has advanced. The Bible, the Constitution, historical figures such as George Washington or Abraham Lincoln, or some current public figures lend emotional impact to any argument, even when they have little to do with the argument's true intent.

9. *Appeal to Tradition.* Some speakers will argue that we ought to do something a certain way because it always has been done that way. In other words, it's traditional. Since time, people, and things constantly are changing, the past often is irrelevant. Tradition is a nice thing, but it is not sufficient reason for neglecting needed changes.

10. *Forcing a Dichotomy.* A misuse of the disjunctive syllogism, this fallacy creates a two-alternative situation where, in fact, several alternatives exist. Such statements as "Either you are for me or you are against me," "Either you elect a Republican or we will have nuclear war," or "Either you don't drink at all or you are an alcoholic" ignore the range of alternatives that exist and instead force the audience to think only in terms of the alternatives the speaker has set out.

11. *Countercharge.* When accused of some wrongdoing, it is not uncommon for the accused to respond not by denying the charge, but by screaming "Well you're one, too" at the party making the charge. During the Watergate scandal, for example, many Republicans responded to Democratic charges by saying, "Well you do it, too." This sort of countercharge really ignores the central issue: whether or not the original charges are correct. But it can distract the listeners from that issue to wonder about the other person rather than ponder the speaker's guilt. As a distractor, the countercharge can be effective; as a piece of logic, it is a fallacy.

12. *Extension.* The old maxim "Give them an inch and they'll take a mile" typifies this sort of fallacy. Rather than worry about the matter at hand, it speculates about future matters that may or may not happen. In one situation observed by your author, a group of corporate executives were trying to decide whether the company benefits should be improved for secretaries and clerks. Several members of this group felt that improvements should not be made. Sure, the benefits were warranted and affordable, but, in one person's words, "If we give this to them, they'll want even more. We could end up giving away the store!" Aside from exemplifying paranoia, this statement also commits the inch/mile fallacy, extending the consideration of the present issue to encompass irrelevant and phantomlike issues.

13. *Bandwagon.* This last fallacy is best exemplified by the little (or not so little) kid who, when his request is denied by his mother, replies, "But Mom, all the other kids get to!" If the Mom is a smart aleck (like at least one I have known), she will respond with something like, "Yeah, and I suppose that if all the other kids were jumping off of cliffs, you would want to do that, too." But she makes the point. Just

because everyone else is on the bandwagon (and often everyone else in fact is *not* on the bandwagon) it does not mean that you should jump onto it as well. But the bandwagon appeal can be effective, and that's why politicians and advertisers will tell you how everyone is voting for them, buying their products, and so on; you are supposed to want to join the crowd.

The 13 fallacies we have just examined should be avoided at all costs. If you use them you might be more effective in persuading (by confusing) your audience, but such fallacies can also backfire. If the audience (perhaps because they have read this book) perceive the faultiness of your reasoning, their estimate of your credibility will drop substantially, and your speech probably will be doomed to failure. Rather than take that chance, you should stick to the solid sorts of argument we saw earlier. Those arguments are every bit as persuasive, and they serve to enhance your credibility rather than endanger it.

SUMMARY

To persuade people, we must give them good reasons. We must present them with (or reasons, or claims, or conclusions) important and believable arguments. In this chapter, we focused primarily upon the believability factor, looking for techniques we could use to make our claims acceptable to the audiences we face. Specifically, we established two secondary objectives—proving correctness and reasoning—that lead to our primary objective, proving our arguments. Then we examined the strategies through which we could achieve those secondary objectives. We saw that, through the use of claims and evidence, we could construct arguments supported by facts, and that, by stringing claims and proofs together either deductively or inductively, we could develop reasons that make sense to our listeners. Through all of this, then, we can appeal to the logical, rational elements of our listeners' minds. In the next chapter, we will turn to the emotional side of our receivers.

REFERENCES

Bostrum, R. and R. Tucker. "Evidence, Personality, and Attitude Change," *Speech Monographs* 36(1969): 22–27.

Brockriede, W. and D. Ehninger. "Toulmin on Argument: An Interpretation and Application." *Quarterly Journal of Speech* 46(1960): 44–53.

Cathcart, R. "An Experimental Study of the Relative Effectiveness of Four Methods of Presenting Evidence," *Speech Monographs* 22(1955): 227–233.

Ehninger, D. and W. Brockriede. *Decision by Debate.* New York: Dodd, Mead, 1963.

McCroskey, J. "Studies of the Effects of Evidence in Persuasive Communication." Mimeographed publication. East Lansing: Michigan State University, 1967.

———. *An Introduction to Rhetorical Communication.* Englewood Cliffs, N.J.: Prentice-Hall, 1968.

———. "A Summary of Experimental Research on the Effects of Evidence in Persuasive Communication," *Quarterly Journal of Speech* 55(1969): 169–176.

Ostermier, T. "The Effects of Type and Frequency of Reference upon Perceived Source Credibility and Attitude Change," *Speech Monographs* 34(1971): 137–144.

Toulmin, S. *The Uses of Argument.* New York: Cambridge University Press, 1958.

Warren, I. "The Effect of Credibility in Sources of Testimony on Audience Attitudes Toward Speaker and Message," *Speech Monographs* 36(1969): 456–458.

EXHIBIT 1

I. Something needs to be done about the problem of handguns.
   A. Handguns and crime are strongly correlated.
      1. Guns, particularly handguns, are used in most crimes.
         a. More than half of all murders were committed by guns.
         b. Nearly three-fourths of all robberies involved guns.
      2. Possession of a handgun actually makes crime easier.
         a. Robberies necessitate threats to gain victims' compliance.
         b. Guns provide the easiest and most effective threat.
         c. Guns require less physical effort to use and thus are psychologically easier to use.
      3. Guns make spontaneous crimes more likely.
         a. Seventy percent of all shootings were unplanned.
         b. Because of their ease of use, handguns are particularly suited to crimes of passion.
   B. Accidents with guns are alarmingly frequent.
      1. Incidents of self-inflicted gunshot wounds have increased every year for the past ten years.
      2. Accidental killings also have increased over each of the past five years.
      3. Last year, nearly 5,000 people died as the result of accidental shootings.
II. Gun control legislation should be passed by the federal government, and we should write to our House representatives and senators individually and sign this petition to support gun control bills.
   A. Only handguns of less than ten inches in length should be banned.
   B. The program must be a national one; local and statewide programs do not work.
   C. Pistols for target shooting will be available at private or public ranges.
   D. Penalties for possession of a handgun should be severe.
III. Several advantages will grow out of an effective gun control program.
   A. Crime will be reduced.
   B. Accidental shootings will be substantially reduced.
IV. The usual objections to gun control are not valid.
   A. Guns are neither safe nor effective as protection for the home.
      1. Safety
         a. A gun is six times more likely to kill a family member as it is to kill an intruder.
         b. Mistaken identity may cause innocent people to be shot.
      2. Effectiveness
         a. An intruder has the element of surprise on his or her side.
         b. The threat of a gun may precipitate violence by the intruder; guns make the situation more dangerous.
   B. Guns are not desirable methods of self-protection.
      1. Only "reasonable force" is permitted by law.

2. Use of a gun is illegal if the danger can be escaped.
C. Gun control is constitutional.
1. The Second Amendment often is quoted as an individual's right to bear arms—to carry a gun.
2. Court interpretations of that amendment have restricted its meaning to organized militia.

Above is a partial outline for the speech on gun control. Analyze the organization, evidence, and arguments used and suggest ways to improve the speech.

EXHIBIT 2

I. Something needs to be done about television violence.
  A. Televised violence encourages violent crimes.
    1. Children learn through imitation.
    2. Recently, children have imitated television violence.
      a. Niemi rape case after "Born Innocent."
      b. Zamora murder case after "Kojak" episode.
  B. Televised violence has long-range effects.
    1. Eron and Rowell study: aggressiveness at age 19 is significantly correlated with television violence observed.
    2. Gerbner and Gross study: prolonged viewing of television violence causes fear of the real world and a distrust of other people.
    3. Skornia study: violence as a means of problem solving is taught as a part of the American value system.
II. We must do all we can to cause a reduction in televised violence.
  A. We should write directly to the networks demanding that violence be reduced.
  B. We should write to and boycott the products of companies that sponsor particularly violent programs.
  C. We should prevent our families from watching violent programs.
  D. We should sign this petition addressed to the FCC demanding control over violent programming.
III. If we reduce television violence, several advantages will result.
  A. Crime will be reduced.
  B. Television can be applied to more beneficial purposes.
  C. The quality of life in America may be enhanced.
IV. Common objections to controlling television violence are invalid.
  A. Restricting violence does not violate the First Amendment.
    1. The First Amendment is to protect free expression of opinion; harmful behaviors like crying "Fire" in a crowded theater are not protected.
    2. Even if the First Amendment did apply, the wide-reaching impact of television demands that it receive special consideration. The framers of the Constitution could never have imagined a medium so wide reaching.
  B. It is not the sole responsibility of parents to monitor and control television viewing.
    1. Seventy-five percent of television's programs contain some violence; avoiding all of them is virtually impossible.
    2. Continual monitoring of children's viewing behaviors is highly impractical.
    3. Parents may not be inclined to monitor television viewing or enforce viewing rules in the first place.

Above is a partial outline for the speech on television violence. Analyze the organization, evidence, and arguments used and suggest ways to improve the speech.

PROJECT

THE SPEECH TO CONVINCE

This sort of speech is designed to have some impact upon the beliefs and attitudes of the audience. Its purpose ultimately is persuasive as the speaker attempts to cause the audience to accept some idea or proposal. However, subpurposes may include informing, entertaining, and so on. In content, speeches to convince consist of logical and emotional appeals designed to produce the desired attitudes in the listeners. Since the goal of that content is to produce changes in the listeners' minds—changes they might resist—such speeches must be carefully prepared. The following stages should be implemented:

1. Select a topic. Choose some issue about which you want the audience to feel differently, and about which you feel strongly. Possible issues might include:

Limiting family size by law	Legalizing gambling
Legalizing mercy killings	Legalizing prostitution
Prohibiting strikes by law	Legalizing drugs
Capital punishment	Gun control
Limiting energy usage	Mandatory military service

   Your topic should be controversial, and it should offer a specific proposition. It should not require action by the listeners; rather, your purpose is to convince them to accept the proposition.
2. Analyze the audience and establish your goals. Determine what beliefs and attitudes presently are held by your listeners and then decide whether you are trying to change (that is, to reverse from positive to negative or from negative to positive) or to reinforce their current attitudes and whether you need to use primarily logical or emotional appeals. Decide, too, whether you need to interest your audience in the topic, whether you need to give them much information, whether you need to deal directly with their value system, and so on.
3. Gather your materials. Decide what arguments you are going to use to support your proposition and then obtain the information and develop the reasoning and emotional appeals you need to support those arguments.
4. Organize your materials. Put your arguments, information, and appeals into some coherent sequence; use one of the organizational patterns described in the preceding chapter.
5. Develop an introduction that gets attention, motivates interest, establishes your credibility, and previews the points you are about to cover.
6. Develop a conclusion that refers back to the introduction of the speech and dramatically asks again that the audience accept the proposition.

7. When delivering the speech, be as dynamic and sincere as you can. The topic itself should help you accomplish that, provided you have chosen a topic about which you feel strongly. Use yourself as a model—let your strength of conviction demonstrate to your listeners the conviction they should experience.

Name _____

Date _____

Speech Type _____

Speech Outline, Project Number _____

Speech Topic: _____

Speech Objective: _____

_____

Speech Title: _____

Introduction

    Attention:

    Motivation:

    Credibility:

      Preview

      Body

      Conclusion

_____

Instructor's Comments:

CHAPTER 10
CONSTRUCTING APPEALS

PRIMARY (PREPARATIONAL) OBJECTIVE:
To adapt to and influence the psychological characteristics of the audience

Secondary Objectives	Corresponding Strategies
To appeal to audience motives	Show utility
	Relate to values
	Create inconsistency
	Appeal to needs
To appeal to audience connections	Problem-solution order
	Reflective-thought order
	Accepted-proposed order
	Climax-anticlimax order
	Motivated sequence order
	Statement of reasons
	Comparative advantages
	Residues order
To appeal to audience reasoning	One- or two-sided messages
	Emotional or logical appeals
To appeal to audience emotions	Humor
	Fear appeals
	Vivid descriptions
	Emotional comparisons
	Emotional display
To close the deal	Action-recommendation step
	Visualization-advantages step
	Rebuttal step

CHAPTER OBJECTIVES

After studying this chapter, you should be able to:

- Construct statements that appeal to audience motives
- Organize persuasive messages so that they establish desired connections in the listeners' minds
- Determine whether one- or two-sided arguments are appropriate in a given situation
- Determine whether emotional or logical appeals are appropriate in a given situation
- Construct messages that appeal to listeners' emotions
- Develop a clear statement of recommended actions
- Develop a list of the advantages that grow out of the recommended actions
- List and answer potential audience objections to the recommended actions

INTRODUCTION

A few years ago, I left university teaching and entered business, accepting a position as an internal consultant in a large manufacturing firm. About four weeks after I had begun, I was called into a meeting in which the personnel manager of our manufacturing plant in Johannesburg, South Africa, presented a particularly vexing problem: Employees were often not obeying the orders their supervisors gave. What, he wanted to know, could he do to improve the motivation of his work force?

When we asked for a little more information, some interesting facts about his problem emerged. It seems that the work force consisted almost exclusively of people in the Zulu tribe. They lived together, came to work together, worked together, and went home together. All of the tribal officials, including the chieftains, were a part of the work force. The supervisors, however, were not Zulu. Thus, what often would happen was this: the supervisor would issue an order; the worker would say, "Hold on a minute," and leave to check with his tribal chief; if the chief said the order was all right, the worker would comply; if the chief said "Aw, don't bother," the worker would simply forget it. In effect, then, the tribal chiefs were running the plant.

After hearing all of this, we gravely nodded, expressed sincere sympathy, and asked to leave the room so that we could confer. Then we went to lunch, had a few giggles, and returned. We reentered the room (again with grave expressions), and after a brief silence, we gave the advice for which he had traveled 10,000 miles: "Promote your tribal chiefs." And promote them he did. Granted, the decision wasn't easy to implement: the chiefs had to be trained in methods of supervision, paperwork, and so on. But the effect was dramatic. Production went up, absenteeism went down, turnover among the work force is now even lower than it had been; indeed, almost every indicator important to business has shown dramatic improvement. We had solved the "motivation" problem in our South African plant.

But was this really a motivation problem? I don't think so. The workers already were motivated. Motivated to do what? Motivated to do as their chiefs asked. And the reason underlying that motivation was twofold. First, the chiefs had credibility—something the supervisors lacked in the minds of the work force. And second, the chiefs had available to them much more powerful motivational and emotional appeals. The supervisors could threaten workers with suspension or firing, or they could promise them increased wages or better benefits. The chiefs could promise life and threaten death. No wonder the workers found the chiefs more persuasive than the supervisors.

Probably you are not a tribal chief. Even so, the principles illustrated in the situation described above apply to you. Certainly, the elements of source credibility we see here are consistent with the things we learned about credibility in Chapter 8. But consider something else. What relationship between appeals to reason and appeals to emotion do you see in this story? I suspect that the supervisors could supply all sorts of good reasons to the workers: that good work would make the business successful, that good performance would keep the worker employed, and so on. But the chiefs could supply something else: emotional appeals. The workers' feelings of fear, hope, pride, loyalty, and so on all were involved in the statements the chiefs made. And the results are clear. Emotion won out over logic; the reasons given by the supervisors were overpowered by the appeals made by the tribal chiefs.

But we need to note something important here. In the previous chapter, we talked about the importance of reasons in persuasion. Really, we are still talking about reasons here. Rather than consider reasons based upon fact and argument, however, we are moving in this chapter toward the realm of reasons based upon emotion. We will consider four secondary objectives, each of which leads to achievement of our primary objective, appealing to the psychology of our audience. First, we will examine the strategies whereby we can appeal to listeners' motives. Second, we will study strategies for appealing to the connections listeners make between ideas or things; that is, we will look at some techniques for organizing our information so that it has maximum influence on our audience. Third, we will consider strategies of argument that allow us to appeal to the reasoning processes of our audiences. And finally, we will investigate strategies for appealing directly to the emotions of our listeners. Through all of these appeals, we will seek strategies that can supplement and add impact to the credibility and argument strategies we saw in the preceding chapters.

APPEALING TO MOTIVES

In Chapter 2, we considered briefly the motives (or drives, or needs) that cause people to behave. We saw that, according to one theory, they act in order to reduce their physiological needs, their safety needs, their social needs, their esteem needs, and their needs for self-actualization. We also considered other elements of people's minds: their values, their needs to maintain consistency, and so on. We come now to the question, How can we use these things? How can we appeal to the beliefs, attitudes, and desires of our listeners. In this section, we will suggest four strategies that may be used individually or in combination to appeal to the things our listeners want.

Show Utility

A general approach to motivation takes into account the consequences of the thing you are offering, whether it is the information you are about to present, the behavior you are about to advocate, the attitude you are about to argue for, and so on. Generally, three such consequences are possible. First is *approach,* whereby people do or think something because they believe it will acquire for them something they want. We already have some idea of what people want—the five needs we previously specified: physiological, safety, social, esteem, and self-actualization. Using this knowledge, we can construct messages that offer to satisfy needs presently unsatisfied or to better satisfy needs now receiving only minimal satisfaction. Certainly, advertisers use these appeals. We are told, for example, that use of a certain toothpaste will give us "sex appeal," presumably allowing us to satisfy a need now unsatisfied or badly satisfied. Similarly, we can suggest to our receivers that we are about to provide them the means for better need satisfaction.

Escape is a second consequence. When undesirable things are happening to us, we look for ways to stop them—to escape from our predicament. We can offer escape to our listeners, of course. Advertisers do it all the time. If we want to escape our dandruff, we have only to use Head and Shoulders; our bad breath can be escaped by using Listerine. Since people without dandruff and bad breath also are more attractive to the opposite sex, advertisers imply, we can even satisfy our needs better. Thus the appeal has double impact.

The third consequence is *avoidance.* Perhaps things are fine now. Our needs are satisfied, and we face no undesirable situations. Still, we can be motivated if someone can convince us that our need satisfaction is threatened and that we must do something to avoid losing that satisfaction. Environmentalists use this sort of appeal: things are fine now, but unless we abandon pressurized spray containers the ozone layer in the atmosphere will be destroyed to the detriment of the entire world. Or antismoking campaigns can be seen to use the same strategy: you are healthy now, perhaps, but if you continue smoking your health may be ruined. And we find the same sort of appeals at stockholders' meetings. The company prospers now, we might be told, but unless federal legislation is passed to protect us from foreign competition, our profits will drop sharply within the next quarter. We do as the speaker tells us in order to avoid undesirable consequences.

In summary, then, utility-based appeals involve two basic stages. First, we must determine what our listener wants, dislikes, or fears (basing that determination upon our understanding of human needs) and, second, we must construct appeals based upon these tendencies. By presenting these appeals early in our message, we can motivate the listener to attend our message and perhaps to modify his or her attitudes, beliefs, or behaviors.

Relate to Audience Values

Earlier we observed that people have value systems concerning what is right, moral, desirable, and so on, and that they wish to think and behave in ways consistent with those values. The value-based appeal takes this tendency into account by proceeding through two basic stages. First, we present the value to which we wish to appeal (fairness, equality, justice, and so on) and note that we and the listener share adherence to that value. In so doing, we have both established common ground with the

listener and laid the foundation for our appeal. Then, second, we offer one of the
following arguments: (1) that what we are about to present is wholly consistent with
that value; (2) that what we are about to suggest violates fewer values than does the
present situation; (3) that urgent need necessitates violation of this value; or (4) that
the value is outmoded and should be ignored. Current examples of each of these
appeals are apparent. Advocates of the Equal Rights Amendment argue that ratifica-
tion of the amendment is consistent with our value system; people who advocate
legalized prostitution and gambling hold that, while these things may violate some of
our values, current enforcement techniques violate even more; those who suggest
drugs or brain surgery to deal with violent criminals concede that these steps violate
values but argue that there is an urgent need to stop crime; and advocates of increased governmental control over business and industry suggest that our values of
free enterprise and government nonintervention are outmoded in the face of today's
economic realities. Thus, we can motivate audience interest by pointing out and
building upon one of the values they hold dear.

Create Inconsistency

In Chapter 2, we saw yet another characteristic of the human mind: the desire to
maintain consistent beliefs, attitudes, values, and behaviors. Again, we can appeal to
this desire through a two-stage process. As in the utility and value appeals, our first
step is to analyze our listener: What does she (or he) believe? What are her attitudes
toward us and our topic? What values does she hold? What does she do? Then we
move to our second step, showing her inconsistency in her thoughts or actions, or
simply arguing for the thing we want. The latter strategy is appropriate if we discern
that the listener thinks us a credible source and that she (or he) will not immediately
reject our viewpoint. Remember, listeners want to agree with sources toward whom
they feel positively. Therefore, if we are a credible source, we can create inconsistency in audience members' minds simply by telling them that they are wrong.

The difficulty with using the inconsistency strategy becomes apparent when we
consider a principle we saw a bit earlier: people want to be comfortable psychologically, and they may avoid information that produces psychological discomfort. To
keep them from immediately turning us off, then, we must choose carefully the
inconsistencies we are going to point out, and after we point them out we must
quickly offer to provide the audience with information that will help them resolve the
inconsistency. For example, in speaking to a group of smokers; you might tell them
that the surgeon general has determined that smoking is hazardous to their health and
that their smoking is in conflict with their desire to remain healthy. But, you quickly
add, in this speech you will tell them how to resolve this problem with a method that
will give them even further benefit in the long run. Thus, we have presented an
inconsistency that is immediately evident to the audience and closely related to their
needs and, therefore, motivates their interest. If we can create an inconsistency that is
both immediately evident and important, then, we can use this strategy effectively.

Appeal to Audience Needs

To some degree, we examined need-related appeals earlier when we discussed utility
appeals. Still, there are three strategies geared specifically to appeal to audience

needs, and it is helpful to study them. Specifically, they are:

1. Promise to help them satisfy unsatisfied needs. When we can use this appeal, it is extremely effective. Consider, for example, most of the advertisements you see on television. Most of them try to sell their products by telling you that, if you use the product, you can satisfy some need presently unsatisfied. Is your need for inclusion not met because no one will accept you? Join the Pepsi generation. Need more excitement because things are dull? Coke adds life. Unpopular, because you are disgustingly flabby? Pepsi Light has just one calorie (as do Tab, sugar-free 7Up, and others). Do you get no affection from the opposite sex (or, for that matter, from the same sex)? Whiter teeth, fresher breath, and odor-free armpits and feet should help enormously. Is your status sagging? A new Cadillac (or Mercedes or Porsche) and some designer bluejeans will take care of that. In fact, no matter what your unsatisfied need may be, someone somewhere has developed a product to satisfy it.

The principle used in these advertisements is the same you should use in your persuasive speeches. First, you should identify something the audience want but are not getting: inclusion, affection, security, or some other need. Then, during your speech, identify that unmet need for your audience and show them how your proposal will help them to satisfy it. Naturally, they have to be convinced that the need truly exists and that your proposal will indeed cause that need to be satisfied; thus, the reasoning techniques we saw in the preceding chapter come into play. Used well, this method of appealing to audience needs can be an extremely effective strategy.

2. Promise to help them satisfy needs better. In our society, most people have most of their needs satisfied to some degree. Thus, instead of promising to satisfy unsatisfied needs, we instead may have to talk about improvements in need satisfaction. Your friendly neighborhood aluminum siding salesperson, for example, can hardly tell you that your house doesn't work; thus, he or she instead talks about improving house performance (it will last longer, look better, and so on). Since people always are looking for ways to improve need satisfaction, they are motivated to hear the salesperson's pitch. Again, this strategy can work for you. Determine what your speech can do for the audience members—what needs it can help them satisfy better—and then tell them about it at the beginning of the address. Then, come through for them.

3. Promise to help them continue satisfaction of threatened needs. This strategy is similar to the avoidance type of utility appeal we saw earlier. In essence, you say to them, "Look. Everything is fine now. You have enough food to eat, water to drink, and air to breathe. But there are storm clouds on the horizon. Danger looms. Unless some changes are made, and made soon, you no longer will have these things." In other words, your needs are satisfied now, but that satisfaction is threatened. In this speech, I will tell you how to overcome that threat and continue need satisfaction. Often, this strategy takes the form of the so-called fear appeal, whereby you try to motivate audience interest by scaring them out of their wits. If the issue is an important one and the threat you describe is credible, this strategy will work; if the issue is unimportant or the threat unrealistic, the audience will tell you to go spin your ghost stories somewhere else. We will speak more of this strategy later. For now, simply note that it must be used carefully in order to be effective.

To appeal to audience needs, then, you can use any of three strategies with

good effect. You can offer to help them satisfy needs presently unsatisfied, better
satisfy needs now being satisfied to a degree, or continue satisfying needs threatened
by some powerful force. Like the strategies we saw earlier, including showing utility,
relating to audience values, and creating inconsistency, these need-related appeals
are effective for motivating your audience members.

APPEALING TO CONNECTIONS

When we considered informative speaking and the principles that underlie giving
information, we saw that people learn by making connections. A bit later, we also
noted that during our speeches, we must use organizational patterns to create the
connections we want our audiences to see rather than allow those audiences to form
connections on their own. These principles also apply to persuasion. In order to
influence our listeners, causing them to make the changes we want them to make, we
must create connections for them that will lead them to the conclusions we want
them to draw. Specifically, we want them to see that there are good reasons for
making the change we advocate, and that our proposed change will meet the needs
described in those reasons. In this section, then, we will examine some of the organizational strategies we can use to appeal to the connections between ideas our listeners will form.

Problem-Solution Order

As its name implies, this pattern first convinces the audience that some problem exists
and then presents the solution the speaker would like the audience to implement.
Probably the most commonly used method of organization in persuasive speaking,
the problem-solution pattern serves as the basis for most of the persuasive strategies
described in this book. As we saw above, you must establish a need for the audience
to change their beliefs, attitudes, or behaviors, and then you must show them how
that need will be satisfied when that change is made. That is, show them the problem,
then give them a solution.

Reflective-Thought Order

Similar to the problem-solution order, this pattern, based upon the method of inquiry
developed by philosopher John Dewey, consists of five steps: (1) define and delimit
the problem; (2) analyze the problem; (3) suggest possible solutions; (4) evaluate
possible solutions; and (5) select the best solution. This pattern is particularly effective
with initially disagreeing audiences, for it both gives the impression of objectivity on
the part of the speaker (even though he or she already has determined what the best
alternative will be) and leads the audience through the speaker's reasoning process
before hitting them with the solution the speaker advocates.

Accepted-Proposed Order

Like the familiar-unfamiliar pattern in informative speaking, this pattern takes the
audience first through arguments with which they already agree and then leads them
into arguments to which they might not be quite as receptive. Ideally, the speaker can
begin with things the audience strongly favor, then move to less favored things, and

finally arrive at the least favored arguments. In so doing, he or she builds momentum and gets the audience on his or her side and makes them more likely to accept the controversial ideas presented later in the speech.

Climax-Anticlimax Orders

A great deal of controversy presently exists concerning the order in which arguments of different strengths ought to be placed. As Applbaum and Anatol (1974) indicate in their summary of relevant research, some theorists believe that the strongest argument should be placed first, while others hold that the strongest should be placed last. But all of the researchers agree on one thing: the best arguments should *not* be placed in the middle of the speech; the audience probably will miss it completely if it is located there. To determine whether the strongest argument should go first (with the second-strongest second, the third-strongest third, and so on in the "anticlimax" order) or last (with the weakest first, a stronger one second, and so on in the "climax" order), we must consider the nature of the audience. If they seem interested and motivated, you probably should start with your weaker arguments and build to your stronger ones, sustaining interest as you proceed. If, however, they seem apathetic, begin with the strongest argument to get their attention; if their attention wanes later in the speech, they still will have heard your most powerful appeal.

Motivated Sequence Order

As presented by Ehninger, Monroe and Gronbeck (1978), this sequence consists of five steps: attention, need, satisfaction, visualization, and action. You should already know what the first three steps are; if you don't, please reread everything prior to this page. Visualization occurs when the speaker asks the audience (and helps them) to visualize how wonderful things will be if only they do as he or she asks. Action, of course, is the final step in which the speaker tells the audience specifically what they should do to satisfy the need identified earlier in the speech. Like the problem-solution pattern, the motivated sequence order serves as the basis for the organizational pattern recommended throughout this book.

Statement of Reasons

The most straightforward pattern of persuasive speaking begins by saying, "There are three reasons why you should . . ." and then presents and proves those three (or four or however many) reasons to the audience one at a time. This approach, of course, can be used in conjunction with other orders, such as climax-anticlimax or accepted-proposed.

Comparative Advantages

This sequence is best suited to speeches in which you intend not to solve some grave problem but to suggest a better course of action. Your task is to prove to your audience that, compared to what they presently are doing or thinking, your proposal is advantageous. Most of your speech thus is devoted to listing the advantages your proposal would provide and proving that they will in fact result.

Incorporating elements of the other patterns listed above, this pattern operates according to a process of elimination whereby you systematically propose and eliminate every possible solution except one (yours) to the problem you and your audience face. Like the reflective thinking pattern, this order is an effective technique for "sneaking up" on an audience likely to disagree with your claim: by the time they hear what you really are advocating, they already have heard your line of reasoning.

Again, all of these organizational patterns are effective under certain circumstances. Your choice of a specific pattern must rest upon your analysis of the audience's characteristics and the sort of material you are going to present.

APPEALING TO REASONING

We already have devoted considerable time to methods by which arguments can be developed in persuasive speeches. Here, we will consider only two more argument-related matters through which we can appeal to our listeners' reasoning processes.

The first is the issue of one-sided versus two-sided messages. The question we face is, Should we present only our own point of view, or should we present and refute other opposing viewpoints as well? Obviously, several of the organizational patterns outlined above automatically cause us to present both sides; however, there will be occasions in which we can choose whether to present one or two sides of the issue. Research by Hovland, Lumsdaine, and Sheffield (1949) and McGinnes (1966), among others, suggests that when deciding which approach to take, we should consider three characteristics of the audience.

1. Attitude. If the audience disagree with your viewpoint, you should present two sides—theirs and yours. Your purpose, after all, is to show them that your ideas or suggestions are superior to theirs, and in order to do that effectively you must draw direct comparisons between the two. Ignoring their views and presenting only your own, conversely, probably will only serve to convince the audience that you are a biased source not worth listening to.

2. Knowledge. If, by virtue of education or experience, the members of the audience probably know both sides of the argument, you must provide them with both sides in your message. As we saw earlier, you must convince them of your competence, and to do that you must show them that you know as much about the topic as they do. Presenting only your own side to a knowledgeable audience might cause them to conclude that you are ignorant or biased or both.

3. Credibility. If you are highly credible, give only your side; that's all the audience want to hear anyway. But if your credibility is low, you might be able to improve it by presenting both sides, showing yourself to be both knowledgeable and objective.

Resolution of the one-side versus two-side problem lies in your analysis of the audience. If they are hostile, knowledgeable, or unconvinced of your credibility, give them both sides. But if they are in agreement with you, not particularly knowl-

To Persuade, Appeal to Audience Emotions

edgeable, and convinced of your credibility, present only your side—they will accept it willingly. But note an important thing in the preceding two sentences: the use of *or* in the first and of *and* in the second. If just one of the three conditions described in the both-sides sentence exists, you must use the two-sided approach; only if all three of the conditions listed in the one-side sentence exist should you present just your own viewpoint. Such situations are somewhat rare; consequently, most of your speeches will take the two-sided approach.

The second argument-related issue is whether to use logical appeals or emotional appeals or both. Considerable research effort has been devoted to answering this question. Hartmann (1936), examining the effectiveness of various appeals made to voters during the 1936 election, found that emotional appeals typically were more persuasive than factual arguments. But Weiss (1960) found the opposite effect, observing that factual arguments are more effective than emotional ones in changing attitudes. Other studies (Bowers, 1963; Carmichael and Cronkhite, 1965) also have found at least partial superiority on the side of logical arguments. Thus, the question remains, Which should we use?

Again, we must look to our audience for the answer. The following characteristics seem relevant:

1. Attitude. If they agree with you, use emotional appeals to whip them into a frenzy; there is not much point in proving to them things they already accept. On the other hand, if they disagree, you must use logical arguments to convince them of the correctness of your views. Then, having done that, you might want to use emotional appeals to stir them into action.

2. Credibility. If you are highly credible, use emotional appeals to arouse the audience who already will accept virtually anything you say. If your credibility is moderate or low, use logic and evidence to raise it and then resort to emotional strategies.

3. Mood. Do the audience seem in an excitable, emotionally charged mood, or do they seem more inclined toward thoughtful, deliberate consideration of issues? Probably you will be most effective if you adapt to the mood you percieve your audience to possess. Part of this, incidentally, is dictated by your topic and the listeners' resultant expectations. Some topics are more geared toward logic and calm, dispassionate reasoning, and the audience will expect that approach. Other topics are more emotionally oriented so that expectations will lean in that direction. Again, you should try to anticipate and adapt to audience expectations.

As with virtually all of the other strategies we have seen in this text, the key here is audience analysis and adaptation. Generally, you will want to use both logical and emotional appeals, but the degree to which you emphasize each and the order in which you use them will be determined by your perceptions of the audiences to which you speak.

APPEALING TO EMOTIONS

Now that we have seen the circumstances under which emotional appeals seem most effective, let's examine some of the actual emotional appeals you might employ.

Humor. Many speakers throughout history have been known for their use of humor to persuade their audiences. Truman and the Kennedy brothers, to cite just four examples, have had some of their political success attributed to their effective use of humor. Happily, scientific evidence tends to support the effectiveness of humor in persuasion. While Gruner (1965) initially found no effects attributable to humor, later studies by Osterhouse and Brock (1970) and Zimbardo et al. (1970) found that the characteristics of the audience seem to make a difference. If they are in agreement with the source, humor seems to make them even more so. Interestingly, though, for all sources, even those with low credibility, the use of humor seems to produce improvements in credibility perceptions. In all situations where humor is appropriate, then, you would be well advised to use it.

Fear Appeals. Would-be persuaders commonly employ fear appeals. As Colburn's (1968) summary demonstrates, a great deal of research has been conducted to assess the impact of fear appeals, with an equally great number of conclusions being reached. Taken together, however, they do suggest some conditions under which fear appeals seem most effective. First, they seem to work best when the source has high credibility. In fact, evidence exists that if a low-credibility source uses fear appeals, his or her credibility drops even lower. Second, fear appeals work best with topics the audience consider important; unimportant topics are too easily dismissed by the audience. Third, the greatest effect is obtained if the threat is real to the audience—if they are unable to rationalize it away. Consider one of the most prominent examples of fear appeals: the message on the side of a cigarette pack telling you that the surgeon general has determined that cigarette smoking is dangerous to your health. A message from a credible source concerning an important topic, certainly, yet ineffective; the smoking rate continues to climb. Why? Apparently, people still can rationalize the threat away, telling themselves, "It won't happen to me" or "I don't really smoke that much." The same thing is true with seatbelt usage campaigns: people rationalize away the life-and-death messages they receive from credible sources. Unless the threat is made real to the audience, the fear appeal will probably not be effective. Finally, such appeals work best when immediate action is called for by the speaker and when specific instructions for carrying out those actions are provided. That is, after you scare your audience, tell them what to do about it, and how. Given all of these things, then, fear appeals can add substantially to the impact of your message.

Vivid Descriptions.   Yet another way to involve audience emotions in your speech is to use vivid, colorful descriptions, which paint in the audience members' minds realistic pictures of the things you are describing. To make your antismoking appeals effective, for example, you might describe in vivid detail the physiological effects of smoking—the black lungs oozing gooey fluids and so on. This would also serve, incidentally, to make your fear appeal more realistic to your audience and enhance its impact. In any case, vivid descriptions do seem to arouse the emotions of your audience by getting their imaginations actively involved in your speech.

Emotional Comparisons.   Being careful to avoid the transfer fallacy, you still might be able to draw comparisons between the things you discuss and other things the audience are emotionally involved in. For example, the hackneyed statement that "Communism is a cancer spreading across the face of the globe" ties together the topic, communism, and something to which negative emotions probably are attached, cancer. By using similar sorts of comparisons, you may be able to stir the emotions of your listeners.

Emotional Display.   If you want your listeners to feel a certain way, you must first show them that you feel that way yourself. In other words, display the emotion you want your listeners to experience. Such a display serves several purposes. It shows your sincerity in asking for the feelings you desire; it serves as a model for the audience, in effect showing them how to act; and it might even be contagious, actually helping the audience to feel the way you do. Obviously, insincere, unconvincing emotional displays will only alienate the audience; you must truly feel the emotions you display, or you must be one heck of a good actor. So if you choose to use this device (and you should use it if you want to arouse emotions), first get yourself involved in the speech so that you feel what you want the audience to feel.

There are other techniques for appealing to audience emotions. Still, when used properly, the methods outlined above are usually effective in producing the emotions that will drive your audience to feel, think, or do as you ask.

CLOSING THE DEAL

In the preceding sections, you have examined strategies for appealing to listeners' motives, connections, reasoning, and emotions. In prior chapters, we studied methods of enhancing credibility and of reasoning clearly. All of these things lead up to this last step of the persuasive speech: closing the deal. It is here that we implement the action-recommendation step, the visualization-advantages step, and the rebuttal step and end our persuasive message.

The action-recommendation step should present as briefly and clearly as possible the exact steps you want the audience to follow (if you are presenting a claim of policy) or the exact beliefs or attitudes you want them to hold (for claims of fact or value). In essence, you ask them to accept your main objective. The most effective action steps; incidentally, ask the audience to do something immediately and provide the audience with the opportunity to do it (for example, "Give blood at the table set up at the back of the auditorium" or "Place your contribution in the collection plate being passed around now") before the impact of the speech has time to wear off. You also might indicate to the audience what you personally intend to do, and thus show your own commitment and act as a behavioral model for them.

The visualization-advantages step seeks to paint for the audience a picture of the future—one in which they will reap the abundant rewards of their actions. At the end of your antismoking speech, for example, you might describe vividly the joys they will experience of breathing freely again, tasting food again, and so on. The key is, use vivid language to create the emotional impact we observed in the preceding section.

Lastly, the rebuttal step occurs when you choose to provide answers to reservations the audience might have. This step occurs as a sort of postscript in which, having completed the main part of your speech, you state and answer the objections you think are most likely to be in your listeners' minds. The success of this step, as with most of the others we have discussed, rests upon your ability to analyze your audience accurately. You should try to anticipate the five most important objections they are likely to have and develop persuasive answers. Then, at the conclusion of your speech, you can present those objections one by one, answering each as you present it. But care must be taken to avoid two problems. First, don't bring up objections your audience are not likely to have thought of already. Should you do that, you will either cause them to think that you are suggesting the objection just so that you can answer it (the "strawman" strategy), or you may provide them with ammunition they can use to argue, if only mentally, against your position. Either way, you lose. Second, don't bring up objections for which you have no reasonable answer. Better to leave the audience wondering whether you could answer it than to prove to them that you cannot.

To close the deal at the end of your persuasive speech, then, you need to do three things. First, tell them specifically what you want them to think or do. Second, project for them how wonderful things will be if they do as you ask. And third, where appropriate, answer any objections they might have to complying with your recommendations. Then, after again emphasizing what you want them to do, quit.

SUMMARY

In some instances, emotional appeals are far stronger than appeals based on credibility or logic. In all instances, the strongest persuasive appeals combine credibility, reasoning, and emotion. Thus, in this chapter we considered some strategies to involve audience emotions in your speeches. We first discussed motive appeals and examined ways of showing utility, relating to values, creating inconsistency, and appealing to needs. Second, we turned to the connections listeners make and studied some patterns to organize persuasive materials. Third, we observed two aspects of listeners' reasoning: one- versus two-sided messages, such as humor, fear appeals, vivid descriptions, emotional comparisons, and emotional displays. And, lastly, we talked about the stages involved in closing the deal. With all of these considerations taken into account, then, we have completed our preparation of persuasive speech materials.

REFERENCES

Applbaum, R. and K. Anatol. *Strategies for Persuasive Communication.* Columbus, Ohio: Charles E. Merrill, 1974.

Bowers, J. "Language Intensity, Social Introversion, and Attitude Change," *Speech Monographs* 30(1963):345–352.

Carmichael, C. and G. Cronkhite. "Frustration and Language Intensity," *Speech Monographs* 32(1965):107–111.

Colburn, C. "Fear-Arousing Appeals," in *Speech Communication: Analysis and Readings,* eds. H. Martin and K. Andersen, pp. 214–222. Boston: Allyn and Bacon, 1968.

Ehninger, D., A. Monroe, and B. Gronbeck. *Principles and Types of Speech Communication,* 8th ed. Glenview, Ill.: Scott Foresman, 1978.

Gruner, C. "An Experimental Study of the Effectiveness of Oral Satire in Modifying Attitude," *Speech Monographs* 32(1965):149–154.

Hartmann, G. "A Field Experiment on the Comparative Effectiveness of Emotional and Rational Political Leaflets in Determining Election Results," *Journal of Abnormal and Social Psychology* 31(1936):99–114.

Hovland, C., A. Lumsdaine, and F. Sheffield. *Experiments on Mass Communications.* Princeton: Princeton University Press, 1949.

McGinnes, E. "Studies in Persuasion: III. Reactions of Japanese Students to One-Sided and Two-Sided Communications," *Journal of Social Psychology* 70(1966): 87–93.

Osterhouse, R. and T. Brock. "Distraction Increase Yielding to Propaganda by Inhibiting Counterarguing," *Journal of Personality and Social Psychology* 15(1970): 344–358.

Weiss, W. "Emotional Arousal and Attitude Change," *Psychological Reports* 6(1960): 267–280.

Zimbardo, P. et al. "Modifying the Impact of Persuasive Communication with External Distraction," *Journal of Personality and Social Psychology* 16(1970): 669–680.

EXHIBIT 1

Perhaps you are unimpressed by these examples and these statistics about death by handgun. Perhaps you think these facts have no relevance to you. Well consider this. Odds are that about one-third of the people in this room will be threatened at least once in their lives by a handgun. And whenever a threat is made, it might be carried out. You might be killed by a gun. You might be wounded by a gun. Do you have any idea what it feels like to be shot? At first, you don't feel anything. Then the wound starts to burn. You feel the blood oozing from the wound and trickling down your body. You may be unable to use the part of you that is shot—perhaps forever. Being shot hurts, and that hurt could last the rest of your life.

Do you own a gun? Does anyone in your family? Nearly half of the wounds that occur by shooting are self-inflicted. Do you have a brother or sister? Imagine him or her lying in a pool of blood, dead because he or she didn't know how to handle the gun he or she found.

These situations are preventable. There is no need for you to be threatened, even shot, by someone else. There is no need for someone you love to be hurt or killed by a gun. The information I am about to present to you could save your life and the lives of your loved ones.

Analyze the motivational devices used in this introduction to the speech about gun control. What devices do you find?

EXHIBIT 2

But what do you care. Television hasn't affected you, right? You haven't committed any crimes under the influence of television. Probably no one you know has been moved to commit a crime because of television. Or maybe television has affected you. Have you ever had anything of yours stolen? Television teaches people how. Has anyone you know been assaulted or robbed? Television offers graduate work in those crimes. Do you own insurance? Whose premiums help to pay people whose losses are covered by insurance companies? Some of those losses were the result of crimes inspired by television. Do you pay taxes? Your tax dollars support law enforcement agencies whose time is devoted to combating the effects of televised violence. Maybe you have not suffered directly from television-inspired crime, but I guarantee that indirectly you have.

I can't stop crime; probably no one can completely. But I believe that crime can be reduced if we stop inspiring and educating potential criminals. And if we reduce crime, we save our money and perhaps our lives. Therefore, I want to discuss something that, I believe, will reduce the crime rate in America.

Analyze the motivational devices used in this introduction to the speech about television violence. What devices do you see?

PROJECT

THE SPEECH TO ACTIVATE

This type of speech has a specific purpose: to persuade the audience to take some specific action proposed by the speaker. Thus, speeches of this sort are primarily persuasive although they also may attempt to inform and entertain. In content, speeches to activate argue that there exists a need for some action, present a plan for that action, list advantages that will befall the audience if they take that action, and then answer any potential objections the audience may have. Such speeches designed to produce changes in listeners' beliefs and attitudes as well as in their behaviors must be prepared carefully. Indeed, the speech to activate may be the most difficult type of speech to perform successfully. As you prepare this type of speech, you should proceed through the following stages:

1. Select a topic. Choose some issue about which you feel strongly, and about which you want your audience to take some specific action. Possible topic areas for speeches to activate include:

   Reducing energy consumption
   Voting for some candidate
   Giving blood
   Donating money for a cause
   Attending an athletic event
   Supporting some legislation

   Going on strike
   Joining some union or group
   Writing to some organization to
     support or oppose their programs
   Buying something

   The topic should be controversial, and it should be relevant to your audience; that is, they should be able to do something about it.
2. State your overall objective for this speech.
3. Analyze the audience and establish your goals. Determine what their beliefs, attitudes, values, and so on are likely to be and then decide what things you must accomplish to achieve your objective.
4. Develop your materials. Gather information about current conditions as they relate to your topic (so that you can prove that some change is needed) and about the change you will propose (so that you can prove your advantages) and develop the reasoning and appeals you will use to support your arguments.
5. Organize your materials. Establish three or four clear reasons why change is needed, lay out a clear plan of action, list two or three advantages coming out of the plan, and develop answers to two or three major objections your audience are likely to pose.
6. Develop an introduction that performs the functions of attention, motivation, and credibility.
7. Develop a dramatic conclusion that demands action, preferably to be taken at that moment, by your listeners.

8. Deliver the speech in a sincere, dramatic fashion. Use visual aids where possible, particularly to make the need for change as dramatic as you can. Use language that is vivid and specific, creating clear images in the listeners' minds. Involve the audience as much as possible, through rhetorical questions, references to specific audience members, and so on.

Name _____

Date _____

Speech Type _____

Speech Outline, Project Number _____

Speech Topic: _____

Speech Objective: _____

_____

Speech Title: _____

Introduction
    Attention:

    Motivation:

    Credibility:

      Preview

      Body

      Conclusion

Instructor's Comments:

PART V
PRESERVATION

I have seen it happen. The speaker has delivered a terrific speech, and now it is time for audience questions. An audience member asks a question. The speaker can't answer. Another audience member asks another question. The speaker answers incorrectly. Still another question is asked. The speaker becomes flustered as he tries to "wing it" through a response. Audience members begin to whisper to each other: "He really doesn't know what he's talking about." "He must have paid somebody to write that speech." "I wonder how much of what he said is also wrong." "What a loser." The effect of the speech and the credibility of the speaker are ruined.

When audience participation is allowed, and after most presentations it is, you must be able to handle it well if the positive impact of your speech is to be preserved. Indeed, a well-managed question-and-answer session can salvage a weak speech or enhance a strong one. While experimental evidence does not exist to prove this conclusion, my own experience suggests that, in many ways, audiences place even more emphasis upon question-and-answer sessions than they do on the actual speech. The reason: speeches are prepared ahead of time while question-and-answer sessions reveal the personality and thought processes of the speaker as he or she stands before the audience. Thus, even if you deliver a very mediocre speech, you can, through an effective audience participation session, leave your listeners with an extremely favorable impression.

In this last part, then, we will examine one final primary objective that leads to achievement of your main objective. Specifically, we will consider how we should handle postspeech audience participation so that it preserves and even enhances the positive impact of our speeches. We will examine the secondary objectives that lead to achievement of this primary objective, and we will study the strategies that seem to promote achievement of the secondary objectives. But remember something important: the strategies we discuss here actually are based upon all of the strategies we have considered in this text. Everything we have said about speakers, messages, audiences, and so on applies to the question-and-answer session. Thus, the things you read in the next chapter are simply principles extracted from our overall knowledge about public speaking by objectives.

As you apply the principles for answering listeners' questions, which are discussed in the following chapter, you should keep in mind many of the things we have seen in earlier sections. For example:

1. Audience analysis. Question-and-answer sessions are both advantageous and disadvantageous in analyzing your audience. They are advantageous in that, by allowing the audience to ask questions, you discover what is important to them, understood by them, agreed with and disagreed with by them, and so on. In effect, they analyze themselves for you. On the other hand, the disadvantage is that, as you formulate your answer, you have only a split second to decide whether they will understand, agree with, accept, or even believe that answer. Thus, you must analyze them instantaneously as you stand there, trying to decide what to say.

2. Delivery. By their very nature, question-and-answer sessions are more informal (and hence less "canned") in their interactions between speaker and audience. Thus, you must take a more casual, conversational approach to your audience as you deal with them. Nevertheless, some elements of good delivery must be preserved. You cannot become "sloppy" in your behavior; propping yourself up on the podium or leaning against a handy wall is no more appropriate while answering questions than while delivering the prepared speech. In addition, vocal variety and fluency continue to be important as you answer questions: monotone responses or a great deal of stuttering and stammering will ruin the professional image you created during the speech. Thus, the nature of your delivery changes, but the quality of that delivery must remain high.

3. Providing information. The principles of getting attention, promoting understanding, and promoting retention still hold true during question-and-answer sessions. Getting attention is particularly difficult, for you are responding to the question of just one person. Nevertheless, you must speak to all audience members, and if their attention seems to be waning, you must use some of the devices seen in Chapter 5 to revive it. Similarly, you must show in your answers that your knowledge extends beyond the information you have in your notes, you must present that information in an organized, coherent fashion so that people will understand it, and you must intensify and associate that information as much as possible in order to help the audience remember it.

4. Achieving persuasion. Credibility, proof, and appeals remain important during the question-and-answer period. Perhaps credibility is the one element most impacted by the question-and-answer performance. After all, this period gives the audience a chance to see you "as you really are," without benefit of notes or preparation. They see your thought processes, they see your personality, they see how you deal with people. And based on all of this, they decide whether the impression they formed of you during the speech was correct or needs revision. In addition, they look for your ability to reason clearly without the benefit of preparation, for your command of facts or opinions that support the arguments you offer, and for reasons (or appeals) why they should feel as you want them to feel or do as you want them to do. Thus, you must continue to persuade them as you answer the questions they ask.

The question-and-answer session, then, provides some unique opportunities

and challenges. The things you do during this session probably will be given greater weight by your audience than were the things you did during the prepared speech. If they like you during the questioning period, they probably will forgive the mistakes you made during the address. If they are impressed by your command of information and argument as you respond to their questions, they probably will forget the weaknesses in your speech materials. However, if they dislike you, or if they discover that your knowledge is limited and your thinking foggy, they will forget all the good things you said in the speech and leave with a poor impression of you as a speaker. The importance of the question-and-answer session thus cannot be overstated; in the following chapter we will consider some techniques to meet the challenges and take advantage of the opportunities the session provides.

CHAPTER 11
HANDLING AUDIENCE PARTICIPATION

PRIMARY (PRESERVATIONAL) OBJECTIVE:

To handle postspeech audience participation in a manner that preserves—even enhances—the positive impact of the speech

Secondary Objectives	Corresponding Strategies
To prepare effectively	Keep objectives in mind Know topic and audience Anticipate question areas Prepare general response strategies
To present effectively	Be considerate of entire audience Respond encouragingly Be honest Avoid confrontations
To generate participation	Use nondirected questions Use directed questions Use redirected questions
To handle questions effectively	Repeat question Rephrase question Postpone troublesome questions Label and rephrase loaded questions

- Prepare thoroughly for question-and-answer sessions
- Present answers considerately, encouragingly, and honestly while avoiding confrontations
- Generate active participation by audience members
- Handle questions effectively

INTRODUCTION

Once upon a time, there was a famous scholar-lecturer and his not-quite-so famous chauffeur. The lecturer would deliver his speeches to packed houses across the country, and the chauffeur would drive him from one engagement to the next. Naturally, the two became good friends, so that each felt free to speak his mind to the other.

One night, after a particularly long, speech-filled day, the scholar remarked to the chauffeur, "Man, I sure wish I had your job. All you have to do is drive this car from one place to the next—no worries, no problems, just drive." "Are you kidding?" the chauffeur exclaimed. "You're the one with the easy job. You just go from one place to the next, delivering the same speech everywhere you go. I have to worry about maintenance, gas, traffic, insurance, and everything else; you just talk." The two argued for a long time, each contending that the other had the easier job. Finally, after much discussion, they arrived at a decision: they would switch places for one day to see which job truly was easiest.

The next evening, the scholar dressed in the chauffeur's uniform and the chauffeur dressed in the scholar's tuxedo. The scholar drove the limousine to the local auditorium, where he parked the car, stepped around to the rear, and opened the car door. The chauffeur stepped out and strode confidently into the hall, making his way quickly to the front, where he assumed the position behind the podium. The scholar, still dressed in the chauffeur's uniform, stood at the back of the auditorium to watch the fun.

To the scholar's amazement, the chauffeur was brilliant! He delivered the speech better than it ever had been delivered before. The audience were completely enthralled, and when the speech ended they erupted in standing applause. But then came the question-and-answer period. The first questioner was a young woman seated in the front row, and her question was incredible. To even ask such a question required at least a Ph.D. in the topic. No one in the audience even understood the question, much less had an answer. But there the question was, hanging out in front of everyone, waiting for the "scholar" chauffeur to prove his expertise by handling it.

The chauffeur was cool. While the question had reduced him to mush internally, on the outside he appeared as confident as ever. For a long moment he looked at the questioner. Then, slowly, he began to speak; "Young lady," he began, "that probably is the most simple-minded question I have been asked on this entire lecture tour. Only a complete moron would ask something like that. Why, to show you what a ridiculous question that is, I'm going to ask my chauffeur to answer it."

The day will come when you will find yourself in a similar situation, having to defend your views and to answer questions posed by your audience. If you handle that question-and-answer session effectively, you will preserve (and perhaps enhance) the positive impact of your speech. However, if you are unprepared to manage this situation effectively (and have no "chauffeur" in the back of the room to help you out), the positive impact of your speech may be completely destroyed. Thus, the purpose of this final brief chapter is to give you some strategies by which you might most effectively prepare for and conduct the audience participation sessions that so often follow presentation of your speech. We will consider some general principles for handling audience participation and then observe some techniques for generating participation when you want it and for handling questions when you get them.

GENERAL PRINCIPLES

In the preceding chapters of this book, we considered the preparation and presentation stages of speaking as we moved toward the achievement of our communication objectives. In this section we will maintain that division, looking first at some principles of preparation that should govern your actions as you anticipate question-and-answer sessions with your audience, and then considering some principles relevant to your actual behaviors during your interactions with audience members.

Principles of Preparation

1. *Keep your speaking objectives uppermost in your mind.* In the speech itself, everything you do or say should be directed toward the achievement of primary and secondary objectives, which in turn lead to the achievement of your overall objective. For example, your speech should be designed to get attention, motivate interest, establish credibility, clarify information, and so on, all leading toward elicitation of the response you want from your audience. In a question-and-answer session, your responses and behaviors must also be directed toward achievement of these goals. If, for example, you have chosen a stately, dignified style of delivery as one means of establishing credibility, you must maintain that style throughout the questioning period as well; to suddenly become informal and "laugh-it-up" in manner would confuse the audience, cause them to mistrust you, or cause them to discount the credibility your speech had established. Similarly, if you have used a great deal of evidence as a persuasive device in your speech, you should be able to continue citing evidence during the questioning; otherwise, the audience might conclude that you have only limited information and that you are "winging it" as you handle their questions. Thus, just as you devised and implemented strategies for goal achievement during your speech, so too should you seek to achieve those goals (perhaps by means of the same strategies) during your responses to audience questions.

2. *Know your topic and your audience.* The first half of this principle is pretty obvious. In the story that opened this chapter, our chauffeur knew his speech, but not his topic. The questioning period quickly could have revealed the limits of his knowledge. Similarly, if everything you know is in your speech, you will probably be pretty unimpressive during the questioning period. It therefore is crucial to know much more about your topic than you initially tell your audience.

Knowing your audience also is crucial, because that knowledge can help you avoid the nasty surprises too often sprung upon unprepared speakers. The key to successful responding is anticipation: if you can anticipate accurately audience members' questions, you can prepare for them; if you can prepare for them, you can handle them easily and impressively when they arise. Through the audience analysis we discussed early in this text, then, you can come to know your audience well enough to make educated guesses about their questioning behavior.

3. *Anticipate question areas.* Really, this third principle grows from the preceding one. Your knowledge of audience members' knowledge, interests, and attitudes should allow you to predict rather accurately the areas of your topic about which they will ask questions. Generally, your listeners will ask questions about things with which they are only slightly familiar, things in which they are interested, and things about which they disagree with you. Usually, questions springing from vague familiarity will seek additional knowledge, questions springing from interests will seek recommendations or deeper knowledge (such as what things you think should be done or what your attitudes are toward specific ideas), and questions springing from disagreement will seek to argue, either defending the questioner's viewpoint, attacking or probing yours, or both. Naturally, you will handle each type of question differently; thus, it is important that you predict both the topic area in which questions will fall and the sorts of questions likely to be asked.

4. *Prepare your general response strategies and gather necessary supporting materials.* That is, decide in general terms what your answer will be, and if your answer is likely to require proof or clarification, gather the information you need to do those things. You may never have to use those answers or supporting materials, of course, but it is nice to have them available rather than having to look frantically at the back of the room for a "chauffeur" who might handle the question.

Principles of Presentation

Whenever you confront the audience in a question-and-answer situation, you should adhere to certain principles as you deal with their comments. If you follow these principles, you will be far more likely to create a positive impression in the listeners' minds; if you violate them, the entire presentation could be ruined.

1. *Be considerate of your entire audience.* At first glance, this would seem to be one of those "Who can argue with that?" statements—the sort of thing one sees offered in support of motherhood, apple pie, the flag, and highway safety. Of course we should be considerate of our entire audience. But the implications of this statement are considerably less obvious and thus demand illumination:

   a. *Do not allow one or two people to dominate the questioning.* Give everyone a chance to participate by calling on a variety of people to ask questions (if in fact you are the person controlling the questioning), by forcing questioners to keep their questions brief and to the point, and by keeping your answers equally brief and relevant.

   b. *Give answers everyone can understand.* If, for example, a particularly knowledgeable listener asks you an unusually complex question whose answer would confuse everyone within miles, postpone the question by asking the questioner to speak with you after the meeting. Alternatively, you might give a brief and simple (although superficial) answer to the question—one which everyone could understand—and then acknowledge the superficiality of the answer and again offer to speak with the questioner afterward. In either case, the principle is followed: do not launch into long, complicated answers likely to lose or confuse the majority of your listeners.

c. *Speak to all audience members.* Remember that when a question is asked, it immediately becomes the property of the entire audience, not just of the person who posed it. Thus, even though the questioner may be seated immediately in front of you in the first row, you should speak to everyone in the audience as you answer the question.

d. *React to all questions.* Invariably, someone in the audience will ask you an "off the wall" question. It may be totally irrelevant to everything that preceded it, it may be hostile or leading, or it may simply be stupid. Your initial inclination might be to ignore the question and call on someone else. Suppress that inclination. It is impolite to ignore someone, no matter how rude, crude, or socially unacceptable he or she may be, and no matter how bizarre the question is; the audience will resent you if you treat the question and the questioner in such a manner. We will note later in this chapter some techniques by which you might handle troublesome questions; for now, keep in mind this principle: react politely to every question, regardless of your opinion of the question or the questioner.

2. *Respond encouragingly to questioners.* Let's assume here that you want audience participation. And you should want it; after all, question-and-answer sessions provide you with an opportunity to discover and respond to issues about which your listeners may be confused or in disagreement. In effect, these sessions allow you to conduct a postspeech audience analysis to determine areas of success and failure, and they give you another opportunity to say the things you ought to have said during your speech. So you have everything to gain in the audience participation sessions that follow your prepared presentation. But if these sessions are to be useful to you in achieving your objectives, the audience must participate. You gain absolutely nothing if the all-too-familiar sequence of asking for questions, getting dead silence, going home is what follows your speech. So you need to encourage participation.

The way you respond to questions encourages or discourages additional questions. Consider, for example, this real-life occurrence: after a particularly complicated lecture about "management by objectives" and "job design" during a training seminar for middle-level managers in a large company, the lecturer asked for questions. Immediately the air was filled with raised hands. The lecturer selected a questioner, who proceeded to ask a reasonably intelligent question. The lecturer's answer, however, was extremely curt, delivered with an underlying tone of "How dare you ask me a question." When the answer had been completed, the lecturer asked, "Are there any other stupid questions?" Not surprisingly, everyone in the room suddenly knew everything they felt they needed to know about the topic. Participation ended.

To encourage further participation, you should respond in a manner that is polite, respectful, and positive toward the questioner. You should make it apparent

When Answering Questions, Avoid Confrontations

that you truly appreciate the question and that you have tried to give the question the consideration it deserves. But note one other thing: avoid falling into the habit of beginning each answer with the statement "Good question." Often they are not good questions, and the audience know it. Such false positiveness serves only to create the impression that you are insincere (or too stupid to recognize a dumb question), and it does not truly encourage further questioning. Encouraging responses are achieved more by *how* you answer rather than by *what* you answer. If your overall attitude is positive toward the questioner and reveals genuine interest in his or her question, other listeners will be encouraged to participate as well.

3. *Be honest.* Too often, our desire to impress the audience causes us to behave in ways that are deceptive. For example, when we are asked a question to which we have no answer, we often are tempted to "wing it" rather than admit ignorance. Or if we are asked for our own plans or ideas, we may be inclined to present "off-the-top-of-the-head" proposals rather than confess that we really had not thought about the issue at hand. Such tactics are dangerous. We can easily be caught by knowledgeable audience members, or additional questioning may illuminate all too clearly the limits of our knowledge or thought. An honest response of "I don't know" or "I haven't really thought about that" avoids those dangers, often with no real damage to your credibility. Naturally, if the question concerns something you really *should* know, your credibility indeed will suffer, as it should. But thorough preparation should minimize the likelihood of such embarrassment, and a confession of ignorance followed by a sincere offer to "find out and get back to you on that" should only contribute to your apparent honesty while inflicting only minimal damage to your apparent expertise.

4. *Avoid confrontations.* Occasionally, you may be asked overtly hostile questions, or you may be confronted by a questioner who obviously wants to argue with you. Do everything you can to avoid such arguments. They will become protracted, so that the rest of the audience will lose interest; they will increase in intensity, making it likely that you will lose your composure and say something you shouldn't; they will cause the audience to take sides, perhaps costing you the good will of those who choose the side of the questioner; they will be unresolved, so that the only outcome possible is hard feelings and loss of credibility. In other words, you have nothing to gain and everything to lose if you enter into an argument with a questioner. Later in this chapter, we will consider methods to handle questions likely to precipitate confrontations; at this point, simply keep in mind that if a confrontation develops, you lose.

In this section, then, we have observed some principles that ought to govern both your preparation for and presentation of answers to audience questions. Again, it is important that you adhere to these principles as closely as possible; the question-and-answer session provides you with a tremendous opportunity to analyze, adapt to, and influence your audience before they leave, but to maximize that opportunity you must handle that session properly. Adherence to the rules offered above will do much to guarantee your success in handling audience participation.

GENERATING PARTICIPATION

We already know that audience participation is desirable and that the way you answer questions can encourage or discourage subsequent participation. But how do you get questions in the first place? That is, when you have concluded your speech, how do you generate participation by the audience? An interesting, controversial speech is the best generator of participation, of course, but beyond that there are some devices you can use to encourage your listeners to ask questions. We will consider those devices now.

The most commonly used device is the *nondirected question,* whereby the speaker asks a question of the entire audience. The question, "Are there any questions?" is a common (and often ineffective) example of this type of participation-generating device, But nondirected questions can be more specific, asking the audience to react to some particular point made during the speech; for example, "Did all of you understand the part about work flow and job satisfaction?" or "Did anyone have trouble accepting my argument that all business in this country should be controlled and operated by the Rhode Island state government?" It is important that questions of this sort be chosen carefully. If they produce only stony silence, you may look rather foolish and face the prospect of answering your own question.

Of the devices with which you can generate audience participation, the nondirected question probably is least effective. Since the question is directed to the audience as a whole, the initiative to answer the question lies with the listeners; no one person has the responsibility to answer, so it becomes easy for all to sit rather than participate. Moreover, if someone truly wants to ask a question but is rather shy about speaking up in front of the rest of the audience, the nondirect question will do little to encourage him or her. Therefore, this type of question really does not stimulate participation. Rather, it serves only to provide already stimulated listeners with an opportunity to speak. Nondirected questions are useful in this regard, but the time may come when you need something more pointed to prod your audience into participating.

Directed questions often are more effective. As their name implies, they are directed toward a specific member of the audience, By asking a particular listener his or her thoughts or ideas concerning a point in the speech, you may be able to stimulate the thinking and participation of many audience members. This strategy is particularly effective in encouraging listeners who are shy or reluctant to ask questions; when communication between you as the speaker and some member of the audience has been established, it becomes much easier for other audience members, who no longer are faced with the prospect of "going first," to speak to you.

As with all of the strategies we have considered in this text, the directed question must be used in accordance with certain principles. First, you should be virtually certain that the person to whom you direct your question can provide an answer. If you make someone in the audience look stupid by asking something he or she does not know, other listeners hardly will be encouraged to participate. Indeed, to be absolutely certain that you do not embarrass an audience member with a directed question, you might contact an audience member prior to the speaking event and tell him (or her) that you intend to ask him a particular question (and tell him what that question is, of course). He then can develop an answer so that he is prepared for the situation as well. This same strategy, incidentally, can be used with nondirected questions. By coaching an audience member ahead of time on the questions he should ask after your speech, you can be certain that your question, "Does anyone have any questions?" will be answered in the manner you prefer.

Second, your directed question should require more than a simple Yes or No. Your purpose, after all, is to establish interaction with your audience. Eliciting a brief Yes from one listener typically is inadequate for that purpose; you need to get the listener talking if the other audience members are going to be encouraged to join in. Suessmuth and Stengels (1974, pp. 46–50) suggest three types of questions useful in eliciting participation:

Convergent: brings together facts to form a unified whole
Divergent: evokes interpretation, explanation, or translation
Evaluative: requests a judgment or opinion

All three of these types avoid the Yes-No response when properly phrased, and each of them is effective in generating discussion.

Third, if you have to use this technique more than once (as when your first directed question does not elicit further participation), try not to call on the same person every time. Certainly, you want to call on people who can answer the question but try to share the burden as much as possible.

Finally, use nonverbal feedback as a cue for determining whom you will ask your directed questions. If you are speaking to a group of complete strangers so that it is not possible to coach one of the audience members, you can try to isolate during your speech someone whom you might call on when the speech is done. If, for example, someone overtly disagrees with one of the points you make during the speech, you might call upon that individual and say something like; "When I indi-

in fact you do?'' Similarly, you might ask someone who overtly agrees with a point whether he or she has had some experience that produced that agreement, or why he or she feels so strongly about that issue. In either case, you use audience feedback as a cue to help you determine who should be the lucky recipients of your directed questions when the speech is over.

The last device for generating participation is the *redirected question*. In using this device, you simply redirect a question to the person who asked it or to another member of the audience (or the audience as a whole). Thus, you might respond to a question by saying, ''That's an excellent question, and I suspect you have given it some thought yourself. What do *you* think about this issue?'' or ''Mr. Jones, you have had some experience in that area. What do you think should be done?'' or ''I think that's a question that concerns all of us. Does anyone have an answer?'' Each of these responses involves the audience even further and prevents you from becoming an answer machine that stops all participation and discussion by providing the definitive answer to everything.

To generate participation after your speech, then, you need both to stimulate the thinking and interest of your listeners and to provide them with the opportunity to talk once they have been stimulated. Asking nondirected questions can provide the opportunity; asking controversial directed questions and redirecting questions can also stimulate interest and thinking. Therefore, to promote active and effective discussions with your audiences, you should employ these devices whenever possible.

HANDLING QUESTIONS

When audience members ask questions following your speech, you should answer them in accordance with the principles we considered earlier in this chapter. But there are some additional procedures you should follow if your answers are to be maximally effective. Those procedures fall into two categories: analyzing the question and giving the answer. We will consider each category in turn.

Analyzing the Question

When someone presents you with a question, you must make several quick decisions and then phrase your answer accordingly. Generally, we can place those decisions in two categories.

1. What is the intent of the question? For example, did the questioner simply not hear you? If so, you need only to repeat the information she (or he) missed. Or, did she not understand what you said because she was unfamiliar with the terms you had used? Then you must explain the terms she did not understand and then check to see if there were other words you used that were foreign to your audience. Or, is the questioner hostile and using her question to start an argument? Is she trying to display her brilliance by challenging you? Is she simply asking for more information because she is genuinely interested in what you have said? You must decide, in literally an instant, which of these motives seems to underlie the question you received.

2. What are the potential effects of answering the question? Several consequences might result depending upon the strategy you choose to follow as you answer the question posed to you. For example, providing an answer might clarify matters and satisfy both the questioner and the audience. If that answer could also be given in a very brief statement, you probably would want to go ahead and respond to the question. However, giving an answer might serve to encourage more, perhaps unwanted, questions. If you are anxious to avoid additional participation at that point in your presentation, you might want to avoid answering the question right then. Similarly, giving an answer might, in your judgment, take the discussion away from the topic of concern, or it might create even more confusion in the minds of the questioner and the audience, or it might create a confrontation between you and the questioner. Again, in situations like these, you might want to select some strategy other than giving a direct answer to the question.

One useful strategy, as we shall see shortly, is to postpone consideration of the question until some point later in the presentation. If you choose this strategy, there is a useful technique you can employ to maximize its effectiveness and to minimize the impression that you are simply putting the question off, hoping that it will go away. Have nearby a blank chalkboard or flip-chart pad. When a troublesome (that is, potentially hostile, irrelevant, or confusing) question is asked and you want to defer consideration of that question until some later time, write the question on the board or pad. In effect, you create an agenda for consideration later on. At the same time, you demonstrate to your audience that you take the question seriously and that you fully intend to talk about it later. Thus, you avoid giving the impression that you are simply ducking the question because, for some reason, you cannot or will not answer it. One note of caution, however: when using this technique, do not leave this growing agenda in view of the audience all of the time. Cover it or turn it away from them until you are ready either to add another question or to deal with the questions written there. If left in full view, this list can easily distract the members of the audience.

At this point, then, you have been asked a question, and you have made several quick judgments about the questioner's intent and about the potential effects answering the question might produce. With those decisions in mind, you next are ready to deal with the situation.

Giving the Answer

When giving a response, you should do several things in order for your answers to be maximally effective. Briefly, those techniques include the following:

1. Repeat the question. This principle is particularly important when you speak to large groups, but it applies to smaller audiences as well. Before answering a question, you always must first be sure that everyone in the audience heard the question and understood it. All too often, speakers neglect to repeat the question, and the listeners are forced to try to reconstruct the question based upon the answer they hear given. Misunderstandings and confusion are the predictable result. Thus, to avoid communication breakdowns you always should repeat the question before you answer it.

2. Rephrase the question when necessary. When a listener asks a particularly long or convoluted question, you should shorten and clarify it to make sense to everyone (including the person who asked it). By rephrasing the question before you begin to answer (and by asking the questioner whether your restatement accurately reflects what he or she was trying to say), you can be certain that you, the other listeners, and the questioner agree on the point of the question and that your answer will be relevant to the questioner's intent. Again, you may not have to do this with every question you receive; only those that require clarification or summarization need to be rephrased.

3. Postpone troublesome questions. As we already have seen, some questions can be potentially dangerous. Those that require long, technical answers, those that are clearly irrelevant, and those that are apparently hostile fall into this category and should be handled carefully. After all, you want to encourage subsequent questions, but at the same time you want to avoid long or irrelevant answers and you want to stay out of arguments. Probably the best strategy you can use when presented with a troublesome question is to postpone it. You might ask the questioner to speak with you privately after the meeting, or you might promise to cover the subject matter later in the discussion. Note, however, that the questioner will expect you to talk about that topic later on if you promise to do so, and if he (or she) perceives that you are going to conclude without having dealt with his concerns he probably will raise them again. If you promise to "cover that point a little later," keep that promise.

4. Label and rephrase loaded questions. Occasionally, a listener will ask a question similar in form to the question, "Do you still put your cat in the clothes dryer and turn the setting to fluff dry?" No matter how you answer the question, you are in trouble. Often such loaded questions are asked deliberately by hostile listeners, but just as often they are asked innocently by listeners who have not thought through the question's implications. You therefore must be tactful in handling such questions (even though you would like to say something like; "You'll never catch me on a leading question like that, you jerk!"), but you also must avoid falling to the trap the question sets. There are several tactics you might use.

First, you need to have everyone in the audience recognize that you have been asked a loaded question. To do that, you can use several strategies: you can pause after the question is asked, giving the listeners time to figure out for themselves that the question is loaded; you can ask the questioner to repeat the question, again giving the audience an opportunity to recognize the question for what it is; you can even label the question openly (but tactfully), saying something like, "No matter how I answer that question, I think I'm in trouble." All three of these strategies call attention to the dangerous nature of the question, and they typically gain you the sympathies of the audience. Once you have accomplished that, you are ready to handle the question directly.

Second, once recognition of the question has been achieved, you should analyze the question. For example, "You asked if I still beat my dog. That question assumes, of course, that I once did beat my dog, and that assumption is false." After delivering a speech, your faithful author once was asked, "Why is it that authors think they know everything when in fact they can't translate their abstract theories into useful practices?" Answering that question required a step-by-step analysis and refutation of the many assumptions the question held: authors do not think they know everything, their ideas have (or at least should have) practical value, and so on. Similarly, you should dissect the loaded questions you are asked and deal separately with the various issues and assumptions those questions contain.

Finally, you must use some judgment in answering these questions in the first place. Occasionally, loaded questions are asked just to harass the speaker. In such situations, the time you spend analyzing and answering the question may be time wasted; the questioner was not interested in having the question answered anyway. If you are reasonably sure that this situation exists when you are asked a loaded question, your strategy should be, first, to label the question and, second, to postpone it by offering to discuss the question with the questioner after the meeting.

When handling questions that arise during your question-and-answer sessions, then, you should seek to employ the procedures discussed in this final section. Briefly, you should repeat the question so that all can hear it, you should rephrase the question if necessary, you should postpone troublesome questions, and you should label and analyze (or postpone) loaded questions. By following these guidelines, and by adhering to the principles described at the beginning of this chapter, you should be able not only to preserve but to enhance the positive impact of your speech.

SUMMARY

Question-and-answer sessions offer you a tremendous opportunity. In them, you can assess the impact of your speech to determine where you have succeeded and where you have failed. But even more importantly, you can try one more time to succeed in those areas where success so far has eluded you. Through the answers you provide, you may be able to convince people who still are dubious, or you may be able to teach people who still are ignorant or confused. But to achieve these last-minute successes, you must handle the question-and-answer session effectively. Our purpose in this chapter was to discover some methods for effectively conducting audience participation sessions.

At the outset, we examined some principles that should govern your preparation and presentation of answers to questions listeners raise. First, we saw that you should keep your objectives and goals in mind, know your audience and topic, anticipate question areas, and prepare general responses during the preparatory stages of your speech, and that you should consider your entire audience, respond encouragingly, be honest, and avoid confrontations when actually dealing with audience participation. Second, we observed some devices useful in generating audience participation, including the nondirected question, the directed question, and the redirected question. And finally, we saw that, when actually handling questions, you should repeat the question, rephrase it if necessary, postpone it if it is troublesome, and label and analyze it if it is loaded. By applying these principles and employing these techniques, you should be able to use audience participation in a manner that makes maximum use of the advantages that question-and-answer sessions offer.

REFERENCE

Suessmuth, P. and M. Stengels. "The Art of Asking Questions," *Training* 26(1974):46–50.

PROJECT

THE QUESTION-AND-ANSWER SESSION

After any speech, you are likely to be questioned closely about the ideas and opinions you have expressed. The questioning may be intended to clarify points that were unclear to the questioner (in which case the purpose of your answer is to inform) or it may be intended to determine why you feel as you do (so that your response is both informative and persuasive) or it may be designed to challenge your viewpoints (so that you must defend your views and persuade the questioner). Thus, your purpose generally is to preserve the positive impact of your speech, but your specific purpose is determined by the nature of the question. As the preceding chapter suggested, your preparation must be based upon careful audience analysis and anticipation of their questions. For this particular assignment, you should proceed through these steps:

1. Select a topic. In two or three minutes, you should make a concise statement of your view on a controversial topic. Such topics should concern some prominent social issue and could include:

Solving racial problems by law	Controlling industry
Controlling television programming	Improving education
National health care	Controlling inflation
Legislating morality	Legalizing victimless crimes
Enforcing the law more strictly	Reducing government size

   Again, the topic should be important to you and your listeners, and you should offer a specific proposition you are prepared to defend.
2. Analyze the audience and prepare response areas. Determine their knowledge, attitudes, beliefs, and values, and then predict their probable reactions to your position statement. Then prepare general responses to those predicted reactions.
3. Gather your material. Obtain the information and develop the arguments that you may need to respond to audience questions. Generally, the more information you possess and the more arguments you have in mind, the more effectively you will be able to respond to your audience.
4. State your viewpoint clearly and concisely, offering two or three reasons why you believe the proposition you are advancing.
5. When answering questions, use the techniques described in the preceding chapter. Employ the general principles described and use the suggestions for answering questions. Above all, maintain control over the situation at all times and retain your composure no matter what happens.

Name _____

Date _____

Speech Type _____

Speech Outline, Project Number _____

Speech Topic: _____

Speech Objective: _____

_____

Speech Title: _____

Introduction

    Attention:

    Motivation:

    Credibility:

      Preview

      Body

      Conclusion

Instructor's Comments:

APPENDIX
KEEPING THE UNIONS OUT

Attention (Silence)   (At the beginning of the speech, the speaker acknowledged his introduction and then stood silently for about 45 seconds.)

(Involvement)   I see that some of you are beginning to get a little restless. You're wondering what's going on; why is this guy standing up in front saying nothing? In fact, you already have gotten the message. I haven't been communicating—at least not in the way you were expecting. And without communication, you don't know what is going on. If I had stayed quiet a little longer, some of you probably would have walked out.

(Expectation reference)

(Recent event)   Interestingly, a situation much like this one occurred in February, 1979, at British Leyland, a unionized British automobile company. About 19,000 of their employees walked out—went on strike—and the reason for that strike is described by *The New York Times* of February

(Quotation)   25 as follows: "The main reason for the strike was that Leyland had not made sure the workers knew what the productivity targets were . . . ." The *Times* article concludes: "Perhaps more than any other factor, the strike here was caused by those clogged lines of communication, mainly—but not exclusively—down from management to its work force. The strike is an object lesson to managers everywhere of the importance of making sure that both the workers on the shop floor and the senior management know what is happening."[1]

[1] Robert D. Hershey, "Labor's Woes in the U.K." (*The New York Times,* February 25, 1979, p. 25).

(Subject reference)	You are attending this conference to learn how you can maintain a union-free environment in your companies.
Motivation (Utility)	British Leyland should give you some idea about the basics of union avoidance right at the start. But in my
Credibility (Competence)	experiences as a management consultant, a businessperson, and a college professor, I have been able to learn some techniques through which you can do much to
Purpose (Statement)	avoid situations like British Leyland. My purpose in this brief talk, then, is to provide you with some techniques for keeping the unions out.
Preview	In this speech, I'm going to consider three questions. First, I'll talk about why we should try to remain non-
Organization (Question-answer)	union in the first place, answering the question, "Why should we stay union free?" Second, I'll answer the question, "Why do employees join unions?" If we know that, we then can consider a third question, "How can we counteract the causes of unionization?" By answering that question, we will have achieved our purpose for attending this conference.
Transition	So let's look at the first question. "Why should we stay
Main Point I	union free?" Probably you have answered this question in your own mind already; otherwise, why would you be
Attention (Involvement)	attending this conference in the first place? But I think it is worth considering just briefly the reasons why a union-free environment is preferable to a unionized situation. There are two such reasons.
Subpoint I.A.	First, unionized situations are more difficult to manage. In union-free situations, you can deal directly with your
Details	people. When a problem arises, you can handle it immediately. When a need for shifts in manpower from one department or area to another arises, you can make those shifts quickly. When people are in danger of becoming bored with their jobs, you can rotate job responsibilities relatively easily. In unionized situations, all of this flexibility is lost. Problems must be handled through grievance procedures; manpower shifts must be approved by the union; job rotation often is prohibited by union contracts. In short, you lose the capacity to manage your people directly.
Transition	This first reason leads to a second: nonunion companies
Subpoint I.B.	tend to be financially more sucessful than unionized companies in the same industry. In a study conducted at
Evidence (Example)	M.I.T., the researchers found that there was a significant correlation between degree of financial success and nonunion or union status. The nonunion companies' average performance for return on capital, return on as-

sets, return on sales, and total investor yield was consistently higher than the performances seen in unionized environments.[2] Nonunionized companies simply are more profitable.

Internal summary

So why should we want to remain nonunion? Because it is easier to manage nonunion companies effectively, and because nonunion companies generally are more profitable.

Transition
Main Point II

Evidence (Opinion)

Internal preview

Our second question is, "Why do employees join unions?" Scott Myers, perhaps the best known student of union and labor relations and the author of *Managing Without Unions*, indicates that there are four basic reasons for joining unions.[3] Let's consider each reason briefly.

Subpoint II.A.

Examples
Attention (Rhetorical question)

First, Myers claims, people join unions in order to protect themselves. When employees fear their bosses, when they think that they are not treated fairly, then they are more likely to join unions. And who can blame them?

Subpoint II.B.

Attention (Rhetorical question)

Second, people join unions for self-respect. When management tells them that they are worthless (and treats them accordingly), employees will join unions simply to reassert their dignity. Again, who can blame them?

Subpoint II.C.

Third, people join unions for self-expression. People want the opportunity to contribute—to have a voice in the things that affect them. They believe that they have ideas, and that those ideas are good ones. If employees are not given a chance to contribute those ideas in a meaningful way, they are more likely to unionize.

Subpoint II.D.

Finally, people join unions to achieve a feeling of solidarity. Everyone has a need to belong—a need for affiliation with other people. Ideally, part of that need will be met by their work situation, as they are given a chance to identify with and feel proud of the company they work for. However, if the management acts in a way that promotes an "us versus them" environment, employees will fulfill their need for belonging by joining something else. Such as a union.

Attention (Rhetorical questions)

Do these reasons tell you something? Do they imply something about communication? Of course they do. If you don't communicate with me, you treat me as a thing, not a person. If you communicate to me in ways that are threatening, or punishing, or inconsistent, I will seek a means by which I can protect myself. If you talk down to

[2] David W. Hunt and Michael R. Bruse, "Communication in Nonunion Companies" (M.A. thesis, Sloan School of Management, Massachusetts Institute of Technology, 1976).
[3] M. Scott Myers, *Managing Without Unions* (Boston: Allyn and Bacon, 1976).

me, I will fight for my self-respect. If you refuse to let me communicate back, I will fight for that right, too. And if you make me feel that you are in the "in crowd" and I am not, I'll try to turn the tables on you. So why do people join unions? To a large extent, they join unions because management, through poor communication practices, forces them to do so.

Internal summary

Transition

At this point, then, we know that we want to stay nonunion, and we know in general terms what causes unionization. Now, we are ready to answer the last question, "How can we counteract the causes of unionization?"

Main Point III

There is, unfortunately, no "sure fire" or infallible method of avoiding unions, but I can suggest four techniques that seem useful in preserving your union-free environment. Again, let's consider each of these four in turn.

Internal preview

Subpoint III.A.

First, to avoid unions, involve your employees. One of the most successful management tools developed recently is *management by objectives,* the process whereby a supervisor and his or her subordinates cooperatively determine what the subordinates' performance goals and measures are going to be. What management by objectives promotes is two things: involvement, as employees are asked to participate in setting objectives and devising performance measures, and communication, as supervisors and subordinates actually sit face to face to discuss these matters. This is the sort of involvement we want. But there are some rules you must follow as you involve employees. That involvement must first of all be meaningful. Don't ask employees what they think and then simply ignore it; that's a bigger insult than not asking at all. If you are going to solicit their input, be ready to implement at least some of their suggestions. But that leads to a second rule: use involvement with some judgment. Employees should be involved in matters that directly affect them, and in matters where they truly can have some impact. For exam-

Examples

ple, employee input concerning appointment of a manager in another facility probably should not be sought, for that decision is not relevant to this particular group. Similarly, their opinions concerning the necessity of company compliance with government health and safety regulations also would not be very helpful; compliance is required by law. However, in matters such as working methods and conditions, for example, employee input could prove invaluable to management, in both developing improvements for those things and improving employee morale by enhancing their involvement.

But there is one other thing concerning employee involvement: we always must remember that no American business is a democracy. Or, to put it another way, we can't let the inmates run the asylum. Managers are managers so that they can manage, and they should have been selected to be managers because of their managerial skills. Thus, employee involvement does not mean that the job of management is turned over to the employees. Rather, it means that when management is dealing with issues relevant to company employees, they should both solicit employee input and, where possible, implement employee suggestions as they make the decisions that govern the company.

Attention (Principle or theory)

Involving employees helps to avoid unionization. But related to involvement is a second union-avoidance method: goal setting and communicating. Again, management by objectives illustrates this technique. If employees are to identify with their company, they must know what goals the company is striving for and what progress toward those goals the company is making. In every company with which I have been involved, employees have expressed a desire for precisely this sort of information. On the employee attitude surveys I have conducted, 85 percent of the respondents have indicated that they want to know more about how their company is doing, about the long- and short-range goals of the company, and so on. They want information about the company as a whole.

Transition
Subpoint III.B.

Evidence (Statistics)

Again, some judgment must be used by management in determining what information concerning company goals is to be distributed to employees. Obviously, any information about company plans and developments that might be harmful to the company's competitive position in the marketplace should not be distributed. But information about desired growth rates or net income can be distributed at the beginning of the year, and periodic reports of progress toward those goals can be provided to employees. However, this raises another issue I've heard all too often from company executives. "What," they ask, "if we are not making our goals? What if we fall short? Then we have to tell our employees that we are failing, and this information might be demoralizing to them." I don't think so. Look at the annual report of any company—even of companies in deep

Attention (Self-reference)
(Quotation)

(Style)
Analogy

financial trouble. They still manage to find a bright side that can provide a silver lining to their corporate cloud. But consider something else. For the better part of ten years, the New York Mets were the sorriest bunch ever to stumble across a baseball diamond. But they didn't give up, and the little successes they achieved were far more rewarding to them than they would have been to any other team. To a large extent, failure motivated the players toward success, and small successes motivated them toward even greater ones, until a world championship was won. Your company could operate in the same fashion. If employees know that the company is falling short of its goal, they probably will be motivated to try just a little harder to promote company success. So while we like to give good news and paint rosy pictures, we still might achieve some benefit by letting our employees know the bad news as well.

Internal summary

To avoid unionization, then, set company goals and then let employees know what those goals and the progress toward them are. In so doing, you demonstrate to your employees that you respect and value them, and that you think them important and adult enough to receive all news, both good and bad, about the company's progress. At the same time, you will promote a feeling of solidarity by stressing the objectives toward which all members of the company are striving.

Transition
Subpoint III.C.

A third union-avoidance technique is related to the second. It isn't enough simply to let people know what company goals are—you also have to clarify their role in achieving those overall goals. Thus, the third technique is to personalize goals. That is, show each employee what his or her role is in working toward the achievement of company success.

Management by objectives also provides a framework for implementing this third technique. In their discussion of the subordinate's objectives, the supervisor and subordinate also should consider the context in which the work occurs. That is, how does the subordinate's job lead to the achievement of some larger goal, which in turn leads to achievement of a still larger goal, and so on, until achievement of the overall company goal is reached? Obviously, if this sort of conversation is going to occur, the supervisor will have to know an awful lot about the objectives and subobjectives of the company. That's why management by objectives must be a top-down process, as each level educates the level immediately below concerning the goals of the company. Ultimately, each level of the company comes to understand it's role in achieving company goals.

Internal summary

We've seen three techniques for union avoidance: involve employees, set and communicate goals, and personalize goals. But there is one last technique that needs to be considered, and it may be the most important technique of all. That is: emphasize face-to-face relations. When communication occurs, it should occur between people meeting face to face as often as possible; written communication should be used only as a support system for face-to-face interaction.

Subpoint III.D.

Attention (Self-reference)

I've worked with a lot of companies that think they have terrific internal communications functions. They show

Narrative

me their annual reports, their benefits booklets, their employee orientation handbooks, their employee newsletters. They sometimes even show me the awards these literary wonders have won. Interesting thing, though. Those awards never come from employees. They come from groups outside the company that appreciate the terrific design, layout, printing, and so on that went into the materials. The impact of the material never is even considered.

When we overemphasize written communications, and when we admire that communication for its beauty and award-winning qualities, we lose sight of the purposes of communicating with employees. And what are those

Attention (Rhetorical question)

purposes? Go back to the reasons employees join unions: self-protection, respect, expression, and solidarity. Communication should promote these things.

Good communication promotes these things. And the best communication occurs in face-to-face interactions between supervisors and subordinates. These encounters provide the best opportunity for a two-way dialogue and they are best for checking to see if the message has been received and understood. It provides a channel for upward and downward communication to occur simultaneously. Regular meetings between supervisors and their immediate subordinates are a good first step toward effective communications.

Attention (Self-reference)

But consider one last thing. A couple of years ago, I was consulting for a company that wanted to institute

Narrative/example

a supervisory training program. As part of my work, I interviewed the first-level supervisors who had been identified on the basis of their department's productivity levels as the best supervisors in the company. There was one supervisor who seemed particularly outstanding. His area had the highest production levels in the company, and turnover and absenteeism among his people was almost zero. So I sought out this man and asked him what he did. The list of techniques was somewhat surprising. The main thing he did, he told me, was communicate. This was not very surprising. But the form of that communication was. While they were working, he sang (and not very well) to them. When someone had some special event (a birthday or anniversary, for example), he sang to them directly. He stopped and talked to each person individually, asking them how things were going and asking if he could do anything. He passed out little awards for people whose attendance or performance was particularly good. In effect, he did everything he could to show his people that he cared about them as people. And they showed their appreciation through their work.

What this supervisor illustrates, I think, is an important element of face-to-face communication. It is crucial that we use that communication channel, but it is equally crucial that we use that channel correctly. We can insult someone face to face just as easily as we can reinforce him. We can demoralize someone just as easily as we can motivate him. We can threaten and intimidate him just as easily as we can encourage and support him. *How* we communicate therefore is the key to effective face-to-face interaction, and such interaction in turn is the key to union avoidance.

Summary So we have seen the answers to three questions. We know that avoiding unions is desirable because nonunion companies are easier to manage and more profitable to run. We know that employees join unions in order to obtain protection, respect, expression, and solidarity. And we now know that the keys to union avoidance are involving employees, setting and communicating goals, personalizing goals, and emphasizing good face-to-face relations.

Conclusion
Example/historical narrative Perhaps you have read Adam Smith's book, *The Wealth of Nations*. That book, of course, is credited with igniting the industrial revolution, which led to the state of industry today. But that book also initiated a style of management that, unfortunately, still exists today as well. Adam Smith owned a needles-and-pins factory and, as was the practice during the eighteenth century, he employed children as his primary labor force. His style of manage-

ment, out of necessity, was one of parent-child interactions in which a domineering parent had to force children to work when those children would much rather be out playing. Sadly, a lot of managers treat their employees in the same fashion. And it is those employees who join (and in my estimation, who *should* join) unions. We conclude our discussion of ways we can stay union free with a final principle: treat your employees like mature adults. After all, that's precisely what they are.

Action statement

INDEX

80 81 82 83 9 8 7 6 5 4 3 2